Strategic Pay

Edward E. Lawler III

Strategic Pay

Aligning Organizational Strategies and Pay Systems

Jossey-Bass Publishers · San Francisco

STRATEGIC PAY
Aligning Organizational Strategies and Pay Systems
   by Edward E. Lawler III

Copyright © 1990 by: Jossey-Bass Inc., Publishers
                      350 Sansome Street
                      San Francisco, California 94104

Jossey-Bass Web address: http://www.josseybass.com

Library of Congress Cataloging-in-Publication Data

Lawler, Edward E.
     Strategic pay: aligning organizational strategies and pay systems/
     Edward E. Lawler III. — 1st ed.
         p.   cm.—(The Jossey-Bass management series)
     Includes bibliographical references and index.
     ISBN 1-55542-262-4 (alk. paper)
     1. Compensation management.   2. Strategic planning.
     3. Pay-for-knowledge systems.   I. Title.   II. Series.
     HF5549.5.C67L383   1990
     658.3'22—dc20   90-37168
                                                       CIP

JACKET DESIGN BY WILLI BAUM

FIRST EDITION
HB Printing   10 9 8 7 6

The Jossey-Bass Management Series

Contents

Preface   xi

The Author   xvii

Part One: The Impact and Design of Pay Systems   1

1. The New Realities of Pay and Organizational
    Effectiveness   3

2. Setting Strategic Objectives for Pay Systems   13

3. Establishing Core Principles   37

Part Two: Paying for Performance   55

4. Using Incentive Pay   57

5. Using Merit Pay   70

6. Using Performance Appraisals to Drive Pay   86

7. Paying for Organizational Performance   108

Part Three: Determining Base Pay   133

8. Paying the Job   135

9. Paying the Person   153

Part Four: Administering Pay Systems   179

10. Setting Total Compensation Levels   181

11. Determining the Total Compensation Mix   202

12. Managing Decision-Making and Communication
     Processes   221

     Part Five: Applying Pay Strategies   **243**

13. A Pay Strategy for Acme Corporation: A Traditional
     Manufacturing Company   245

14. A Pay Strategy for HiTech International: A Global
     Technology Company   260

15. Strategic Pay and Public Policy: The Need for Change 273

     References   289

     Index   297

Preface

Because pay systems represent a significant cost for most organizations they receive considerable attention—but often with the wrong emphasis. Too much attention is focused on reducing pay costs and too little is focused on increasing the benefits of the pay system. A well-designed pay system can be a very important contributor to an organization's effectiveness.

The challenge is to align an organization's pay system with that organization's strategic direction. This is not easy to do—if it were, it would be common practice—but it *can* be accomplished. It is important to begin with a careful analysis of the objectives of the pay system as they relate to the strategic plan of the organization and the kinds of behaviors needed to accomplish the organization's strategic objectives. Once the objectives of the pay system are identified, the pay system can be developed by choosing among the available approaches.

The major focus of *Strategic Pay* is identifying the choices that need to be made in order to develop a strategically designed pay system. The process can be simple if an organization can identify what it wants the reward system to accomplish and if it has an idea of the pay system alternatives that are available. Unfortunately, all too often organizations establishing or revising pay systems simply look at what their competitors are doing and follow their example. This tendency is supported by the extensive information available on competitive practices. However, the key to fitting pay effectively with business strategy is a willingness to look beyond what competitors are doing and to identify pay as a potential source of competitive advantage.

I have no doubt that pay, because of its ability to affect individual and organizational behavior, can be an important source of competitive advantage. Indeed, it can be a relatively long-lasting source of advantage for the firm that takes the time to implement and develop pay strategies. In many respects innovative strategies are hard to copy because they are more than just technology: they are a social system, a management philosophy, and a way of operating that permeates the entire organization.

Strategic Pay is aimed at managers who are interested in pay system issues. It contains neither large amounts of jargon nor extensive reports of research studies. Instead, it presents general principles and points concerning the impact of pay systems and the various pay system options that are available. I have written the book in this way because I believe that pay system design issues should be addressed by *all* members of an organization. These issues are too important to be left just to compensation experts. Because they can be the source of an organization's competitive advantage, pay systems need to be understood and designed by employers who have general business responsibilities and who understand how competitive advantage can be achieved.

Overview of the Contents

Strategic Pay begins by discussing the competitive challenge that is faced by businesses today. Most organizations are already quite aware that the changing business environment places them in an increasingly competitive situation. The old question, "Are we as good as or better than our U.S. competitors?" is no longer sufficient. New competitors have entered international markets. As a result, if organizations are going to be effective, they have to be sure that their management systems provide them with a global competitive advantage. The traditional practices in the United States in areas such as pay do not always do this. In many cases these practices were designed simply to match what other U.S. corporations were doing, so that no corporation was at a disadvantage. This was all right as long as competitive advantage could be found elsewhere. Unfortunately, it is no longer all right; competitive advantage cannot always be found elsewhere. Given the high cost of labor in developed countries such as the United States, it is important to look at both how pay dollars are being spent and what is being received in return for them.

Chapter Two looks at the impact that pay systems can have in an organization. This chapter focuses on the benefits that are derivable from a pay system and urges organizations to decide what benefits they want from their pay systems. It provides a framework for understanding the impact of pay systems in organizations as well as a set of criteria against which any pay system can be evaluated.

Chapter Three explores the core principles that need to be developed as a first step in designing a strategic pay system. Core principles are crucial because they help form the perceptions that are the major link between pay system practices and individual and organizational behavior. An approach to developing these principles is also discussed.

How to pay for performance is a major focus in virtually every organization. Chapters Four, Five, Six, and Seven address different ways of paying for performance and point out the strengths and weaknesses of each. A broad range of approaches is covered, including merit pay, gainsharing, and employee ownership. Because of the common practice of linking bonuses and merit-based salary increases to performance appraisal outcomes, an entire chapter is devoted to performance appraisal and its relationship to pay. Taken together, these four chapters provide a complete discussion of the potential ways of paying for performance; they should help an organization decide which (if any) of these approaches fits best with its strategy.

Chapters Eight and Nine deal with determining an individual's base pay. Chapter Eight looks at the traditional approach of focusing on the job and determining an employee's base pay or pay rate by measuring the "size" of that job and then pricing it in the external market. Chapter Nine presents an alternative to this approach—paying the person. This approach offers some compelling strategic advantages in situations in which a participative culture is desired and an organization's key assets are its human assets. Taken together, these two chapters should allow an organization to determine whether its best approach is to pay the person or to pay the job.

Chapter Ten looks at a variety of issues involved in setting total compensation levels. Its focus is on how high these levels should be relative to the market and on what market should be used in determining compensation levels. The total compensation level is a critical issue, because it strongly affects the attraction and retention of human resources as well as organizational culture.

Chapter Eleven focuses on the elements of a total pay package. Important strategic decisions are involved in determining how much of an individual's pay package is made up of such things as benefits, cash, base pay, and incentive pay. Practices such as flexible benefits and pay for performance—practices that can have a powerful impact on who is attracted to and retained by an organization as well as on its culture—are considered here.

The "process" issues involved in designing and administering pay systems are discussed in Chapter Twelve. Here communication issues and participative management practices are examined in detail. Process is often as important as structure and pay technology in determining a pay system's impact on organizational effectiveness.

Chapters Thirteen and Fourteen present cases that show the development of a strategic pay approach for organizations. Two radically different hypothetical organizations are described, and a set of core pay principles, practices, and processes are prescribed for each. This is done to synthesize the discussions of the previous chapters and to illustrate why strategic choices in pay system design need to be based on an organization's need for particular kinds of performance and behavior. In these chapters the key decisions— how to pay for performance, whether to base pay on the job or on the person, where and how to set total compensation levels, what type of total compensation mix is appropriate, and what decision-making and communication practices are used—are brought to life through their application to particular cases.

The final chapter, Chapter Fifteen, considers public policy and how it relates to the types of pay practices organizations need in order to be competitive. The chapter concludes with a number of recommendations for change in some current laws favoring pay practices that do not always allow organizations to gain competitive advantage.

Why This Book Was Written

My interest in pay research goes back to the early 1960s, when I was a doctoral student at the University of California, Berkeley. My earliest research focused on pay, and I have never lost my interest in the topic. There are always new issues to research; and, because of the changing environment, there is always a need for new pay practices and policies. Thus I have continued to be intrigued by the role of pay in organizations and by pay practices. Indeed, my interest increased during the 1980s, because during this decade organizations became more willing to try new pay practices. This willingness to deviate from traditional pay practices undoubtedly stemmed from the fact that, because the old ways were often inadequate, organizations sought new approaches to management. In the search for new ways to manage, pay was one of a number of practices that underwent scrutiny and, in some cases, important change.

For someone like myself, who for decades has tried to encourage organizations to change their pay practices, the 1980s proved to be an exciting decade. Suddenly organizations were willing to try new practices. Their innovation gave me a chance to refine my thinking: it became possible to study issues that previously had been beyond my ability to research simply because there were no examples available to study.

This is my third book on pay and organizational effectiveness. The first two were research-based books that summarized the existing knowledge about how pay affects organizational effectiveness and how it can be used to support organizational development and change. Missing from the two earlier books was a framework for helping organizations choose the right pay practices for their respective situations. As I have done more and more work with organizations, helping them choose the right pay practices, I have become acutely aware of the need for a book that helps identify the key choices and clarify how an organization should make these choices.

This book is a result of my thinking and of my work with a number of organizations that have faced strategic choices in the pay area. Although it is research-based (and certainly has been enriched by the increasing amount of research on pay), it is not a book that primarily reports recent research.

I wrote it because I wanted to demonstrate how important pay system design choices are to the ultimate effectiveness of an organization. I hope that it will put to rest the idea that pay is simply a cost for an organization, make it clear that making the right choices with respect to pay practices and processes is vital to an organization's effectiveness, and establish that pay practices can provide a definite competitive advantage.

I owe a large debt of gratitude to the many organizations that have allowed me to work with them and that have ventured onto new ground in the area of pay system design and administration. In some respects these organizations are the real authors of *Strategic Pay*, for they provided me with material and kept me interested in the area of pay system design and administration.

Los Angeles, California   Edward E. Lawler III
June 1990

The Author

Edward E. Lawler III is research professor and professor of management and organization in the Graduate School of Business Administration at the University of Southern California. He joined the university in 1978 and during 1979 founded and became director of the university's Center for Effective Organizations.

After receiving his B.A. degree (1960) from Brown University and his Ph.D. degree (1964) from the University of California, Berkeley, both in psychology, Lawler joined the faculty of Yale University. He moved to the University of Michigan in 1972 as professor of psychology and program director in the Survey Research Center at the Institute for Social Research.

Lawler has been honored by many professional associations for his research work. He has served as consultant to more than 100 organizations on employee involvement, organizational change, and compensation and is the author or coauthor of more than 150 articles and 18 books. His most recent books include *Pay and Organization Development* (1981), *Managing Creation* (1983), *Doing Research That Is Useful for Theory and Practice* (1985), *High-Involvement Management* (1986), *Designing Performance Appraisal Systems* (1989), and *Employee Involvement in America* (1989).

Strategic Pay

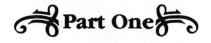 **Part One**

The Impact and Design of Pay Systems

 Chapter One

The New Realities of
Pay and Organizational Effectiveness

The world of business has changed dramatically in the last several decades, yet the pay practices of most organizations have not. Fundamentally, they differ little from the practices of the 1950s, when American companies dominated the world's economy. Employees are still paid according to the worth of the job they hold, they are still given a fixed set of fringe benefits, they are still eligible for small merit increases, and they are still told little about how their company's pay system works.

Why are these approaches still in place? Is it because they are so effective and robust that there is no need to change them? Or is it because most organizations have become so wedded to or mired in their traditional practices that they are unable to make badly needed changes?

I believe many organizations are more concerned with doing the wrong things right than with searching for the right pay practices. They have pay systems that are driven more by history and what other organizations do than by a strategic analysis of organizational needs. The simple fact that reward systems have changed very little over the years, despite enormous societal and business change, suggests the power of history. In addition, most organizations seem obsessed with finding out what other organizations are doing in the pay area; they are constantly gathering and studying comparative pay rate and pay practice information. In my experience these data tend to be used as a check on what is "good" pay practice. There is an implicit assumption that if something is not being done by other companies, it probably is not worth doing and if it is, it is okay. Instead of trying to gain competitive advantage by doing different things, most companies seem happy to copy what other companies do and thereby to avoid being at a competitive disadvantage.

Ultimately, the wisdom of an organization's sticking with traditional pay practices—or, for that matter, adopting new practices—must be assessed by looking at the *results* that these practices produce. When all is said and done, pay practices are only as good as the impact that they have on organizational effectiveness. The tremendous amount of money that organizations spend on compensation needs to be carefully evaluated in terms of a cost-benefit analysis. A look at the annual reports of manufacturing companies shows that payroll expenses often account for 40 percent or more of the total cost of doing business. In the growing service sector, the number typically is much higher. What are the potential benefits of these costs?

I believe that pay systems can make a significant contribution to organizational effectiveness. If an organization makes the right choice, it can gain a competitive advantage through its reward system. This view is supported by considerable evidence showing that effective pay practices can produce a number of positive results (Lawler, 1981). Organizations do not have to settle for pay practices that simply minimize the dissatisfaction of employees and yield costs that are comparable to those of other organizations.

Pay programs can motivate employees to perform more effectively. They can create a culture in which people care about the organization and its success. They can provide the fringe benefits that individuals want in a cost-effective manner. They can attract and retain the kind of talent that an organization needs in order to be effective. They can encourage people to develop their skills and abilities in areas that will best aid the organization. Finally, they can create for an organization a cost structure that is realistic given the kind of environment that it faces.

Achieving the positive results that can come out of effective pay systems may require more than simply revising and improving the kind of traditional pay programs that corporations have operated for decades. The simple fact of the matter is that the approach to pay practiced by most U.S. corporations is deficient in many respects. It is an approach that in many situations has lost its applicability and effectiveness, because it is no longer in concert with the realities of organizational life in a globally competitive economy (Grayson and O'Dell, 1988).

What is needed is not just a new approach to merit pay or a better approach to job evaluation. Doing the old better is simply not good enough in most cases. Rather, what is needed is a set of fundamentally different approaches to conceptualizing and structuring pay systems, because the traditional practices do not score well when evaluated against the kind of results that a pay system should produce. They do not, for example, tend to motivate effective behavior. Rather than unifying the organization, they tend to split it into groups of people interested more in protecting their own jobs and perquisites than in improving the performance of the organization. They tend to attract and retain average to below-average performers while often alienating the best performers. They tend to produce high fixed costs, which make organizations inflexible and noncompetitive in the international marketplace. From a cultural point of view, they tend to produce hierarchical, rigid cultures with low levels of teamwork and cooperation. Finally, because they are so often based on surveys of what other organizations do, most pay systems have a vanilla, me-too flavor that provides no competitive advantage.

Research over the last twenty years has gone a long way in establishing the effectiveness in today's business environment of various new pay practices. Admittedly, many of the administrative details of these new pay approaches need further development, but it is not too early to specify their broad structure and to talk about how they can be implemented. Indeed, many of the new approaches are already being practiced by some of the best corporations.

Not every organization has been doing business as usual: two recent surveys of American business practices have found that a significant number of corporations are trying such "new" pay approaches as skill-based pay, gainsharing, and flexible benefits (O'Dell, 1987; Lawler, Ledford, and Mohrman, 1989). There also are organizations such as Herman Miller, Procter & Gamble, and Lincoln Electric, which have done a number of things right with their pay systems for a long time. In many ways we can learn more about pay practices from what has gone on in exemplary organizations such as these than we can from theory and research. Important new practices have been invented and developed by these pioneering companies.

Although these companies are a rich source of ideas and practices, simply copying their strategies is not the right thing to do. What works for them will not necessarily work for other organizations. Pay practices must fit how an organization is managed and structured and follow its strategic agenda. Thus the same pay practices are not right for all organizations.

The Traditional Approach

The traditional approach to compensation is based on a particular view of how an organization should be structured and managed. This view, often called the *bureaucratic model*, is based on a set of assumptions about the willingness of people to take orders and the effectiveness of a hierarchical, control-oriented approach to management. In this approach, which is well known to everyone who has worked in a large organization, much of the thinking activity is separated from the doing. Individuals at the top of the organization are assigned the task of conceptualizing and directing the overall activities of the organization. Most of the individuals in middle and lower management end up implementing those ideas and controlling the behavior of those at the lowest level of the organization. Finally, at the lowest level, individuals are assigned carefully prescribed, well-laid-out tasks that require little problem solving or thinking. They are expected to execute these tasks in a consistent, conscientious manner, with little use of their mental capacities.

Senior executives in the hierarchical approach tend to be paid extremely well. Charged with the overall direction of the organization, they have a great deal of responsibility. It follows that they deserve extraordinarily high levels of compensation and that their pay should be directly tied to the success of their organization. Their effectiveness is key to the competitive advantage of their organization in the marketplace. In large organizations senior executives are typically paid over $1 million a year (over fifty times more than the pay of the lowest-paid employees). Individuals in the middle are also seen as warranting high levels of compensation, because they have several levels of management reporting to them and are responsible for large budgets and large numbers of subordinates.

The lowest level of individuals are often also well paid in the

United States and western Europe—not because their work is particularly responsible, meaningful, or important, but because it takes that to get them to perform the work. People at this level are paid for their dissatisfaction rather than for their high levels of responsibility and performance. Their abilities to think, plan, problem-solve, and control are underutilized. They often do work that requires little talent or training. Thus, even though this work should perhaps be paid at a relatively low rate—as it is when done in such low-wage countries as Mexico, Malaysia, and China—the realities of the American economy dictate that it cannot be (Grayson and O'Dell, 1988). There are minimum-wage laws and, in many situations, active unions that bargain for relatively high wage rates.

Over the years wage rates have risen in such industries as automobile, glass, and steel manufacturing to the point where they are substantially above what individuals in much of the rest of the world are paid for doing the same type of work. For decades this did not place American companies at a serious competitive disadvantage, because the products involved simply could not be made elsewhere and/or the U.S. markets were not sufficiently open to outsiders to allow for serious international competition. Clearly, this has changed. In many industries the United States has been invaded by goods and, in some cases, services from abroad. Because of a combination of high wage costs and low performance effectiveness, American companies are often noncompetitive in the face of the invasion.

The simple fact of the matter is that most U.S. corporations—with their high wage and benefit costs and the current productivity levels of their workforce—simply cannot compete effectively. Something needs to change: either the performance of the organizations needs to improve radically or labor costs need to go down. The latter can be accomplished by devaluing the dollar and reducing wages through concession bargaining and unilateral wage cuts, but this means a lower standard of living. The preferable solution is to use pay to improve organizational effectiveness so that organizations can maintain their present wage rates and still be competitive. In many cases doing this requires more than simply administering pay programs better: it requires new, strategically appropriate approaches to pay.

One final word about the issue of the competitiveness of U.S. wages. For a long time the high wage structure in industries such as steel and auto manufacturing was not a problem, because all companies had the same high wage costs. Thus they were able to pass on the high wage costs in the price of the products they produced; in other words, the costs were borne by the consumer. The auto industry and the United Automobile Workers (UAW), for example, fell into a pattern of bargaining that ensured that no auto company would be at a competitive disadvantage because of its wage costs and work structures. The UAW essentially guaranteed that all companies would end up with the same wage structure. Thus, although no company gained an advantage over the others as a result of pay practices, none ended up at a disadvantage. This standoff was a satisfactory one for most U.S. auto companies until they began to meet foreign competition. Then, and only then, did they start talking about how their wage costs were dramatically out of line with what was going on in the rest of the world and how their pay practices limited their productivity.

Although they do not talk about it much, the problem for many U.S. corporations is much deeper than just the cost of hourly labor. Their compensation costs at all levels in the organization tend to be higher than those of their foreign competitors. In addition, their wage costs tend to be fixed, because they come primarily in the form of benefits and salary, while those of many of their competitors are variable. Japanese companies, for example, have low wages, but pay large bonuses. This allows them to reduce their labor costs without laying people off and causing the kind of workforce stability problems that are endemic to such cyclical industries as steel and auto manufacturing.

Finally, there is the issue of how much the workforce in bureaucratic organizations actually contributes to organizational performance. To the degree that workers are asked only to be a pair of hands, they are being underutilized in the workplace. The Japanese recognize this and involve their employees in problem-solving activities and work-improvement approaches. Clearly, this is happening in the United States too and represents a possible way to utilize employees that can justify the higher wages built into the U.S. political and economic structures (Lawler, 1986b). Ironically, the Japanese-owned and -managed auto plants in this country have been very effective in utilizing their American workforce. They seem to be able to pay standard U.S. wages and yet produce quality cars at a cost that is so competitive that the cars can be exported.

Societal Changes

In addition to the dramatically changed competitive situation that most U.S. corporations face, there are other changes that contribute to the outdating of the traditional approach to pay. The nature of the work in the U.S. economy has also changed dramatically. Not only has manufacturing declined and service work increased: even the *kind* of manufacturing that is done has changed considerably. Manufacturing today is much more complex. In some ways it could be described as *knowledge* work: many manufacturing employees are programming computers and monitoring production processes in remote control rooms. They are doing work that is a radical departure from employees shoveling coal into a furnace or standing at an assembly line doing highly repetitive tasks every few seconds.

The rate of change in the business environment has accelerated tremendously. There is no question that few products have long life cycles, and stable production and service processes are therefore disappearing. Today's organizations need to be able to adapt quickly and flexibly to a turbulent environment. This turbulence is produced by a number of factors, of course, including the global interdependencies that have appeared and the rapid advances in technology. The dramatic growth in the service sector has led to an ever-increasing number of workers doing work that is neither controlled by the pace of machines nor programmable in the sense of traditional production work.

The workforce has also changed dramatically, and it will continue to change (Johnston, 1987). It is much better educated than it was a decade ago, for example. Increasingly, the U.S. workforce has at least a high school education (and often a partial college education). In 1910 only 3 percent of Americans over the age of twenty-five had a bachelor's degree; by 1970 the figure was 11 percent; and by 1988, 20 percent. During the 1990s over one million Americans are expected to earn college degrees each year. Although there have been many questions raised about the quality of American education, everyone agrees that it is producing a large number of graduates who have high expectations about their careers.

Attitudes have also changed toward authority and control. Increasingly, today's workforce expects to have a say in decisions that affect them. They also expect that many of the democratic rights available in society will extend to the workplace, and in fact the legal situation has already changed to provide support for these rights. For example, it has given employees the right to sue when they feel wrongfully treated in organizational decisions that affect their employment status. This is particularly relevant to pay, because it means that many individuals can and may contest a pay raise, a promotion, or even an unfavorable performance review.

Finally, the United States workforce has changed its composition dramatically in ways that have strong implications for compensation. It is no longer a workforce made up of male heads of households. In fact, these represent less than 15 percent of the workforce. Today most women are in the workforce, and there are many single-parent families represented. Finally, the ethnic mix of the workforce has changed and will continue to change because of the influx of immigrants and minorities into the workforce.

In summary, the competitive situation faced today by organizations is dramatically different from the one faced by organizations just a few years ago. The workforce differs in terms of its expectations, skills, education, and background, and the very nature of the work that is done in most U.S. corporations is different. Given these changes, it is hardly surprising that the traditional approaches to management and pay are increasingly inadequate. What is needed in many situations is a new approach to management that includes new pay system assumptions and practices.

The New Management

The elements of a new management are already taking form and have been written about in such books as *In Search of Excellence* (Peters and Waterman, 1982), *Vanguard Management* (O'Toole, 1985), and *High-Involvement Management* (Lawler, 1986b). These books tend to agree that new approaches to management must be based upon employee commitment and employee involvement rather than upon top-down control. In terms of organizational functioning, this means decidedly less hierarchy, the making of decisions at the lowest level possible, and a greater emphasis upon employee development.

This new management approach also needs to include the ability to change rapidly and adapt to new environments and new technologies. It needs to be clearly focused on the external competitive environment so that organizations are constantly able to score themselves against both past performance and the outside environment. Finally, it needs to fully utilize its human resources so that it can be competitive in an increasingly difficult business environment.

This new approach to management clearly calls for some new approaches to compensation as well, simply because it calls for a different relationship between people and their work organization. As I have noted, many of the old compensation practices assume a hierarchical organization in which thinking and controlling are separated from doing. Once this assumption is abandoned, not only do managers need to behave differently, but many new pay and reward policies need to be developed.

Choosing a Pay Strategy

Even though the new management approaches are attractive to and successful in many organizations, they are not right for all situations. There are some kinds of organizations that are best managed in a traditional way, with traditional pay practices. Thus the challenge is to develop pay programs that support and reinforce the business objectives of the organization and the kind of culture, climate, and behaviors that are needed for the organization to be effective. As will be discussed next, this can be done if organizations begin with an analysis of the outcomes or results they need from their pay system and then develop a core set of compensation principles and practices that support these directions. The key is finding those approaches to pay that fit the organization's strategy and management style. As will be shown in the chapters that follow, this can be done by aligning the basic structure of the pay system with the way the organization is managed.

Pay system design is much like the design of a new building. The architect needs to start with an understanding of what the building will be used for. Once this is determined, some basic design decisions can be made about height, size, materials, and so on. In the case of a pay system, we also need to know what it is supposed to accomplish. Once this has been determined, we can make the basic design decisions and establish core principles. In the chapters that follow, we will first consider what a pay system can accomplish and then review the basic design decisions that need to be made.

Setting Strategic Objectives
for Pay Systems

The starting point for any reward system design process needs to be the strategic agenda of the organization. Once the organization has decided on its approach to gaining competitive advantage, then—and only then—is it possible to talk about the specifics of the reward system. Thus the first step in designing the reward system for an organization is to focus on the individual and organizational behaviors that are needed in order for the organization to be successful. Organizations that strive to be low-cost producers, for example, often need dramatically different reward systems than those firms that target leadership in technology. Organizations that have unrelated businesses and do not need to coordinate the performance of their different divisions need to take a different approach to reward system design than do organizations focused on one business.

In my strategic compensation system design work I focus on six areas in which the reward system impacts organizational behavior. We will want to look at each of these in order to develop an understanding of what impact pay and reward systems can have. Once this is clear, we can first consider how different pay system designs impact organizational effectiveness and then point to those practices that support particular strategies.

Pay Systems and the Individual

Motivating Performance. The vast majority of the literature on motivation strongly supports the view that rewards such as pay can have a significant impact (Vroom, 1964; Lawler, 1971). Study after study has shown that an effective pay system can increase the motivation of individuals to perform by as much as 40 percent (Nalbantian, 1987; Kerr, 1975; Blinder, 1990). Everyday observation also points to money as a motivator of performance: baseball players

13

perform better when their contracts are expiring than when they have just signed multiyear contracts; commission salespersons in retail stores such as Nordstrom sell more than salespersons in non-commission stores; and people change jobs, make investments, and break the law in big ways and small in order to obtain more money!

Even though there is evidence everywhere of the motivating power of money, it is not always easy to design a pay system that motivates performance. Indeed, designing one can be an extremely difficult process and is one that organizations often fail to execute effectively. Many organizations that talk about having a policy of pay for performance in reality offer little more than pay for seniority, and as a result they do little to motivate performance.

Let us look for a moment at what is required if an organization is to motivate performance. First and foremost, the organization needs to be able to identify and measure the performance that it wants to motivate. Performance in an organization can be measured in a number of different ways. It can be measured by the subjective views of others, for example, as it often is in performance appraisal systems. It can also be measured by hard operating results, as is often done at the executive level for the purpose of determining bonuses.

Performance can be measured at different levels of aggregation as well. The performance of individuals can be measured, or performance can be measured at the group, plant, or company level. These different approaches to performance measurement have very different implications for pay practices, as might be expected, and none is necessarily better than the others. The key issue concerns which is the best way to measure performance *given the strategic objectives of the business.*

Effective pay systems can use a wide range of these various performance measures. To be motivating, however, the measures must have certain characteristics: they must be seen as both credible and susceptible to influence by those individuals whose performance is being measured and whose pay is being determined. The "influenceability" of a measure is often referred to as *line of sight* or *line of influence.* Both terms capture the idea of an individual's being able to affect his or her performance measure through behavior.

Strategy should drive decisions about the kinds of performance to reward and about how to measure performance. Unfortunately, organizations do not always have the type of clear strategy that supports pay for performance. Several years ago I was asked by a bank to help put a group of branch employees on a pay-for-performance system. I was interested in the project because the branches were small and in many ways seemed to be ideal locations for group performance–based pay systems. The problem was that management did not know what kind of performance it wanted from the branch. Executives argued long and hard about the purpose of a branch in the bank's overall strategy but were never able to come to a decision.

One group saw each branch largely as a collector of assets and wanted to encourage an increase in deposits through checking accounts and other approaches that brought cash into the bank. Another group saw the branch as a profit-generating retail store that was to sell a variety of products. Another saw the branch as something of an albatross and simply wanted to reduce the operating costs; as these particular executives looked at it, there was no way that branch banking could be a profitable business for the organization. Given these widely divergent views of the role of a branch, it was impossible to design an effective pay-for-performance system. It simply wasn't clear what to measure and reward.

Sometimes the issues are not so much what to measure as how to measure it. In some work I did with a hotel chain, the issue was how to motivate employees to increase customer satisfaction and reduce operating costs. This seemed to call for measures that looked at cost per room night, customer satisfaction, and customer willingness to use the hotel chain again. Measuring cost was no problem, but measuring satisfaction and willingness to return was difficult. Finally we decided to use two survey instruments to measure customer satisfaction: we used the postcard checklists that are found in many hotels, and we mailed questionnaires directly to the customers. The purpose of the latter was to get more complete data and to check on the validity of the data coming from the returned postcards. In this case the measurement approach worked, and a successful bonus plan was created.

Identifying Valued Rewards. Once it has been decided what the strategically correct performance is and how it can be measured, the issue is identifying valued rewards. A reward system that does not offer something of significant value is unlikely to be effective, even though good measures are in place. There is nothing inherently valuable about many of the things that people seek in organizations. They are important only because they lead to other things or because of their symbolic value. A particular kind of desk or office, for example, is often seen as a reward because it is indicative of power and status.

Pay is important because it leads to other things that are attractive, such as food, job security, and status. If money were to stop leading to some or all of these things, it would decrease in importance. Pay is important to most people; but because it typically leads to a variety of other rewards and may therefore satisfy a variety of needs, it may be important to individuals for quite different reasons. This means that in order to understand how an individual will respond to a particular pay action, management must understand both how important pay is to the individual and why it is important. Finally, because it leads to such rewards as status, pay can remain important when the material needs of individuals are satisfied. For many individuals pay is a way to keep score and measure their success. This is an important point, because it refutes the often-made statement that once people's basic needs are satisfied pay is unimportant to them. The simple fact is that pay *can* remain important as a way to measure status and keep score.

Historically, one of the most frequently and hotly debated topics in the literature on motivation concerns how important different rewards are to employees. One group says interesting work is of utmost importance, while another argues that money is. Both groups, of course, are able to find examples to support their points of view, because for some people money is most important, and for others job content is most important. This confusion is compounded by the fact that some studies have found pay to be rated first in importance, while others have found it to be rated much lower (Lawler, 1971). These differences seem to be accounted for by a variety of factors, including how the research question is worded (for example, "high" pay is rated lower in importance than is "fair" pay) and the characteristics of the people who are asked (for example, their organizational and pay levels).

People differ substantially, and in meaningful ways, in regard to what is important to them. Some groups, because of their background and present situations, value extrinsic rewards like pay more than other groups. My earlier summary of the research on pay gave the following description of a person who is likely to value pay highly: "The employee is a male, young (probably in his twenties); he has low self-assurance and high neuroticism; he comes from a small town or farm background; he belongs to few clubs and social groups; he owns his own home or aspires to own it; and he probably is a Republican and a Protestant" (Lawler, 1971). On the other hand, there are people with different personal and background characteristics who typically value an interesting job more highly.

There is no exact formula that leads to specifying how valued a reward will be, but monetary value can give a good indication. In the case of cash, for example, a reward of $2,000 is always valued more than a reward of $1,000, although it may not be valued twice as much. Generally speaking, people value amounts of money in proportion to the amount that they and others receive (Varadarajan and Futrell, 1984; Giles and Barrett, 1971). The relative value of money was clearly illustrated by a comment made by Danny Cox, a baseball pitcher. Bemoaning his $600,000 salary, he is quoted in *Sports Illustrated* as saying, "Hopefully, I'll get a lot of wins and some big bucks in the future." Thus the common organizational practice of giving merit raises in percentages makes good sense, except that the amounts are usually too low. Evidence suggests that in order to be motivating, changes in pay ought to be 10 to 15 percent rather than the often-seen 2 to 6 percent. The simple fact of the matter is that an increase in pay of 2 to 6 percent generates little excitement for most individuals.

There are some other things that help determine how important a reward will be. For example, rewards that are in the public domain tend to be valued much more than those that are not. The reason for this is simple: rewards in the public domain have much more status value than do rewards that are secret. It is hard for people to receive acknowledgment from others if their good performance and rewards are secret.

A good example of a reward system that lost its impact because of secrecy is provided by one company I studied. They had a special award plan that gave very large amounts of money—as much as $100,000—to individuals for outstanding performance. The problem was twofold. First, no one knew about the program except for the reward recipients and a few executives; thus it was impossible for people to see a pay-for-performance relationship in advance of the reward. Second, the recipients of the reward were kept secret; they got no public recognition. The organization further reduced the motivating power of the program by asserting that no one could receive the reward twice. Thus, the only people in the organization who knew about this very costly reward were the ones who could no longer receive it. The result was that no one was motivated by the reward system, even though people who received the reward were pleased to have received it. This system, better than any other I have encountered, proves the point that a pay system can be rewarding without being motivating.

Scarcity is another factor that can contribute to the motivational importance of an award. The Nobel Prize, for example, is valued partially because it involves a large amount of money—over $400,000—but also, and perhaps more important, because it is a rare reward.

The Nobel Prize has another feature that contributes to its importance. The selection process is highly credible in the eyes of the recipients. Respected scientists and other contributors choose a winner in their respective fields and thus when individuals are honored by the program they are honored by people whose opinions they value.

In summary, the importance of rewards is a function of their monetary value—but much more. How the recipients are selected, the degree to which the rewards enter the public domain, and scarcity of the rewards all enter into determining their importance.

Relating Rewards to Performance. Individuals have to perceive a connection between their pay and their performance in order for any pay change to impact motivation (Lawler, 1973). Believing that pay and performance are related is an act of faith or trust, however. An individual must be willing to accept on faith that, when an organization promises a pay reward for a particular kind of performance, it will deliver on its promise.

Close timing of the tie between the reward and the performance can help make the relationship between the two clear and credible. Long delays between behavior and reward do little to clearly establish that there is in fact a relationship.

An extreme example of a slow reward system is provided by the federal government. In one particularly bad case three federal employees who won from $25,000 to $35,000 for cost cutting received the rewards eight years after they were initially considered. As one recipient noted, "Awarding the money so late is anticlimactic." Another noted that "you never know that you're going to get it. There's always uncertainty."

Delays can be a particular problem in organizations that give salary increases. Because of an organization's desire to slow down its spending rate, management sometimes stretches out the time between performance and reward substantially. Executives may justify this on the basis of wanting the reward to be large enough to make a difference—as if an 8 percent raise after two years is somehow more valued by individuals than a 4 percent raise after a year. Another justification for delay is the old argument that pay actions should be separated from performance reviews. As will be discussed later, the evidence fails to support this widely held view. In any case, programs that stretch performance reviews and "consequent" pay changes out over more than a year are unlikely to impact motivation.

In many respects an effective formula-driven pay-for-performance system is the most credible, because it is an automatic way to ensure that pay and performance are in fact related. The challenge in producing this kind of system, of course, is figuring out the right things to measure and developing a formula that will stand the test of time. The highly unstable environment that most organizations face today can make it extremely difficult to come up with a formula that will have long-term validity. Formulas that are frequently changed may have little credibility, because they raise questions about management's intentions and trustworthiness. Such instability is particularly problematic for an employee when changes are made after a good payment is received.

The credibility of the link between pay and performance can be enhanced by making information about the pay system public. In most cases openness contributes to trust; thus an organization that wants to establish the principle that pay and performance are related needs to be as open as possible about how the pay system works. Putting the system in the public domain allows individuals to do their own audit of how it operates. They do not have to rely on the all-too-familiar "trust me" assurances that accompany secret plans.

Of course, openness helps establish the credibility of a pay-for-performance system only when it in fact pays for performance. If, as is often true with merit-based pay systems that rely on subjective performance measures, little pay-for-performance connection actually exists, making the system public may harm its credibility. On the other hand, with formula-driven gainsharing and profit-sharing plans, openness is almost always necessary. Such plans produce a weak "line of sight" because they cover so many individuals. If in addition the details of how they work are kept secret, it is hard to imagine how they could be motivating.

Setting Performance Goals. One final factor needs to be considered in thinking about whether a reward system will be motivating. For a reward to motivate performance, the performance level that leads to the reward has to be seen as achievable. This might seem like an obvious point, but it is an extremely neglected one. The Nobel Prize, for example, is motivating only to the small number of leading research scientists and authors who feel that they can in fact win it. It is not motivating to most people—even, for example, to most research scientists—even though they would very much like to receive it. The problem is that they see no probability of receiving it; therefore, it does not impact their behavior. The same kind of problem exists with the reward systems in many organizations. In large organizations, for example, Nobel-like awards for outstanding achievement often fail to impact the behavior of most individuals simply because the awards are so far away from what they can aspire to. Most individuals have no chance to impact organizational results dramatically and therefore they are unlikely to be singled out for large rewards.

A more common example of why reward systems fail to motivate because of performance expectations exists in the area of sales quotas. Time after time I have studied sales programs that are not motivating, and one of the most common reasons is that the goals set are not realistic in the eyes of the salespersons. They agree that if they could accomplish the goals they would get the rewards, and that they want the rewards offered. Who wouldn't be happy to take the typical trip to Hawaii or Europe that goes to a sales incentive winner? The problem is that they often perceive that there is simply no way that they can achieve the necessary performance level given their territory, product line, pricing policy, and so on.

A somewhat different weakness exists in most profit-sharing and group bonus plans. Employees may believe that if the company achieves its profit goals they will get a payout, but they do not believe that they can influence the company's performance. Thus, like the salesperson with too high a goal, they do not feel that their day-to-day behavior can influence their pay; thus pay is not a motivator for them.

Motivation and Punishment. Finally, in talking about motivation in organizations it is important to discuss the issue of punishment, which can take many forms in addition to the obvious one of firing. Pay reductions, missed promotions, poor job assignments, and loss of power are just a few of the possible punishments that organizations can and do utilize. An individual's motivation to perform a task is influenced by the consequences of failure to perform it successfully. If the consequences of performing unsuccessfully are particularly negative, an individual may well decide not to try to tackle a given challenge even though the rewards for successful performance may be great. This point is particularly pertinent in organizations that say they want individuals to engage in entrepreneurial and risk-taking behavior.

Part of the secret of getting individuals to take risks concerns the upside of success—that is, the rewards for successful risk taking. The other part, however—which is equally important—concerns the consequences of failing to perform successfully. If the consequences for failing to perform successfully are severe punishment— for example, firing or a dead-ended career—individuals may decide not to take the risk even though the rewards on the upside are high. I remember well a series of interviews I did in a company that was concerned about the lack of entrepreneurial behavior on the part of its managers. Manager after manager told the same story: rewards for success were small and uncertain, while punishment for failure was fatal and sure. Not surprisingly, few individuals took big risks (Lawler and Drexler, 1981).

One organization that I worked with had a very interesting culture with respect to failure. Failing—"getting a bloody nose," as the firm called it—was an important part of demonstrating a willingness to take risks. That willingness was a precondition for promotion to senior management, because the organization wanted only "proven risk takers" in management. This particular firm has had an extraordinary growth record. In my opinion its success is at least partly due to a reward system that not only does not punish failure but actually rewards "good" failure.

Another good example of an organization that protects and rewards its risk takers is Minnesota Mining and Manufacturing (3M). It has a career track for individuals who are very successful as managers of new ventures. Both their pay and their security in the organization grow as they successfully manage new ventures. Thus individuals are rewarded based on a long-term track record rather than on the immediate success or failure of their most recent venture. This approach, which has allowed 3M to retain many of its better managers in entrepreneurial ventures and activities, is quite different from what all too often happens in large corporations: individuals seek the security of staff and management positions in well-established ventures because they know that it is risky to be associated with new ventures.

Motivating Skill and Knowledge Development. The reward system in an organization is one of the most powerful determinants of the kind of skills an individual will try to develop. Again, there is no "right" type of skill; rather, the key issue is developing the right mix of skills for a particular set of business objectives. An organization that is in a knowledge-work field needs a much different set of skills than an organization in a relatively simple service business such as fast-food or gasoline sales. The key, from a reward system point of view, is to develop a pay system that reinforces the development of the right skill mix. And the reward system needs to do this not just at the senior management level but at *all* levels in the organization.

The pay issues associated with motivating skill development are essentially the same as the ones associated with performance motivation. The key is to tie valued rewards in a credible way to the development of the right mix of skills. As we shall see in the discussion of skill-based pay in a later chapter, appropriate kinds of skills are very much determined by the management style used in the organization as well as the type of business it is in. An organization that is managed in a participative way needs very different skills than one that is managed in a top-down, autocratic way, just as a high-technology firm needs different skills than a relatively low-technology manufacturing firm.

The reward systems in most organizations have a strong, although somewhat unanticipated, impact on skill development. Traditional pay systems vary the pay rates of individuals based upon their position in the management hierarchy. Without question, the way to maximize income in most organizations is to rise to the top level of management. As was noted earlier, in large corporations the pay at the top level is often at least fifty times greater than it is at the bottom level. The impact of this pay gap is to encourage individuals to develop those skills associated with being promoted to higher and higher levels of management. This consequence—not necessarily good or bad—is often unintended and sometimes inappropriate. For example, it may not make as much sense in a high-technology or knowledge-work organization as it does in a traditional bureaucratic organization.

My point in focusing on skill development at this point is not to criticize the typically hierarchical organization but to stress that reward systems can be used to target and influence the skill-development activities in an organization. If an organization has a clear sense of its strategy, it can specifically target the kind of skills that the organization needs (Lawler and Ledford, 1985). It can go beyond simply paying people for the jobs they do; it can offer incentives that clearly develop the skills that will give the organization a competitive advantage in the marketplace. This need not cost more than the traditional approach to pay, and it can yield better results.

Fostering Attraction and Retention. The pay and reward system practices of an organization can have a major impact on the attraction of individuals to work for it and on the retention of those individuals. Just as pay and other rewards can motivate performance-oriented behavior, they can also motivate membership-oriented behavior. Simply stated, those organizations that offer the most valued rewards tend to have the best attraction and retention rates (Mobley, Hand, Meglino, and Griffeth, 1979; Mowday, Porter, and Steers, 1982; Mobley, 1982). While motivation is determined by changes in pay and their relationship to performance, the key issue in attraction and retention is the amount of total compensation and its position in the market. People make choices about where to work by comparing the rewards offered by different organizations.

Level of pay satisfaction is one indicator of how likely individuals are to leave a job. It turns out that people's feelings about the adequacy of their pay are based upon comparisons they make between their pay and that of others. It is more critical how their pay compares to the pay of others than what they make in absolute dollars and cents (Lawler, 1973; Adams, 1963; Adams, 1965; Lawler, 1968). When it compares favorably, individuals are satisfied and tend to remain in their jobs; when it compares unfavorably, they tend to be dissatisfied and look for ways to make more money.

There are two primary types of pay comparisons that individuals make: internal to the organization and external to it. Of these two, external market comparisons are most critical, because they are the ones that primarily determine whether an individual will leave the firm. If external comparisons are poor, an individual will usually leave as soon as he or she can find another job. If the external comparisons show that the individual's present pay is close to the external market, that individual is likely to stay. A good rule of thumb is that it takes at least a 10 percent pay increase to persuade someone to change jobs for pay reasons alone.

Even if internal pay comparisons are felt to be bad, an individual is not likely to leave an organization as long as the external comparisons are favorable. Thus the individual who complains that

others in the company are paid too much may not be ready to quit.
Rather, that employee will probably stay, continue to complain,
and/or try to do something to change the internal comparison (for
example, organize a union). Overall, then, dissatisfaction with external equity is usually a more severe problem than is dissatisfaction
with internal comparisons, although the latter can have negative
effects.

One final thought about pay satisfaction is in order here.
Sometimes it seems that individuals are never satisfied with their
pay, and to a degree this is true. Attitude-survey data from most
companies consistently show pay to be one of the least satisfying job
areas. Similarly, national survey data tend to show it as an area of
high dissatisfaction. One of the reasons for low pay satisfaction
seems to be that individuals seek out unfavorable comparisons. First
they look externally; if those companies are favorable, they then
focus on internal comparisons. Only if these are favorable as well
are they likely to feel satisfied. The range of comparisons internally
and externally is virtually limitless. If individuals cannot find an
unfavorable comparison with others doing their type of work, they
can always look to other types of work. For example, highly paid
baseball players not only compare their pay to that of other athletes;
they compare it to the pay of entertainers. Because so many comparisons are possible, it is very difficult to create high levels of pay
satisfaction.

Our discussion of pay satisfaction leads to an important
point about how organizations should interpret pay satisfaction
data collected from their employees. A finding that employees are
dissatisfied with pay is, in effect, a nonfinding. It is to be expected.
The key thing that the organization needs to focus on is whether
its employees are more dissatisfied with their pay than are employees in other organizations. If they are, the organization may
have a problem: such dissatisfaction is an indication that employees
are looking for jobs elsewhere, and they may find better-paying
ones. It is also important to focus on who is dissatisfied. In many
respects it is desirable to have a situation where the poorer performers are dissatisfied and the best are satisfied. This has the effect
of causing turnover among just those employees the organization
can afford to lose, the poor performers. Accomplishing this takes a

very effective pay-for-performance system because higher performers have to be paid much more in order to be satisfied with their
pay.

One recent study I did helps to highlight just how complex
and difficult it can be to influence pay satisfaction. I studied a
professional service organization that paid its employees almost
twice what other organizations paid for similar types of work. On
the surface it seemed that everyone would be satisfied with their pay.
Wrong! When interviewed, many employees mentioned unfavorable internal comparisons: "Joe doesn't perform as well as I do, yet
his pay is the same." Some even mentioned that they could make
more with other firms. When I asked what firms, they all cited
examples outside their industry. My conclusion was that if this firm
had a pay problem, it was that it paid too much.

There is some research that suggests that high pay rates can
lead to high motivation. However, motivation from this source
seems to be very short-lived. Most individuals quickly decide that
they deserve whatever pay rate they receive and do not try to perform
better in order to deserve it (Lawler, 1973). They tend to find something that justifies their pay—often the high pay of some other
person or group—and conclude that they are fairly paid. This
brings us back to the point that was made earlier about motivation:
it is the *anticipation* of high pay that is motivating. Thus an organization that pays well will not necessarily have a highly motivated workforce.

Because pay level in part determines turnover, there still may
be a payoff from the policy of being a top-notch payer. Such organizations as IBM and Hewlett-Packard have for a long time recognized that if they pay well, they will have very little turnover and
be able to pick from among a large number of job applicants.

The cost of turnover was graphically demonstrated to me a
few years ago during a research project for a semiconductor firm in
Silicon Valley. The organization prided itself on paying low wage
rates and yet still being able to fill its jobs. The problem with this
strategy was that the turnover rate approached 100 percent a year.
Further investigation revealed that many of the individuals who
quit went to work for IBM and Hewlett-Packard. They had joined
the firm we studied simply to get the kind of work experience they

needed in order to be eligible for jobs at Hewlett-Packard and IBM. This might not have been a problem except that training costs are high in semiconductor manufacturing, as are the costs of the poor quality that often results from having inexperienced employees. Thus, although the company was a low-cost producer from a wage point of view, it ended up as a high-cost producer overall and gained a reputation for poor quality. One executive estimated for us that each individual who quit cost the organization well over $100,000 in quality, training, and other costs. Despite this, the organization maintained its policy of being a low payer and eventually went out of the business.

A final word about the impact of selection on organizational performance. The research on selection clearly shows that for a selection process to be effective there need to be many more applicants than positions to be filled (Ghiselli and Brown, 1955). Thus even an organization that has *enough* applicants to fill its open positions is not in a good position to fill them unless it has enough applicants to allow it to choose carefully from among them. If all it has is a minimal number of applicants for a position, the most it can do is screen out a few extremely unqualified individuals and hope that, through training and other programs, it can get by.

Finally, it is important to comment on the costs of turnover. Study after study has shown that turnover is extemely expensive to an organization (Mirvis and Lawler, 1977, 1984). This is particularly true at the senior management level, where turnover costs are often estimated to run as high as twenty-five times the monthly salary. Costs are high for senior management positions because of the training time required and the cost of having an executive operating at less than peak proficiency while learning the job. Given these costs, it is not surprising that some organizations choose to pay top wages. Paying low wages, and suffering high turnover rates as a result, is often a penny-wise, dollar-foolish strategy. The strategic issue, of course, concerns just how expensive turnover is.

In a situation where individuals are easily replaced and there is little difference between the experienced and the inexperienced job performer, it may make sense to pay low wages and live with high turnover rates. One industry that has clearly chosen this approach is the fast-food industry. It pays low wages and has high turnover—as much as 300 percent a year—but it has worked to reduce its turnover costs by creating simple jobs that require minimum skills and little training.

An important factor in the issue of retention versus turnover is the question of *who* is attracted and retained by the organization. The type of people drawn to an organization is determined in part by how individuals are paid as well as by the mix of rewards that are offered. For example, an organization that offers a straight base salary with no chance for incentive earnings typically ends up attracting and retaining very different individuals than one that offers large amounts of incentive pay and stock. One need only look at the type of individuals who work in entrepreneurial ventures and those who work in large bureaucracies to get some sense of just how dramatic an impact the type of payment offered can have on who is attracted and retained by the organization.

Again, there are no right answers to the question of who should be attracted or retained by an organization. The issue very much depends upon the strategic objectives of the organization. A relatively stable, well-established organization may want predominantly to attract and retain individuals who are security-oriented and dislike a lot of risk in their rewards, while just the opposite can apply to an organization that is entrepreneurial in its objectives and strategy.

Basing rewards on seniority can help with the retention of individuals. Most large organizations base benefits and pay increases (often called "merit" increases) partially on seniority. The effect is to reward people simply for remaining a member of the organization. This in turn can produce a "familylike" culture; people spend their entire careers in the organization and expect the organization to look after them in return for their loyalty. This approach represents a good fit for organizations that need stability and are in a slowly changing business. It does not fit well in a more dynamic situation because the costs of retaining the wrong individuals by rewarding seniority rather than performance can be great. It worked well for AT&T during its years as a monopolistic telephone company, for example, but does not fit as well now that the company is in more competitive and dynamic businesses.

The degree to which an organization pays for performance

can very much influence the attraction and retention of good performers. As noted earlier, good performers require higher levels of reward than do poor performers if they are to be retained by an organization. A good performer's market value is simply higher than the market value of a poor performer. This is, of course, most dramatically apparent in activities where performance is highly visible to the outside world, as it is in sports, sales, and research jobs. In sports, for example, stars command a much higher market value (300 percent or more) than do most players even though they play the same position or fill the same job. This means that an organization that fails to pay effectively for performance runs the risk of losing its best performers to those organizations that do. On the other hand, it will rarely lose its poor performers, because they cannot do as well on the outside. Over the years this can have an exceedingly negative effect on the organization's performance; it leads to an organization of average to below-average performers.

To repeat, the issue of attraction and retention is not just an issue of turnover rates and number of job applicants; it is an issue of who is attracted and retained by an organization. An organization that does not do a good job of rewarding the individuals it needs to attract and retain can end up with the wrong mix of employees. Specifically, it can end up with employees who are poor performers and whose behavior does not fit the strategic objectives of the organization. Finally, a satisfied workforce is not necessarily a productive workforce, but it is likely to be a low-turnover workforce.

Pay Systems and the Organization

Influencing Organizational Structure. Pay and reward systems are not typically thought of as having a major impact on organizational structure. My experience and research, however, suggest that they strongly influence the structure of an organization. They do this because they influence the degree to which individuals in different parts of an organization are treated alike with respect to rewards. Reward systems that cover everyone in an organization and treat all people equally serve to integrate the organization. Those that treat individuals or groups differently tend to differentiate the organization and may cause individuals and groups to behave differently. Let us look at two examples that illustrate how reward systems affect integration and differentiation.

Organizations vary widely in the degree to which they are hierarchical in nature. Large bureaucracies, such as General Motors and AT&T, historically have had many levels of management, each with increasing demands, responsibility, and power. Their reward systems have reinforced this hierarchy in a number of ways. First and foremost, of course, they allocate more rewards to individuals at higher levels, helping to contribute to the power and desirability of those positions. But they also provide numerous visible perquisites and symbols of office for each succeeding level, reinforcing the incremental importance of each level. These perquisites are a constant reminder to subordinates that the person above them is more important and should be respected and listened to. Thus the distribution of rewards reinforces the basic organizational design, with increments in power and prestige assigned to each higher level in the organization. In effect, it differentiates the organization on a hierarchical basis.

Organizations also vary widely in the degree to which they are decentralized. Typically, those in a variety of businesses are decentralized, while those in single or multiple but related businesses are centralized. A reward system can contribute to integration or centralization just as it can contribute to decentralization or differentiation. For example, a pay system that dictates the same benefits, rates of pay, and pay practices throughout a corporation will contribute to an overall perception of organizational centralization; thus it can help produce a strong sense of corporate identity and integration. On the other hand, a reward system that allows different business units to develop their own pay practices and reward systems strongly differentiates the organization, creating a focus on the specific line of business for which the employee works. The same effect can occur when organizations develop different reward systems for different functions. For example, having different reward systems for sales, research and development (R & D), and production can differentiate those areas so that employees identify with and have their careers primarily focused on only one function.

These impacts of the reward system on centralization and on the degree to which the organization is hierarchically structured are just two examples of how the reward system influences structure. There are numerous other ways in which the reward system can help to reinforce or negate the intended structure of an organization. One of them deserves particular mention here: when organizations reorganize and ask individuals to pursue new strategic objectives, failing to change the reward system can hamper the change. All too often organizations expect dramatic changes in behavior because of an announced reorganization, when in fact the reward system is communicating to individuals that change is undesirable. The organization that fails to change the reward system often finds that the new structure and objectives are not implemented. The reason: individuals are still driven by the reward system that measures them on traditional measures and rewards them according to what they accomplish on those familiar measures.

For example, if a manager is asked to devote considerable energy to introducing a new product but is still measured on cost relative to volume, she may focus more on existing products and costs than on getting the new product up and running. Similarly, individuals who are asked to reorganize and reduce their staff may not be motivated to do this if the pay rate for their job depends on the number of subordinates that they have and the amount of budget that they control.

The right fit between structure and rewards can be found not in a single reward system practice or set of practices but in targeting the reward system to the kind of organizational structure and practices that are desirable from a strategic point of view. For example, if the strategy calls for an integrated organization with everyone focusing on common objectives, a common reward system is needed. If the organizational strategy depends upon very decentralized units maximizing their own performance effectiveness, each unit needs its own reward system.

Shaping Organizational Culture. The reward system has a strong impact on the culture of most organizations. The impact of rewards on culture is often most evident in the early days of the organization. The early rewards that are given and the early structures that are put in place cause beliefs to develop about what is rewarded in the organization, what is valued, how fair the organization is, how open it is, and how individuals are treated. Over time, reward system practices become an integrated part of the culture, and as a result they may be difficult to change.

In many cases the reward systems and cultures that develop in organizations are the product of the actions of a founder or an early leader. Some of my favorite examples include the impact of Tom Watson on IBM, the impact of Ken Olsen on Digital Equipment Corporation, and the impact of Fred Smith on Federal Express. All of these founders had strong views about how people should be rewarded in their organizations, and they put in place policies and practices that were congruent with their views. These policies and practices have helped shape the strong cultures of these organizations. IBM's policy of putting everyone on salary has helped create a culture in the organization that says there are no second-class citizens; every employee is expected to contribute in a mature, adult way. Digital's policy of giving stock options to people at all levels in the organization has helped create an egalitarian climate. It has also contributed to the view that everyone in the organization is expected to worry about doing the right thing and to try to make a significant contribution to the organization's performance. Federal Express has developed a culture of teamwork and commitment in part because of its egalitarian reward system.

In one organization I studied, pay secrecy was an important part of the culture. When I asked someone how the secrecy had evolved, I was told that it had been an unchallenged part of the culture since someone had asked the founder a question about pay practices during a management meeting. The founder had responded that he was not there to talk about pay and had walked out of the room—this marked the end of the discussion and the beginning of a culture in which pay is not discussible.

The reward system practices in large organizations are particularly prone to creating the feeling that the organization is highly bureaucratic and that individuals are cogs in the system rather than drivers of the organization. For example, job evaluation systems—with their many rules, scoring procedures, and review processes—often clearly send the message to employees that the system is more important than they are and that there is little they can do to make a difference in their pay. Similarly, the extremely hierarchical pay plans that are prevalent in large organizations can create a culture in which individuals greatly value getting to the top of an organization and see the organization as made up of different classes of employees rather than as a team of employees striving to improve the performance of the organization.

Another feature of an organization's culture that can be strongly driven by reward system practices is the attitude toward risk taking and entrepreneurial behavior. An organization that gives large rewards to risk takers tends to develop a culture that values and supports risk taking. An organization that severely punishes failures, on the other hand, tends to produce a culture in which individuals feel that big risks are too dangerous. Employees in such organizations tend to produce large volumes of defensive materials, support documents, and explanatory memos; in general, they operate from a position of fear.

Finally, some organizations pay well in the belief that doing so can contribute to an organizational culture of excellence. IBM, a good example of this, tells employees that they are well paid and that the organization expects excellent performance. Paying well does not guarantee a culture of excellence, of course; many well-paying organizations are seen as little more than country clubs and as operations that waste money and talent. On the other hand, an organization that pays well and places high demands on individuals often develops a strong culture of excellence. Employees believe that they are the best simply because they have been chosen to work for what they see as an outstanding organization—one that, in part due to high pay, does indeed have a chance to get the best employees. It is hard for anyone to make this argument in an organization that pays poor wages and has relatively few job applicants.

Changes in pay practices are often difficult to implement, because those individuals who have stayed with any organization have done so in part because they like the reward system. Thus, when somebody threatens change, much of the organization may be resistant. It is not that the new practices are necessarily worse; they may in fact be better from an organizational point of view. Rather, it is that the new reward system practices represent a whole new set of rules about how the game will be played, and this can be extremely threatening to individuals who have been winners under the old rules. As one AT&T employee commented when asked how he liked a new bonus plan designed to make AT&T more competitive, "I didn't sign up for this cruise ship." Those individuals who might have liked the new rules probably left years earlier, dissatisfied with the way the organization was being operated then.

The resistance of people to major reward system change was highlighted for me when I tried to help implement merit-based pay programs in the federal government. (When Jimmy Carter became president, he championed legislation that called for performance appraisals and merit bonuses for senior managers. The idea was to reward excellence and motivate better performance so that the government would be able to motivate, attract, and retain the best managers.) Although some managers worked with us to implement pay for performance, many strongly resisted. In hindsight this is hardly surprising. If they had wanted merit pay in the first place, they probably would not have gone to work for the government, notorious for its seniority-based pay. Most of those who did join the government, despite liking the idea of merit pay, probably left if they were good enough to land a job elsewhere. If they were not good enough to get a job elsewhere, they were probably fearful of merit pay because they were unlikely to prosper under it. Thus the typical manager was someone who either did not like the idea of merit pay or feared the consequences of it. Not surprisingly, the effort to change the merit-based pay programs failed.

The other side of the change coin is that if a major pay system change *can* be accomplished, it often dramatically changes the culture of the organization. Because pay change is an important and high-leverage intervention, it can be a good place to start a change process despite the difficulties (Lawler, 1973). As will be discussed later, gainsharing plans, skill-based pay plans, and a host of other pay practices can play an important role in cultural change efforts.

Meeting Cost Objectives. As was mentioned earlier, payroll costs are significant in most organizations; therefore, it is critically important to think of them strategically. Specifically, it makes sense to consider how the labor costs of an organization compare with those of its competitors and how an organization can control its labor costs (Weitzman, 1984; Kerr, 1985; Kerr and Slocumm, 1987; Gomez-Mejia and Welbourne, 1988). Most strategies try to position labor costs so that in the worst case they do not put an organization at a competitive disadvantage and at times may even give it an advantage. It is important to note, however, that this does not always mean that wage costs per employee need be lower than those of a competitor. The key issue is labor costs relative to the volume and quality of the products or services produced.

It may even be possible to lower labor costs by paying more to each employee! As will be discussed later, this has been done in many new plants that pay people for their knowledge and skills rather than for the job they do. These plants tend to operate with lower numbers of individuals, and as a result they end up with lower total labor costs even though they pay higher wages to each individual. In essence, they end up with lower total costs because they get more performance out of each individual.

Control over labor costs is a particularly important factor in determining how well a pay system supports organizational objectives. Traditionally, American companies have paid people largely in terms of fixed fringe benefits and cash compensation. Annual increments have adjusted the total amount of pay to fit performance, seniority, and market conditions, but radical changes in an individual's pay rate have not been possible, because past increases become annuities. In addition, the percentage of most organizations' total pay costs that is committed to benefits has increased over the years; now benefits account for a major part of total labor costs. In large corporations benefits typically run at least 35 percent of cash compensation (and in some cases exceed 50 percent).

In highly stable industries and in growth situations, a fixed-cost approach may be defensible. This approach has real problems in cyclical businesses, however, because it makes it difficult for an organization to reduce labor costs when the revenue is not there to cover them. Typically, organizations handle this by laying individuals off or assigning shorter hours. This reduces labor costs, of course, but it has severe negative consequences for the commitment of an organization's workforce, the stability of the workforce, and the productivity of the organization.

In some cases it clearly makes sense to strategically structure pay plans such that they vary the labor costs of an organization according to its ability to pay. This flexibility can allow an organization to avoid layoffs, and the negative consequences associated with them, while at the same time reducing its labor costs to meet its ability to pay. There is no right or wrong answer here. The key consideration is the business situation in which an organization operates. If it finds itself needing to adjust its labor costs significantly and regularly, it may need to put in place an overall labor-cost structure that is quickly and immediately responsive to changes in its ability to pay. Stable organizations that do not have to cope with rapid, frequent changes in their ability to pay do not need to have variable labor costs.

Conclusion

We will consider pay system design issues next. Before we do so, however, it is important to once again stress that the design process needs to start with the organization's business strategy, as translated into pay system objectives. Without establishing strategic objectives in areas such as the kind of behaviors to be motivated, the kind of people to be attracted and retained, and the type of structure that an organization wants to operate with, it is impossible to design a reward system that adds value to the organization. The most that can be hoped for without strategic objectives is a neutral reward system—one that does not get in the way of the organization's effectiveness.

Even neutrality may be difficult to achieve, however, in the absence of a thorough analysis of the strategic direction of an organization. The very fact that rewards are being given causes behavior to change and impacts the effectiveness of the organization. Even the systems that appear the most neutral—such as ones that simply pay everybody doing the same job the same amount—are not neutral. Such systems affect an organization's ability to motivate, attract, and retain good performers; they send a clear message about what is valued and what rewards an individual can expect to secure. Thus it is very important to focus on the intended results of the reward system before the design process begins.

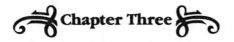

Chapter Three

Establishing Core Principles

The strategic management of pay requires the design and building of a basic reward structure. Creating this structure involves deciding how the organization will position itself on key reward system issues. Decisions about the structure of the reward system should take the form of core principles that indicate how the organization intends to operate. As was indicated earlier, I like to compare the development of a reward system structure with the decisions involved in designing a building. The decision making needs to begin with the purpose of the structure—in the case of a building, what it will house; in the case of a pay structure, what type of business strategy it should support.

Once the basic purposes of a structure have been decided upon, consideration needs to be given to two factors: the environment in which the structure will be placed and affordability. In the case of buildings, this process involves looking at land availability, local codes, budget, and a host of other issues. In the case of pay systems, it involves looking at competitors, the business environment, the legal environment, and affordability.

The next design step is to make some basic decisions about the characteristics of the structure. Is it going to be a high-rise or a bungalow? Is it going to be open, with office "landscaping," or is it going to have interior walls? What size is it going to be? Once those basic design decisions have been made, details of how the space is laid out, decorated, and utilized can be decided. In the case of reward system design, the basic decisions involve pay for performance, setting base pay, market position and pay comparisons, the role of benefits, and process issues concerned with communication and decision making. These issues are basic to the structure of any reward system and need to be decided upon before specific practices are chosen. Pay practices are important, but they need to be driven by basic decisions about how the organization wants to position itself. These decisions are best expressed in the form of a statement of core principles. These statements are intended to be used as a basis for developing specific pay programs and practices.

Managing Beliefs

Reward systems affect organizational performance and individual behavior largely through the impact that they have on people's beliefs and expectations about how they are and will be rewarded. Expectations are particularly important in influencing motivation, but they also have an important influence on organizational culture, the ability of an organization to attract and retain the right members, and organizational structure. In order to be effective, a pay system must impact perceptions and beliefs in ways that produce the desired organizational behaviors.

The perceptions and beliefs that individuals develop are partly a product of the practices and behaviors of the organization, but they are also influenced by the statements that an organization makes—or fails to make—about its values and intentions. Regardless of what an organization says or does not say about its reward practices, individuals will form beliefs about how rewards are administered. They develop these beliefs after considering their experiences with the organization, what they are told by others, and what they are told by the organization. Individuals try to make sense out of their world so that they can develop action plans to cope with it. In the world of business, coping means developing a satisfying and rewarding work situation for oneself.

If the organization is silent in terms of what it is doing, it may cause individuals to develop less functional beliefs than they would have if the organization had stated principles that effectively guided individual beliefs. The key issue from an organization's point of view is how it can influence the beliefs that individuals develop.

When I interview the members of an organization, they often tell me what they think the core principles of the organization are. Often these are negative: "There's no pay for performance," "Pay for performance is a joke," "This is a low-paying organization,"

"They try to keep benefits low," "Nobody ever gets ahead here," "The organization always looks for a chance to screw you," and "They're always trying to save a dime." These negative views are often held and stated even in organizations that deserve a more positive image in the eyes of their employees—that is, even in organizations that pay reasonably well and have sound pay practices.

The problem is that organizations often fail to do a good job of explaining their pay practices. At times—in meetings about changes in benefits, for example—they talk about the details of their pay practices, but they rarely talk about the overall commitments that guide individual pay practices. The result is that individuals make their own sense out of isolated actions. In most cases, the sense they make creates a more negative perception than is warranted. It is not inevitable that this negativism will develop: it happens only when organizations fail to develop an effective communication system based on firm commitments to principles of reward administration.

Once the statement of core principles of reward administration is developed, it should drive and guide the reward system practices of the organization and be a relatively permanent piece of the organization's culture, history, and policies. The principles should not change, except in those extraordinary circumstances where major strategic changes need to occur in the way the organization is managed and run. Once they have been established, they should be frequently and publicly stated by the organization, communicated on every possible occasion.

There are some good examples of organizations that over the years have effectively communicated their core principles. IBM, for example, first communicates its beliefs on pay and how the organization rewards employees when an employee applies for work, and then regularly thereafter. Similarly, Hewlett-Packard has supported its profit-sharing plans with regular communications. One Hewlett-Packard manager told me that the company has developed over thirty ways to state the principles that underlie the profit-sharing plan and to communicate the operating characteristics of the plan.

The core reward system principles that an organization develops should represent a standard for the organization—that is, the organization should always test its behavior against them. They are something that the organization gives to the employee that allows the employee to trust and depend upon the reward system commitments of the organization. Individuals should feel that they can count on these principles' remaining in place until the organization makes major strategic changes clearly demanded by large business and environmental changes.

Developing Core Principles

Now that I have argued that core principles are an important part of an organization's reward system, we need to look at where they should come from. There are two major factors that should influence the core principles of an organization: the business strategy of the organization and the core values of the organization. Given what has already been said about the strong impact of strategy on the appropriateness of reward system practices, it follows that strategy ought to drive the development of the core principles. For example, if the organization wants to emphasize a strategy that calls for teamwork and flexibility, the core principles need to call for rewards that are based on these behaviors. Similarly, if the strategy calls for a great deal of entrepreneurial behavior, the reward system needs to state a strong commitment to giving rewards to individuals who take significant risks and succeed.

Less obvious, but in many cases equally important, is the point that reward system principles need to take into account the core values of the organization. Relatively few organizations have done a good job of developing and stating core values, but those that have have profited handsomely from doing so. For example, Digital, Federal Express, Procter & Gamble, Johnson & Johnson, Nordstrom, and others have stated values not only about how they will deal with their employees but how they will deal with their customers. These values are important in times of crisis as well as in guiding individual and organizational behavior on a day-to-day basis. Sometimes these core values make direct statements about the reward system and how it will be administered. In these cases, of course, the implication for the reward system principles is direct and clear. In other cases, the core values are not directly related to the reward system but still need to be considered in establishing the reward system principles.

A good example of a core value that has direct implications for the reward system comes from Digital. An important core value of that organization is that social distance between people at different hierarchical levels in the organization should be minimized. In other words, the firm is strongly opposed to any organizational practice that differentiates individuals in terms of organizational level. Thus the reward system at Digital has a core principle that rules out organizational level as a driver of the perquisites, benefits, and status symbols an individual receives.

In much of the work I have done, core reward system principles have been developed by task forces that represent key individuals and groups in the organization. Typically, these task forces come from multiple levels and functions in the organizations. I find that the task of developing principles that will guide the reward system for at least the next twenty years is a challenge that most individuals are eager to take on. It typically takes a group at least six months of work, however. Participants must develop a good current understanding of the business strategy of the organization and debate long and hard its implications for the reward system.

The desired product of such a task force is a relatively short list of principles that can be widely distributed and easily understood by everyone in the organization. Surprisingly, it is often more difficult to get a short list than a long report. The fact of the matter is, however, that a short list is much more useful than a long polemic. Principles can be easily communicated; long documents cannot be. Exhibit 1, which outlines core principles for Honeywell developed in the early 1980s, shows the results of one such task force with which I worked. A much shorter list of core principles was developed by Dow Chemical in 1988 (see Exhibit 2).

Key Core Principle Issues

There is no magic number of core principles needed by an organization, nor is there a definitive list of issues that core principles

Exhibit 1. Honeywell's Pay Philosophy.

Honeywell is one company made up of many different businesses. These businesses are united by a common set of values and by common technologies. Yet they differ in respect to their products and services, size, customers, locations, and competitors.

The company's pay philosophy reflects who Honeywell is—both its diversity and its unity. It allows each individual business to design pay systems responding to that business's own requirements. It also means that each system must contain certain assurances of Honeywell employment. These assurances are expressed as four basic pay objectives and four basic pay principles.

Pay Objectives

These objectives are the products of Honeywell's management philosophy. They apply to all Honeywell pay systems.

- To attract the best person available for each Honeywell job.
- To encourage growth both on an individual basis and as a participant on a work team.
- To recognize the importance of high-quality work performance and to reward it accordingly.
- To encourage a career-long commitment to Honeywell.

Pay Principles

In support of these objectives, four basic pay principles also apply to all Honeywell pay systems:

- First, pay must be fully competitive in the market, as defined by each business.
- Second, each individual's pay must be fair in relationship to the pay other employees receive within the same Honeywell business.
- Third, pay must be communicated. That communication must explain general pay principles, the specific pay system applicable, and the process used to determine individual levels under that system.
- Fourth, each Honeywell business has the basic responsibility for establishing and maintaining its own pay system.

Source: Reprinted by permission of Honeywell.

must address. There are, however, some critical areas that demand attention when core principles are being developed. These are areas in which beliefs almost inevitably develop, regardless of what the organization does. In the absence of well-developed core reward system principles in these areas, informal beliefs develop and are

Exhibit 2. Dow's Corporate Compensation Philosophy.

We intend to provide our employees with a career opportunity that can be more financially rewarding than our competition. Making the most of that opportunity is largely dependent on the employee's contribution to Dow's success.

We will provide compensation that is responsible to, and reflective of, the quality of performance of both our employees and our business.

In managing our compensation programs, we will look at total compensation—base pay, variable pay, benefits, and postemployment compensation.

We will provide compensation that is appropriately competitive with various industries and employers with whom we compete for human resources.

Our compensation programs will be developed in the context of national economic and social conditions.

Our programs will always be in conformance with applicable laws and regulations.

Source: Reprinted by permission of Dow Chemical.

communicated throughout the organization. They often gain high levels of stability and acceptance—in effect, becoming part of the organization's culture. Let us look at these areas and discuss some of the strategic issues that are involved in setting core principles in each.

Pay for Performance. In the United States and western Europe, the issue of pay for performance is almost always front and center when it comes to establishing what an organization stands for in the area of pay and rewards. Virtually every major U.S. corporation states a core principle of pay for performance—it supports virtually any business strategy and it feels so right. In addition, research in this area clearly shows that individuals believe that pay for performance is a good idea (Lawler, 1966; Yankelovich and Immerwahr, 1983). They do not have a strong preference with respect to the kind of pay for performance they receive, however. Research also shows that individuals usually see a significant gap between the degree to which they *want* to be paid based upon their performance and the degree to which they *are* (Lawler, 1966). Simply stated, most organizations fall far short of fulfilling this core principle. In later chapters we will discuss why this typically happens. The point here is simply to identify the issue as one that needs to be dealt with by a core principle.

A good set of reward system core principles usually goes beyond simply saying that pay for performance is the organization's policy. It also says something about what kind of performance is rewarded. For example, is it individual performance, plant performance, or total organizational performance? The Dow Chemical principles, for example, mention both individual performance and business performance. Organizations such as Donnelly Mirrors and Herman Miller, which for a long time have based pay on organizational performance, have a strong commitment to individuals' sharing in the performance of the organization. This commitment fits well with their organizational core values, which stress participation, involvement, and equity. Hewlett-Packard and Lincoln Electric have traditionally emphasized both pay for individual performance and pay for organizational performance. IBM, which places strong emphasis on individual pay for performance, stresses the importance of the performance appraisal and has regular and thorough performance appraisals as an important part of its pay-for-performance system. This fits well with IBM's core values, which stress individual accountability and responsibility.

In summary, dealing with pay for performance is a must. The most effective principles go beyond the simple statement that the organization is committed to pay for performance; they reflect the business situation, the core values, and the management style of the organization. When done well, a core principle in the area of pay for performance can indeed help to cement the belief that pay is performance-based, which in turn can produce positive effects in the areas of motivation, attraction and retention, and culture.

Basis for Pay. Because in most U.S. organizations pay structures are job based, the first step in determining an individual's pay typically involves an assessment of his or her job. If this is true it needs to be stated in a core principle. The principle should also state what determines the relative worth of jobs. The alternative to basing pay on the characteristics of jobs is to base it on the characteristics of individuals. Performance is only one of several characteristics that can play a role. In some cultures age plays a major role because it is valued. As will be discussed in later chapters an intriguing possibility is to base pay on the skills an individual has. Many organizations do this in some situations (for example, R & D labs) but don't make it a core principle. In certain types of organizations it may make sense to do it for all employees and to make it a core principle. It particularly makes sense for organizations that are critically dependent on a skilled workforce and those that require a highly flexible workplace. If this approach is chosen a core principle is needed that stresses paying employees on the basis of the skills they have.

Market Comparisons. A second major area in which it is important to have a core principle is market position. The issue here is essentially how well an organization rewards its people relative to other organizations. It is important to avoid meaningless phrases such as "pay the market," "match the competition," or "be a good payer." What is needed is an effective stake in the ground with respect to how well people will be paid.

Principles concerning market position are particularly important in managing perceptions. There is no doubt from the research in this area that people have a tendency to see their own pay as worse than that of others, even though they may be relatively well paid (Lawler, 1971). This tendency results in part from the information vacuum that most employees are in. In the absence of complete data, they tend to see and hear about only the most favorable pay conditions in other organizations. They hear about individuals who leave their positions for higher-paying jobs elsewhere, for example, often not taking into account the need of the hiring organization to pay a little extra to get someone to leave a good job. They also tend to hear about those in their own organization who get large raises or high starting salaries.

The issue of market position is complicated by the problem of defining the market. It is important that this definition be clear and that the resulting choices about market position be driven by considerations of what the organization can afford. Let me illustrate this point with some consulting work that I did with a manufacturing organization that opened two new plants in the 1970s.

One was in a southern city and the other was in a heavily unionized northern city. Management in the southern city said that employees in the plant would be paid at the top of the local market. This translated into being one of the top three firms on a year-to-year basis. Management in the northern city said that employees would be paid comparably to unionized employees in other company locations.

As a general rule, over the next ten years the company lived up to these core principles and did a good job of communicating to employees just how well they were paid. Several unusual things were done to facilitate communication and to assure the credibility of the pay practices. Salary surveys were done by nonmanagement task forces that reviewed the data from other organizations, and meetings were held to communicate competitive salary data to all employees.

Because of market differences, the employees in the southern plant were paid much less than those in the northern plant. Ironically, though, they ended up being better satisfied because they were paid as well as or better than others in their local market; for them this represented a fair pay level. The individuals in the northern plant were much better paid than other manufacturing employees in the local market, but they were not satisfied. They compared themselves to unionized company locations that paid high wages, and they were constantly concerned about keeping up with them. Keeping up proved difficult because pay rates at the northern plant were progressing at an extremely rapid rate and putting it at a competitive cost disadvantage when compared to the southern plant.

Ultimately, then, the organization ended up in the ironic position of paying more in the north but getting less satisfaction there. It has always been my belief that if management in the northern plant had established a core principle that stated that employees would be paid as well as the local community's wage rates, they would have been satisfied with lower pay rates.

The kind of comparison that should be made to determine market pay rates for managers is also a crucial issue, and one that will be discussed further in later chapters. At this point I simply want to note that this comparison can, over the years, make a big difference in both how fair individuals feel their pay is and how much an organization spends on its compensation. The simple fact of the matter is that some industries pay more than others, and organizations that try to match the best companies in *all* industries may end up in trouble if they happen to be in a relatively low-wage industry.

Some companies go beyond saying that their wages will be competitive; they say that they will be among the best-paying companies or even be *the* best-paying company. Large corporations such as Hewlett-Packard, IBM, and Exxon, for example, have taken similar stances, as have small growth companies such as Apple and Sun Microsystems. There are some obvious competitive advantages in doing this, particularly in the area of attraction and retention.

Taking a leading position in compensation and publicizing that lead can contribute to an organization's being seen as the best company to work for in the industry. This desirable effect can discourage individuals from looking elsewhere for work, because they perceive it as unlikely that they will find a better-paying situation elsewhere. It can also, of course, dramatically increase the number of applicants that an organization has, because people are attracted to better-paying situations. Finally, it can lead to the feeling among employees that the organization demands the best, gets the best, and will tolerate only the best. In short, it can lead to a culture of organizational excellence and command significant respect for the organization.

There is a major problem with implementing a strategy of being a leading payer, however. In most industries more than one company usually attempts this strategy, although only one can be the best. Thus implementing it can be difficult and expensive, while failing to implement it can be seen by employees as breaking faith with an important commitment.

One final point about market position. A few organizations—TRW is the best example I know of—have clearly defined market position strategies that relate to their performance as an organization. In essence, these firms state that their market position will reflect their organization's performance. They promise that when organizational performance is better than the competitors', the total pay of individuals will also be better; on the other hand, when their performance is worse than the competitors', total pay will reflect this.

This interesting core principle is a partial resolution of a problem that organizations have with respect to pay-increase budgets. Pay-increase budgets in many organizations are cut back in times of economic difficulty, but they rarely increase in times when profits are high. This tends to lead to considerable mistrust on the part of the employees concerning what will lead to their being treated in an above-market way. A core principle that states that organizational performance is the key driver deals with this.

Internal Comparisons. Individuals have a strong tendency to compare their pay with the pay of others in their immediate work location. Research on equity and social comparisons shows that this is the first comparison many individuals make (Adams, 1965). Organizations need to think long and hard about how important they want internal comparisons to be and how broadly they want comparisons to be made within the organization. Many organizations do stress internal equity in their core principles, stating that pay rates will be guided by this factor. Practically, this often means that individuals anywhere in the organization doing similar work are paid equally. Extensive internal equity comparisons may be made through the use of job evaluation technology to be sure that comparable pay levels exist across the total organization. As we will see in later chapters, the issue of internal equity is a crucial one in determining the overall cost structure of an organization and has clear implications for the kind of pay practices that an organization adopts.

The alternative to a strong commitment to internal equity is a commitment to external equity. That is a commitment that stresses to individuals that their pay will be based upon what individuals in other organizations are paid rather than on what goes on elsewhere within their own organization. In the extreme, this may involve arguing that jobs in the immediate work area are not relevant comparison points for determining what a job is paid. The only driver in this extreme case becomes the external market.

The key decider between an internal and an external equity orientation should be organizational structure and strategy. For example, an external strategy fits particularly well in those organizations that operate a series of unrelated businesses and develop a differentiated approach to pay. Internal equity, on the other hand, generally fits best when an organization is in a single, integrated business. Finally, an organization making the equity decision needs to consider the core values of the organization and weigh how important the organization feels it is to have one set of practices and a single organizational culture.

Benefits. Because benefits account for such a large portion of an individual's total compensation in most U.S. corporations, it is important that any statement of core compensation principles address them. As in other areas, there is no "right" core principle with respect to benefits, but let me say something about what individuals are concerned about in the area of benefits. Typically, they worry about the adequacy of the safety net provided by their benefits and how this safety net compares to that of other corporations. They are also concerned about the degree to which individuals in the organization get differing levels of benefits. Thus the issue of whether moving up the hierarchy leads to more benefits is important, as is how the overall benefit level in the organization compares to that of other companies.

Some organizations take a strong stand, committing themselves to benefit levels that at least equal those of other corporations. This commitment can certainly play an important role in attracting and retaining people—particularly those who value benefits. It plays into people's need for a sense of security as well as the organization's desire to be a responsible corporate citizen and to see that its employees are looked after well. In short, it fits a set of core values that emphasize long-term employment relationships, stability, and concern for employees. It fits a strategy that calls for a stable group of employees and fixed labor costs. On the other hand, it does not fit a strategy that calls for short-term employment relationships, flexible labor costs, high levels of entrepreneurial behavior, and large amounts of pay at risk. Thus, Apple Computer, which wants to retain an entrepreneurial spirit, has no retirement plan.

An interesting alternative to fixed benefit levels, to be discussed in detail in Chapter Eleven, is the use of flexible or "cafeteria" benefits (Gifford and Seltz, 1988). In these plans organizations commit to giving individuals a choice in how their benefit dollars are spent. This can move the organization away from a paternalistic relationship and toward a supplier-customer relationship in which employees are expected to make important and intelligent decisions about their benefits. This approach fits well with a general set of core values that emphasize employees being responsible, mature adults who manage their own careers and personal lives.

Process Issues. Communication and decision making are important parts of the reward system practices in any organization. Organizations vary widely in the degree to which they openly communicate with employees about the reward system. An often-unspoken core principle in many organizations is that pay and everything about it will be secret. For example, some organizations fire individuals for talking about their individual pay raises, and others strictly forbid employees from gathering and distributing data about their company's pay practices. A few organizations at the other extreme openly distribute salary information and encourage employees to talk about it.

Decisions concerning pay systems can be made in either a top-down or a participative manner. As will be discussed later, there are some definite advantages to making pay decisions participatively. Historically, most decisions have been made top-down, but change is occurring (Lawler, Ledford, and Mohrman, 1989; O'Dell, 1987); increasingly, organizations are adopting participative decision-making practices. For example, representative task forces are being used to design pay systems. Employees are also getting more involved in operating decisions. In some skill-based plans they evalute each other's skills in order to determine raises, and they participate by conducting salary surveys. In organizations adopting these participative practices, openness exists in order to facilitate employee involvement. Without openness it is hard for employees to participate in decisions concerning pay.

There is no right or wrong answer to how participative and open pay system decision making should be. Organizations can operate effectively at either extreme on openness and participation.

The important issue is whether individuals have a clear picture of what they can expect and what is okay in the organization. This, of course, is why core principles need to be stated.

In many cases what happens in this area is less the product of an organization's business strategy than the product of the core values of the organization and its management style. Organizations committed to openness and participative decision making inevitably seem to end up practicing openness and participation in the area of pay in order to be consistent. Similarly, organizations that are not generally participative are rarely open and participative in the area of pay practices.

Due Process. Many organizations have a core principle concerning due process in reward system administration. This principle typically commits the organization to providing internal appeal and review processes concerning individual grievances about pay administration. This means going beyond existing legal requirements (simply having a principle that says the organization will live up to legal requirements is a nonprinciple) and providing an effective internal hearing system that individuals feel can be safely used.

A core principle concerning due process is not an absolute necessity, but in the highly legalistic climate of the United States it is hard to argue against it. It makes sense from a legal point of view, and it also makes sense from an employee relations and cultural point of view. Those organizations that have strong commitments in this area usually have them because they have a core value focusing on employee rights. Polaroid, for example, has a long history of providing individuals with meaningful chances to have their complaints heard and resolved. Admittedly, sometimes these "values" exist in order to prevent the formation of unions, but they often simply reflect management's desire to be fair and reasonable in dealing with employees.

Overall, due process is an area in which most organizations should make a strong statement. It is also an area in which society virtually demands practices that protect individuals from unreasonable behavior on the part of supervisors, pay administrators, and others in positions of power. Organizations are subject to legal

penalties if they are guilty of discrimination and other unfair actions. It makes sense to resolve issues internally instead of letting
them become the subject of court actions.

Fit Between Core Principles and Practices

The development and communication of a set of core principles by
an organization is merely the very first baby step toward having an
effective reward system. Indeed, it may be a step backward if subsequent steps are not executed effectively. The key to success is easy
to state but often hard to execute. Essentially, the core principles
must drive the practices and policies of the organization. If they do
not—that is, if there is a significant discrepancy between the core
principles of an organization and its policies and practices—the
organization may be worse off because of its development and statement of core principles. In essence, it has committed itself to something that it has not delivered. The result of this failure may be that
the management of the organization loses its credibility, the trust
that the organizational members have in the organization is decreased, and it becomes more difficult to deal with employees on
other issues.

A classic example of organizational failure to live up to
stated principles concerns pay for performance. As was mentioned
earlier, organizations almost always claim that they pay for performance. In reality, however, most organizations either do not do so
or do a very poor job of it. I think that a good case can be made
that firms that fail to pay for performance are worse off if they have
a stated core principle in this area. If they had not committed to
paying for performance, the absence of such payment would not be
such an irritating and visible sign of low credibility.

The basic point is a simple one but one that is easily violated.
Stated in the terms of a number of the organizations that I have
worked with, it is this: "Walk like you talk" or "Do what you say
you're going to do." In an organization that fails to execute what
it commits to, future commitments have less impact and management loses its ability to lead and influence the organization. Thus,

although developing core reward system principles can be power-fully positive, it does have a downside. Failure to implement and act upon the principles stated moves the whole activity from the positive category to the negative category. It is better to have no principles than to have principles that are not lived up to.

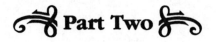 Part Two

Paying for Performance

Chapter Four

Using Incentive Pay

Incentive pay calls for paying individuals predetermined amounts of money for each unit produced. More than any other pay-for-performance system, incentive pay has the potential to create a clear line of sight between an individual's pay and performance. The 1920s and 1930s saw a tremendous growth in the installation of piece-rate and other individual incentive plans (Lawler, 1971). These were used to motivate performance at least partly because the simple, repetitive manufacturing jobs of the day lacked the ability to motivate workers intrinsically (Hackman and Oldham, 1980). For several decades, however, the popularity of incentive plans has been in a steady decline. Fewer and fewer new ones are put in place and those that do exist are being eliminated.

Incentive plans have definitely not disappeared entirely, however. A survey of the *Fortune* 1,000 companies (500 industrial and 500 service firms) found that only 13 percent had no one on incentive pay (Lawler, Ledford, and Mohrman, 1989), while 49 percent had from 1 to 20 percent of the employees on incentive pay. The definition of incentive pay used in the survey was rather inclusive—"all bonus plans that are based on individual performance"— thus it covered sales incentive plans and executive bonus plans as well as factory piece-rate plans. This breadth of the definition probably accounts for the large number of companies reporting at least some individuals covered by incentive pay plans.

The low use of incentive pay shows up in the attitudes of the American workforce. A 1983 study by the Public Agenda Foundation found that only 22 percent of American workers say that there is a direct link between how hard they work and how much they are paid (Yankelovich and Immerwahr, 1983). As was noted earlier, there is a cost associated with pay systems that do not directly link pay to performance. Studies tend to show productivity increases of between 15 and 35 percent when incentive pay systems are put into place (Lawler, 1971; Nalbantian, 1987; Guzzo, Jette, and Katzell, 1985; Blinder, 1990). The Public Agenda Foundation survey itself reports that 73 percent of the workers surveyed attributed decreased job efforts to the lack of incentive pay.

Given the effectiveness of incentive pay systems, their decreasing popularity is at first glance both hard to understand and troubling. There are, however, important reasons for the decline of incentive pay. Once these have been considered, we can determine when and where incentive pay is the right way to pay for performance in those organizations whose strategy calls for performance-based pay.

Problems with Incentive Pay

The literature on incentive plans is full of vivid descriptions of the counterproductive behaviors that piece-rate incentive plans produce. One of the first books I read in compensation provided story after story about how employees were outsmarting and defeating piece-rate systems (Whyte, 1955). Indeed, as I read this classic book I marveled at the ingenuity of the worker and found myself wondering what could be done to see that this talent was used to make better products. It was clear that the systems were motivating behavior—but unfortunately they were motivating the *wrong* behavior. It was also clear that the talents of the employees far exceeded the demands of the work they were doing.

I recently interviewed a manager who told of an event in his company that once again pointed out how incentive plans can limit performance. His company was in the middle of a strike, and in order to keep production going they had assigned his secretary to do a factory job that was covered by an incentive plan. She learned the job quickly and started turning out parts. A few days later the supervisor in her area reported that she was breaking production records by 375 percent. The worker who normally did the job had been doing it for ten years and had often complained that the standard was "too tight." Clearly, he was playing games and attempting to get the standard reduced.

Often the negative behaviors associated with incentive pay

are not caused so much by the concept itself as by the way it has been put into practice. For example, in some cases management has unfairly and without explanation changed an incentive plan or otherwise destroyed a plan's integrity. Nevertheless, it is difficult to separate the practical problems with the plans from the general idea of incentive pay. Let us briefly review the major problems with incentive plans.

Beating the System. When incentive plans are put into place, an adversarial relationship usually develops between the system designers and the employees who work under the plans. Employees engage in numerous behaviors in order to get rates set in such a way that they can maximize their financial gains relative to the amount of work that they have to do. For example, they work at slow rates in order to mislead the time-study expert when he or she comes to study their job. As new work methods or new procedures are developed, they hide these from management so that the job will not be restudied.

A classic case of hiding information occurred in the baby-food industry. One company's sales force in Florida found that they could increase their sales dramatically by appealing to the senior-citizen market. Because they were on an incentive plan, they kept this information from management so that their sales standard would not be raised. Each year they turned in the best results in the country, but they kept their performance low enough to avoid arousing suspicion and having their standard raised significantly.

Informal norms tend to develop in the organization about how productive people should be. In this way the workers set a limit on production. Anyone who goes beyond this limit is often ostracized or even physically punished. Unfortunately for the organization, this limit is often set far below what people are capable of producing.

One of the clearest cases of production restriction that I have seen occurred in a ball-bearing plant. Over the years the workforce had decided that the approved production level was 140 percent of standard. Virtually everyone produced at this level except for the union officers, who were "allowed" to produce at 180 percent. I visited the plant at the request of management, who wanted to put in a gainsharing plan. After doing some initial research on the plant, I convened a joint union-management meeting. I explained to those attending that gainsharing would work to their mutual advantage but that they would have to give up the incentive plan, because among other things it was inhibiting productivity. Management readily agreed, but the union resisted. Employees wanted to be paid for giving up the plan. When directly asked, they said that they could produce at least 25 percent more than they were currently producing. A gainsharing plan could have been structured to reward them for greater production, but the trust level was so low between union and management that the union would not agree to installing one without cash up front.

The fear of job loss because of high productivity can also lead to production restriction on incentive jobs. Individuals reduce production because they are afraid that if they produce too much, they will work themselves or their co-workers out of a job. The macro issue of international competitiveness gets overlooked because of the short-term need for a job.

Other forms of "gaming" include producing at extremely low levels when employees consider standards too difficult to reach and initiating union grievance procedures both to eliminate rates that are seen as too difficult and to harass management by tying it up in paperwork and hearings. Finally, in order to gain leverage in negotiating incentive rates, employees will organize unions so that they can deal from a more powerful base. When unions do exist in the workplace, they are often able to negotiate piece-rate plans that allow workers to work "off standard" while being paid at a rate that represents a previous high level of performance. Thus organizations end up with the undesirable combination of high pay and low performance.

Even though it was over fifteen years ago, I remember well being asked to consult with a tire company that was in just this situation. Over the years the union had negotiated a contract that allowed employees to work off standard most of the time but to be paid at a rate that represented their previous rate of on-standard production. Any problems with the availability of raw materials or the operation of the equipment provided grounds for working off standard. The employees worked hard during the first few hours of each week to set their on-standard weekly rate of production; from then on, most of their time was spent working off standard but at on-standard wages. The solution? Under the contract all that the company could do was buy out the incentive plan by making large cash payments to the employees. Procter & Gamble found itself in the same situation in some of its paper plants in the 1960s. The firm finally bought out the plans and to this day will not allow incentive plans in its plants.

In summary, then, incentive plans often set up an adversarial relationship between those under the plan and those designing and administering the plan. The result is that both sides often engage in practices designed to win the game or war at the cost of organizational effectiveness. In many cases the winner is the employee, which is hardly surprising. Employees know their jobs better than management, and they stay around longer than most managers. After a while managers tend to be rotated and promoted; but the employees are still there, and they know the system best.

Dividing the Workforce. Because many support jobs and nonproduction jobs do not lend themselves to incentive pay, the typical organization that has incentive pay has only part of the workforce on it. This often leads to a we-they split in the workforce that can be counterproductive and can lead to noncooperative work relationships. In one plant I studied, the conflict degenerated into open warfare. Occasionally the support people would purposely delay their work, thereby holding up incentive workers, so that the workers on incentive would not make more than they themselves did. The incentive workers, on the other hand, would constantly complain to management about the support workers and at times even threaten them. I have seen the same behaviors develop in sales situations; there the conflict is between the incentive sales personnel and the clerical support employees.

This split, interestingly enough, is not a management-worker split, but a worker-worker split. In its most severe case it can lead to open conflict among employees who need to cooperate in order to make the organization effective. This split can also lead to dysfunctions in the kind of career paths people choose. Often individuals will bid for and stay in incentive jobs that do not fit their skills and interests because of the higher pay that those jobs offer. The higher pay of established incentive jobs also often causes individuals to be inflexible when asked to change jobs temporarily, and it can cause them to resist new technology that calls for a rate change.

Compounding Maintenance Costs. Because incentive plans are relatively complicated and need to be constantly updated, a significant investment needs to be made in the people who maintain them. The problem of maintaining incentive systems is further complicated by the adversarial relationship that develops between employees and management. Because employees try to hide new work methods and avoid having changes in their rates made—unless, of course, those changes are to their advantage—management needs to be extremely vigilant in determining when new rates are needed. In addition, every time a technological change is made or a new product is introduced, new rates need to be set.

Finally, there is the ongoing cost of computing peoples' wages relative to the amount of work and kind of work they have done during a particular performance period. All this takes engineers, accountants, and payroll clerks. Added together, the support costs of an incentive system are significantly greater than those associated with a straight hourly pay or a traditional pay-for-performance salary-increase plan.

Limiting Behaviors. Incentive plans are usually very specific about what they reward. Because they are usually based on formulas, they are often limited in the number and kind of behaviors they motivate and reward. This can be a great strength of the plans if all an organization wants employees to do is a few simple, *measurable* things. Unfortunately, many work situations just are not that simple. Take the case of retail employees. It is relatively simple to put them on an incentive plan based on how much they sell. But this can lead to their doing nothing but selling. Peripheral tasks such as stocking shelves, wrapping packages, and handling refunds may be ignored. What can be even worse, employees may use sales methods that make the sale but alienate customers so that no further sales are made.

Souring Organizational Culture. The combined effects of dividing the workforce into those who are and are not on incentive pay and the adversarial process of rate setting can create a very negative organizational culture. In particular, it can produce a climate characterized by low trust, lack of information sharing, poor support for joint problem solving, and inflexibility. Because individuals want to protect their pay rates, incentive pay works against creating a climate of openness, trust, joint problem solving, and commitment to organizational objectives.

In summary, it should be clear at this point that the installation of incentive pay is, at best, a mixed blessing. Although it may be very effective at motivating improved work performance, the counterproductive behaviors, the maintenance costs, the splitting of the workforce, and the poor culture that it leads to may make it a poor choice. Many organizations have dropped incentive pay or decided not to put it in place because they believe that the negative effects and maintenance costs outweigh the potential advantages that come from the increases in performance that it typically produces.

Societal Changes

The decreasing popularity of incentive pay probably cannot be understood solely by looking at the problems it causes. Some important societal changes have taken place since it gained its greatest popularity. Because these changes, mentioned earlier, have in many ways led to the declining popularity of incentive pay, let us review them here. We will look at how the nature of the work, the nature of the workforce, and the nature of society have all changed and examine how those changes relate to incentive pay.

Nature of the Work. In the early 1900s many of the jobs in the United States were in the manufacturing and agricultural sectors of the economy, and they involved the production of relatively simple, high-volume products. Today the United States is moving rapidly toward work that is increasingly based on the service sector, on knowledge, on information processing, and on high technology. Many of the simple, repetitive tasks in the manufacturing sector have either left the United States for less developed countries or been automated. Instead of simple, stand-alone tasks that an individual could do singlehandedly, many jobs now involve the operation of complex machines or the delivery of services that require the integrated work of many individuals, or they take place in continuous-process plants.

The type of work that exists in the United States today is therefore less amenable to individual measurement and to the specification of a "normal" level of production. Instead, performance can be measured reliably and validly only when a group of workers or even an entire plant of workers is viewed. In many knowledge-based jobs, it is even difficult to specify what the desired product is until it has been produced. Work of this nature simply does not lend itself to incentive pay.

Where knowledge work is dominant and where high technology is prevalent, the nature of jobs and technology is often subject to rapid change. Because stability is needed to set incentive rates and to justify the start-up costs of an incentive system, rapid change conflicts directly with incentive pay.

There are still work situations in which simple, repetitive, stable jobs lend themselves to piece-rate pay. However, the research findings on job enrichment have led some organizations to try to make these jobs more complex and to create conditions under which employees will be intrinsically motivated to perform them well (Hackman and Oldham, 1980). For example, in some cases self-managing teams have been given responsibility for whole pieces of work. In many cases, enriching jobs makes them poor candidates for incentive pay: first, because a different kind of motivation is present, and second, because the enrichment process makes the simple, measurable, repetitive, individual nature of the jobs disappear.

In summary, then, the nature of work—at least in the United States—is less and less amenable to individual incentive pay.

Nature of the Workforce. When incentive pay was introduced in the United States, the workforce was composed primarily of poorly educated immigrant workers who were for the first time entering factories and manufacturing environments. Individuals such as this still exist, but the changing demographics of the workforce have made them a much smaller portion of the total workforce. Today the workforce is much more highly educated and diverse (Johnston, 1987), and there is evidence to indicate that it has different values and different orientations toward work. An increasing percentage of the workforce is interested in influencing workplace decisions, desires challenging and interesting work, and hopes to develop skills and abilities (Lawler, 1986a). Incentive pay plans, because of their top-down nature and the kind of work they are typically associated with, do not suit this type of workforce. Indeed, it is the nature of the workforce that is often used to support the call for more enriched jobs and for the elimination of standardized, specialized, highly repetitive work (*Work in America*, 1973).

Nature of the Society. The rate of societal change in the United States has been accelerating. Particularly in the last ten years, the United States has seen an expansion in employee rights, employee entitlements, and the kind of legal avenues that are open to employees who feel unfairly treated in the workplace. This has made incentive pay plans subject to grievances and to the kind of challenges that make them difficult and expensive to maintain.

Today we have extensive fringe benefits and high base wages in many industries that used to have incentive pay. In many respects this trend does not fit with the increasing national awareness that workplaces in the United States need to be more productive, but it does fit with the idea of increased entitlements and the elimination of incentive pay plans.

Overall, the United States has become a society in which the profits of companies are at risk as an incremental function of performance, but the pay of individuals is affected only at the extremes of performance (Weitzman, 1984). That is, an employee loses only when the company is in such poor shape that it has to lay the individual off, and the employee gains only when growth is such that the employee has the opportunity to be promoted. Society seems to have evolved to a state where individuals consider that they are entitled to a fair wage and extensive fringe benefits simply because they are employed by an organization. This kind of thinking is represented in the union contracts that have eliminated piece-rate pay and in companies that, in order to stay nonunion and attract the best employees, have simply given high base wages to all employees. In this kind of environment it is hard to "sell" incentive pay to many members of the workforce.

Future Developments

There are no indications that changes likely to tip the scales in favor of incentive pay are occurring. Indeed, the trends that have led to widespread abandonment of incentive pay seem to be continuing; thus the next ten years will probably see a continuing decline in the use of incentive pay plans. There is, however, one important trend that seems to call for the increased use of pay as a motivator: the lack of growth in national productivity and the strong international competitive situation with respect to productivity and economic growth.

Given the competitive situation, it seems foolish for any organization to abandon such a potentially powerful motivator as incentive pay. Just this point was made by the 1983 White House Conference on productivity; in fact, it recommended the *increased* use of pay as a motivator. The Public Agenda Foundation study mentioned earlier also supports pay for performance; it found that 61 percent of the employees surveyed wanted pay tied to performance (Yankelovich and Immerwahr, 1983). On the other hand, the analysis so far suggests that piece-rate and other incentive pay plans are not a good answer in many cases. However, where they are appropriate, these pay systems should still be used and can play a positive role.

Let us spend a moment outlining the conditions in which incentive pay is appropriate. As was mentioned earlier, it fits situations where the work is repetitive, paced by the worker, stable, and simple, and where the results of the work are easily measurable. Incentive pay is often badly needed with highly repetitive work because there is no other incentive to perform; the work is simply not motivating in and of itself. It also fits work that can be designed for individual employees and situations in which interdependence and the need for cooperation are at a minimum.

Because of the international economic trends mentioned earlier, much of the work appropriate for incentive pay is leaving or has left the United States. It is simply too expensive to do work in the United States that can be done equally well by low-wage employees in developing countries. But not all such work can be exported. Particularly in the service sector, some of it must be done in the United States. For example, many sales jobs, such as running a cash register, are of this nature.

Nordstrom Inc. is one organization that seems to have made incentive pay work. The salespersons in its department stores are on commission plans that pay from 5 to 10 percent of the sales price after a standard or quota is met. This has created a very entrepreneurial and competitive work environment in Nordstrom stores; but most retail selling is basically an individual task, so this is not necessarily dysfunctional. In fact the major problem that Nordstrom has had with their plan stems from its being "too successful." In order to earn a commission and show a high rate of sales per hour employees have underreported the number of hours they have worked. Hours spent doing such extra service work as delivering purchases to customers' homes and writing thank you notes to customers have not been reported. The problem with this is that according to federal law these hours must be paid for and as a result Nordstrom has been subject to complaints that it owes employees for unpaid hours of work. In order to be sure that service quality remains high, Nordstrom gives numerous individual and storewide awards for service quality. The company has also developed a strong service-oriented culture; for example, executives tell all employees that there is only one rule, "Satisfy the customer," and the corporate culture is full of stories about salespersons who have gone out of their way to heroically serve a customer.

The processing of paperwork by banks involves some highly repetitive tasks. For example, individuals have to encode checks with the amount for which they were written. In one bank with which I consulted, individuals encoded thousands of checks an hour at a machine. They controlled the pace of their work and were asked to do no more or less than key in the amount of the check. When the bank first approached me, it was interested in putting a group bonus or gainsharing plan in place. After we went through an analysis of the work to be done, executives agreed that individual incentives made more sense because they offered the best line of sight and because the bank wanted individuals to maximize their individual performance; teamwork and cooperation were not needed. In addition, there were few opportunities for employees to problem-solve or develop better work methods and equipment. The bank installed a piece-rate plan, and it quickly led to a 30 percent increase in productivity.

There are many other examples of situations in which incentive pay fits. For example, telephone reservation work and some repair jobs fit incentive pay very well, because they are individual jobs that have easily measurable results. And in the manufacturing world I still run across situations in which repetitive tasks that lend themselves to incentive pay exist. The manufacture of many electronic instruments, for example, requires individuals to do very routine jobs, such as connecting hundreds of pieces of wire an hour or inserting hundreds of components in a board every hour. There are a number of good reasons why these jobs are not sent to low-wage countries. Sometimes it is just too inconvenient; in other cases the shift cannot be made because the work involves military products.

If incentive pay is used, it is important to avoid making the mistakes that have characterized the history of incentive plans. Many of these mistakes have their roots in unilateral management actions that are seen by employees as unfair. A common problem area is the changing of standards and setting of rates. All too often management comes to the conclusion that employees are making too much, so they raise the standards or reduce the rates. When this is done unilaterally, it almost always builds mistrust and the counterproductive behavior mentioned earlier. Most organizations do not have the option of running incentive plans on a unilateral basis; if they do not involve employees, there is a good chance that the employees will find a way to get involved—for example, by organizing a union.

An alternative that I have seen work well is to make the design and ongoing management of the incentive system a participative process. Employees trained in rate setting can sit on task forces used to establish and revise incentive plans. This process can be successful when employees feel that they can have a real influence and are not just token members of the task force.

Obviously, the conditions that need to be in place for incentive pay to work well mean that in most work situations it should not be used. Overall, we can expect to see a continuing decline in the uses of incentive plans in the United States and other developed countries. As will be discussed in the next chapters, this does not mean that pay for performance cannot or should not be used. It can still play an important role, but it needs to take a different form.

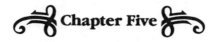

Chapter Five

Using Merit Pay

The idea of merit pay is so widely accepted that almost every organization claims to have a merit pay system that allocates pay increases based upon individual performance. A survey of the *Fortune* 1,000 found that 96 percent had merit pay (it is unclear what the rest had in its place); 31 percent of these companies reported covering all their employees with it (Lawler, Ledford, and Mohrman, 1989). Even the U.S. government calls its pay system a merit pay system; and, as was mentioned earlier, legislation (the Civil Service Reform Act) was passed during the Carter administration calling for the system to be more dependent on merit.

The major reason for the popularity of merit pay is the belief that pay can motivate job performance and increase organizational effectiveness. As was noted earlier, research evidence clearly shows that pay *can* be a motivator of performance when (1) it is important and (2) it is tied to performance. For most people pay is important, so typically this first factor is not a problem in using pay as a motivator. In most instances the critical issue is whether a perceived relationship exists between a significant change in pay and performance; in other words, significant changes in compensation must be clearly related to performance. The emphasis here is on significant *changes* in compensation rather than on *total* compensation because changes are what can produce a motivating link between current performance and pay.

Merit pay can play a major role in attracting and retaining particular employees. As was noted earlier, total compensation levels influence people's decisions about where they work. There is no secret to what is key here: total compensation relative to the market. Individuals who are well paid relative to what they can receive elsewhere are particularly likely to stay with an organization; those who are poorly paid are likely to leave. If an organization wants to attract and retain good performers, it may have to pay them more than other employees are paid. The only alternative is to pay everyone—good performers and bad—more than the market. I have seen a few organizations do this, but it is a very expensive way to manage pay. Thus some form of pay for performance is needed if an organization is to retain its best performers and have salary costs that are in line with its competitors' costs. Paying poor performers less can have the desirable effect of causing them to leave. Overall then paying for performance can lead to the right kind of turnover— good performers staying, poor performers leaving.

Despite widespread support for the policy of merit pay, there is considerable evidence that in most organizations merit pay systems fail to create a perceived relationship between pay and performance and fail to pay better performers more in total compensation. Thus they fail to produce the positive effects that are expected of them. In addition, there is reason to believe that in the future it is going to be harder to design effective merit pay programs. But before we consider what the future holds, let us briefly review the problems with using merit pay as a motivator of performance.

Problems with Merit Pay Systems

Fundamental to an effective merit pay system are credible, comprehensive measures of performance. Without these, it is impossible to relate pay to performance. There is a great deal of evidence that in most organizations performance appraisal is not done well and that, as a result, no good measures of individual performance exist (Mohrman, Resnick-West, and Lawler, 1989). Sometimes the problem is that managers simply lack the skill to appraise performance. In other cases the problem is that the appraisal system is defective. These problems are correctable, but there is one common problem that is not: the fact of the matter is that work performance is sometimes simply not easily measured by focusing on individual job performance. In situations where teamwork is needed because no one individual can offer a service or make a significant part of a product, measuring the performance of an individual may be impossible and counterproductive.

In the absence of objective measures of performance, most

organizations rely on the subjective judgments of managers. These judgments are often seen by subordinates as invalid, unfair, and discriminatory. Because subjective performance measures are not trusted, when pay is based on them little is done to create the perception that pay is based on performance. Indeed, in the eyes of many employees merit pay is a fiction—a myth that managers try to perpetuate. Thus, rather than contributing to motivation and a positive culture, it can nourish a distrust of what the organization says.

Finally, there is the issue of whether merit pay is effective in retaining the best performers. For merit pay to affect retention, the best performers must consistently get the largest raises so that their total pay exceeds that of others. This can happen only if valid performance measures exist. Thus the entire usefulness of merit pay rests on the performance appraisal system. Yet all too often, rather than providing a firm foundation, it is the weak link.

The problems with merit pay are not limited to its dependence on often-defective performance appraisal systems. The policies and procedures that make up a merit pay system often lead to pay actions or pay changes that do little to relate pay to performance for another reason: the typical merit-based salary-increase system allows for only small changes in total pay to occur in one year. This is particularly true in times of low inflation, when an organization's budget for merit increases may be only 4 percent. This means that for someone to have a big increase—say, 18 percent—many other individuals have to get a zero or close-to-zero increase.

Merit pay further compounds the problem by making past "merit payments" part of the individual's base salary, thereby creating an annuity. As long as someone stays with an organization, he or she is paid for past performance. This means that an individual can be a poor performer for several years, after having been a good performer, and still be highly paid.

Further problems are introduced by changes in the inflation rate. In times of high inflation it is quite possible for someone to get a large increase simply because the budget is high. This substantial raise then gets built into his or her pay forever. Just the opposite happens in times of low inflation: outstanding performers have trouble getting a significant increase and increasing their total compensation. The difference between the raises given for poor performers and those given for good performers can end up being so small that their financial impact is minimal, although they may still be important to some individuals for ego or status reasons.

The effects of inflation were brought home to me during some interviews I did after inflation had been very high. One employee pointed out to me that he had it made because he had "won at inflation roulette"—that is, he had been a good performer during a period of high inflation and as a result had been able to achieve a high base pay. He went on to add that his present performance made little difference, because it had little effect on his total compensation. He was correct, of course, because he had a high market position and the raise budgets were very small.

Relating pay increases to current performance is made more difficult by the pay-range systems most organizations use. These systems typically specify a pay range for each job that includes the starting rate and the top rate that the organization is willing to pay. This approach makes sense from an expense-control point of view but, when combined with merit pay, it means that the new people on a job will almost always be poorly paid. It also means that individuals who have performed well will eventually "top out" (that is, reach the top of the range); after that, no matter how well they perform they can get only a small increase, which effectively eliminates pay as a motivator for them.

The combined effect of year-to-year differences in salary-increase budgets and the annuity feature of merit raises almost always creates a situation in which the total compensation of individuals is unrelated to their performance at any point in time. Time after time, in analyzing the pay practices of companies, I have found that the best performers are equally likely to be paid at a below-average rate as an above-average rate. Indeed, the best-paid individuals in any salary range are often individuals who have simply been around for a long time and have performed adequately. Over time, they have worked their way to the top because of the compounding effects of annual merit increases.

Average and poor performers rarely quit because of how they are treated by merit pay systems; the problem is with the best performers. If they are newly in a job, they are usually poorly paid, and it can take years for them to reach a top pay rate. Not only does this do little to motivate them; it also creates a high risk of their leaving the organization for a higher-paying job elsewhere. To counter this, organizations often "promote" their best performers frequently in order to give them the large increases that are required to keep them. This works from an administrative point of view, because promotion pay increases come out of a different budget and can be large, but it may be a case of the tail wagging the dog. There are many good reasons for promoting someone, but giving a pay increase is not one of them. Promotion for pay makes especially little sense in an organization that is trying to reduce overhead and layers of management, although it is a somewhat more practical approach in an organization that is rapidly growing.

In one organization I studied, the managers had found a way around the merit pay system limitations on pay increases. They recognized that they could not give their best young engineers large enough raises to keep them, because as they gained experience their market value increased rapidly. They simply let them go to other organizations, and after nine to twelve months they rehired them at much higher rates. This was possible because (1) the engineers had established a higher market value by working somewhere else and (2) the managers were not limited by a merit-increase budget in setting salaries of "new" hires.

Some organizations try to improve the relationship between pay and performance by developing charts that call for the size of raises to depend on individual performance *and* the position of an employee's total pay in the pay range. The effect is to give good performers who are low in total pay high increases while giving good performers who are highly paid low increases. This makes sense from a retention point of view, because it causes pay-increase money to be spent to retain good performers who are low in the range. It also prevents pay-increase money from being spent on those individuals whose total pay is in line with the market.

It is a disaster from a motivational point of view, however. It in effect says to the highly paid good performer, "Your performance doesn't make any difference." I have seen a number of pay administrators try to argue otherwise in explaining this "merit" practice to employees, but I have never seen one succeed. The higher-paid individuals simply do not accept that they are paid for their performance when changes in their pay do not depend on their current performance. Calling such a system a *merit* system simply harms the credibility of management; it does nothing to motivate performance.

The simple fact of the matter is that with a merit-based salary-increase system there is no way to have both total compensation and changes in compensation reflect current performance. Because of this, it is impossible to have a merit pay system that does an effective job of both motivating performance and retaining the best performers. One of these two highly desirable objectives has to be sacrificed because of the annuity feature of merit pay. Annuities create base salaries that cannot be significantly changed to reflect current performance, unless of course the budget is unlimited—an unlikely situation. I know of one organization that has handled this problem by abolishing pay ranges so that it can continue to give large raises to its best employees. This approach works there, but it is expensive.

Managers who administer merit-based salary-increase systems often do a number of things that negatively affect the perceived connection between pay and performance. Perhaps the most serious is the failure to recommend widely different pay increases for their subordinates when large performance differences exist. Some managers are simply unwilling to recommend very large and very small pay actions, even when they are warranted. One reason for this is the unpleasant task of explaining to subordinates why some got a low raise.

The difficulty of explaining low raises often leads to a second destructive behavior on the part of managers: disowning the pay decision. Despite the fact that they may have made a recommendation for a small raise and believe that it is appropriately given, supervisors sometimes deny or discount their role in determining a subordinate's pay. They may, for example, say that they fought hard for the subordinate to get a good raise but lost out. Or they may say that their hands are tied by the budget or by the personnel department's policies. This clearly communicates to the subordinate that pay increases are beyond his or her control and thus not based on performance.

The existence of any one of the common problems that plague the administration of merit pay programs is usually enough to destroy for most employees the belief that pay is related to performance. And in reality, the merit pay systems of most organizations suffer from all or most of these problems! As a result, at best the policy of merit pay fails to achieve its intended objectives; at worst it also becomes an embarrassment that undermines management's credibility.

Given the rather questionable performance of merit pay, is there any reason to believe that things can or will get better? To answer this question, let us look at those forces and trends operating in the environment that threaten merit pay and those that favor it.

Forces That Threaten Merit Pay

More and more organizations seem to have fallen into the practice of giving everyone increases in order to keep employees "whole." In times of high inflation, many organizations seem to feel obliged to give everyone something because inflation is affecting everyone so negatively. This serves to keep people from losing real income, of course, but it fails to relate pay and performance. The situation is no better in times of low inflation, because then there is little money available to reward good performance.

It seems that merit pay is ineffective in times of both high and low inflation. No one can predict what future inflation rates will be, but in view of recent history it seems likely that periods of both high and low inflation are likely. Given this, it is hard to see how organizations can effectively use merit programs to reward good performance.

In large organizations it is often particularly difficult to tie pay to individual performance. A large organization is more likely to have many jobs that lack both a direct interface with the external environment and clear performance goals and measures. Needless to say, as performance becomes more difficult to measure, so does tying pay to it. There is also a clear tendency for more and more jobs to be in organizations that provide services, use process technologies (for example, the chemical, oil, and food industries) or do knowledge or high-technology work. This represents a serious problem for tying pay to individual performance, because it is more difficult to measure individual performance in service, knowledge work, and process production settings. As performance becomes more difficult to measure, measuring is less likely to be done well. The result: pay is less likely to be effectively related to performance.

In addition, new forms of organization are developing. Some of them are complex structures created to handle the complexities of competing in global markets that require being a leader in technology as well as being responsive to local market conditions. Probably the most popular is some form of matrix or network structure, in which individuals have multiple reporting relationships and several bosses (Davis and Lawrence, 1977; Miles and Snow, 1986; Johnston and Lawrence, 1988). There are a number of advantages to these structures, but not in the area of tying pay to performance. On the contrary, a complex structure may make it more difficult to measure individual performance and, as a result, to tie pay to it.

Organizational structures designed to increase employee involvement are also becoming more common. In many cases these structures are built upon teams that are highly interdependent (Lawler, 1986b; Walton, 1980). The practice of allocating a budget amount to a supervisor and asking him or her to divide it up among team members on the basis of merit can be very disruptive of teamwork. It very clearly puts the team members in a competitive situation in which team performance does not matter but individual performance does. Thus measuring and rewarding the performance of individuals in a team structure can be both difficult and counterproductive, because it can detract from the sense of shared responsibility and accountability. At the very least, cooperation and teamwork must be measured in assigning merit pay to team members; otherwise, the reward system can pull a team apart.

The many quality-improvement programs that are being adopted by U.S. corporations raise serious problems for merit pay. Deming, the best known of the quality experts, says that performance appraisal simply should not be done in an organization that wants to improve quality (Mohrman, 1989; Deming, 1987). He gives a number of reasons for this. The two most compelling are that the performance appraisal causes competition among individuals and causes attention to be diverted away from those organizational systems—such as the information system—that are usually responsible for poor quality.

The increase in fringe-benefit costs over the years has had, and promises to continue to have, a negative impact on the cash available for merit pay. Compensation dollars that could be spent on merit pay end up getting spent on fringe benefits, many of which some people do not even want and none of which are based on performance. The impact of this, of course, is to reduce further the tie between pay and performance, because the cash is simply not available to distinguish between the better and worse performers.

There is clear evidence that employee expectations concerning due process and public accountability in decision making are increasing (Ewing, 1977, 1983). Further, there is evidence that individuals are willing to go to court when they feel that they have been unfairly treated and denied due process in the area of salary decisions. One answer to this is to move toward open salary decisions, public accountability, and appeal processes; but the more openness there is, the more some managers seem to back off from making tough decisions that reward performance. Another way of saying this is that the more managers are held accountable for their pay decisions, the more they tend to engage in the homogeneous treatment of individuals in order to avoid the discomfort of defending differential treatment. In the past this discomfort might have been only interpersonal discomfort in confronting an unhappy subordinate. Today, of course, it may involve court appearances, a financial loss for the organization, and considerable loss of face for the manager. The result is that more and more managers seem to be thinking two or three times before they withhold a pay increase or give a very large one.

Overall, the future of merit pay looks pretty bleak. Does this mean that we should forget about the whole idea of merit pay and concentrate on keeping pay rates equitable in order to attract and retain the best employees? In some situations this may be the best approach, but not in all. The situation for merit pay is not entirely negative; there are some positive trends that need to be mentioned.

Forces That Favor Merit Pay

More than ever, organizations need the performance motivation that can be generated when pay is successfully tied to performance. Many organizations face tough international competition, and they need the motivation that pay can produce. Organizations are being "flattened" in order to reduce costs; promotion opportunities are therefore disappearing, leaving pay increases as the most available individual reward. People are likely to stay in their jobs for longer and longer periods of time, and organizations that are not careful can end up with a large percentage of their workforce topped out with respect to pay and promotion—and as a result poorly motivated.

Clearly, paying for performance cannot solve all the motivational problems associated with the new workforce and strong international competition. However, it can be an important part of a total management system that is designed to create a highly motivating work environment. The realization that pay-for-performance systems can help makes efforts to develop effective merit pay systems both likely and important.

Inflation does not have to be a negative force in tying pay to performance; it can be a strong positive force. Because a larger pool of money is created when inflation is high (in fact, even when it falls in the 4 to 6 percent range), inflation makes it possible to give substantially varied pay increases. For organizations that have not paid for performance in the past, inflation can represent a unique opportunity to get total compensation levels more in line with performance. In some respects it is harder to make these differentiations when the failure to get an increase means a loss in real income for the individual, but for an organization that is strongly committed to paying for performance, inflation can provide an opportunity to tie pay more closely to performance.

There is a continuing belief on the part of the U.S. workforce that pay *should* be related to performance. Despite the fact that there is a growing mistrust of the way rewards are distributed in society, there is no evidence that the historically strong belief that pay and performance should be related is going away. Indeed, as was noted

in Chapter Three, most surveys shows that employees at all levels
in organizations still think that people should be paid for their
performance and that pay for performance is a valid principle for
salary administration (Yankelovich and Immerwahr, 1983). Individuals typically also see a large gap between the degree to which their
pay and performance are related and the degree to which they feel
they *should* be related.

The growing measurement capability of many management
information systems can be a positive force in relating pay to performance. These systems can help make up for many of the inade-
quacies of today's performance appraisal systems and thereby
increase the validity of pay-for-performance systems. What is needed
is a set of comprehensive, objective measures that focus on the var-
iances in performance that are under the control of the individual
or group being measured. Systems that measure things that cannot
be controlled are not particularly helpful in this respect.

The tendency of some large organizations to decentralize—
to organize around products, customers, and lines of business—can
provide a strong basis for improving the relationship between pay
and performance. Decentralization has the effect of breaking up the
organization into a number of mini-enterprises. This allows for
better measurement of group, unit, and sometimes individual performance, and this in turn makes it easier to relate pay to performance. In short, decentralization can improve the organization's
ability to measure performance in objective and valid ways.

Some organizations have combined more openness and employee participation with better pay-for-performance systems. The
latter is not a necessary or inevitable consequence of openness and
participation, but it is a possible one when the openness and participation are handled effectively. In some organizations, in fact,
peer groups measure performance and determine rewards in an
open discussion (Lawler, 1986b). Where this has been tried, it has
often proved to be more effective in relating pay to performance
than the typical superior-subordinate pay-administration decision
process. Peers have better information; and when they are motivated
to do a good appraisal, they can often make better judgments than
the supervisor can alone (Kane and Lawler, 1978). They are partic-

ularly good at judging performance in the areas of teamwork and cooperation.

Xerox has developed an interesting program that helps get everyone involved in measuring and rewarding performance. The "X award"—X stands for *excellent*—may be given by anyone to anyone at any time. It is a piece of paper that can be redeemed for $25. Wells Fargo Bank has instituted a similar award. Each employee is given a check for $35 at the end of the year to give to another employee who has been particularly helpful to him or her.

Finally, it is worth noting again that there is research evidence that pay is becoming more important to people in American society. This means that efforts that *do* successfully tie pay to performance are likely to pay off in the area of motivation, because the more important pay becomes, the more motivational potential it has. There is no convincing evidence as to why pay is becoming more important, but it is not hard to guess at reasons. With inflation eroding incomes, and economic instability producing feelings of insecurity, people are becoming more concerned with their pay and the purchasing power it provides.

Merit Pay in the Future

What should organizations do in the future with respect to merit pay? One clear implication of the discussion so far is that they should not automatically say that they have a merit pay policy. It seems clear that the concept of merit pay has been bought by a number of organizations that are unaware of what is needed to make a merit system work, and for them merit pay probably will *not* work. Many organizations, after full exploration of merit pay, should conclude that it does not fit all or part of their operation. For organizations that do not have a work situation that lends itself to individual performance measures, merit pay is inappropriate and should be abandoned—a step that could have some very positive results in the area of culture. At the very least, the abandonment of ineffective merit pay should increase the credibility of management, and it may also serve to eliminate unneeded superior-subordinate conflicts and save administrative time.

For those organizations that decide to have individual merit pay, the following points warrant serious consideration.

1. *Use a bonus system.* As a delivery system, bonuses have a number of advantages, and there is increasing evidence that bonus plans of a number of different types can be effective. Particularly effective in relating individual pay to individual performance are annual bonuses or lump-sum merit payments over a market-driven base wage rate.

The basis for any bonus plan needs to be a base wage or job rate that is effectively positioned in the market—that is, at or below market. In a pure performance bonus system, everyone doing a particular job gets this rate, which is adjusted annually to reflect market changes. For maximum bonus impact the rate should be set below market in order to free up more money for bonuses. The key is in determining how much variability in pay the organization and the employees can live with. My feeling is that at the lower pay levels a 0 to 20 percent bonus range is usually appropriate, while at the higher levels a 0 to 40 percent bonus range is appropriate. Adjustment of the base wage rate is possible if the organization wishes to reflect seniority and past performance in the pay of individuals. But the more this is done, the less effective the merit bonuses are likely to be and the more the culture stresses loyalty and service rather than current performance.

A merit-based bonus approach need not cost any more than a salary-increase system, but it can produce true pay for performance. Just as with a salary-increase system, a fixed number of dollars can be budgeted and spent on salaries. The difference is that no portion of each year's budget, through a compounding base salary, has to become an annuity. Rather, the bonuses are awarded on an annual basis and as such they can reflect current performance. The advantages of this approach are significant. The primary one is that pay can vary significantly with current performance. Both total pay and bonuses can be related to current individual performance. This is ideal for both motivation and retention. It means that the individual who is a good performer can immediately be paid at the top rate for a job. It also means that there are no annuities, so the individual who has performed well in the past has to continue to do well in order to be well paid. In short, employees have to earn their bonuses each year—a crucial point as far as motivation is concerned.

The base pay rate can be adjusted annually to reflect market movement. Thus individuals get an annual increase most years, but the increase in job rate is not presented as a merit increase. This represents a significant advantage over merit-increase systems, which combine market changes with performance-based changes and falsely call the total a merit increase. Changing from a merit-increase system to a bonus-based system can be difficult, but it is possible. Instant conversions can be accomplished by simply reducing everyone's pay to the job rate. Kodak, DuPont, and Dow Chemical have all done this. It might be described as "shock therapy" and is appropriate only when an organization needs dramatic change. When gradual change is appropriate, base wages can simply be frozen until they reach the desired market position. The money saved by not giving salary increases can be used to fund the bonus payments. At first the bonuses are likely to be small, but eventually they will be significant.

2. *Pay attention to the process issues involved in merit pay.* A good system of bonuses and base rates is important in any merit-based plan, but so are good communication policies and proper decision processes. Without these, the best merit pay system will fail, because employees will not see the relationship between pay and performance. This point is particularly pertinent in light of the changing nature of the workforce. It is quite possible that, in the future, due process and open communication will be necessary if merit pay systems are to operate at all. The evidence on participation in pay decisions suggests that the use of participation can make decisions more credible (Lawler, 1981). In any case, considerable attention needs to be devoted to a description of the system and an explanation of the decision process.

3. *Take performance appraisal seriously.* As will be discussed further in the next chapter, in order for appraisal to be effective people need to be trained, systems need to be developed, and time needs to be spent by both the appraiser and the appraisee. Having an untrained appraiser spend a few minutes reviewing the performance of a subordinate and then making a pay recommenda-

tion is simply not acceptable—particularly when large bonuses are involved. Performance measures need to be mutually agreed on, results jointly reviewed, and pay actions discussed. If these practices are not acceptable or possible, pay should not be based on performance appraisal results.

4. *Focus on key organizational factors that affect the pay system.* Often a poor merit pay system is a symptom of other problems and cannot be improved until those problems are solved. It is impossible to have an effective merit pay system if, for example, an organization or its jobs are poorly designed. With these conditions it is simply too difficult to measure performance and assign responsibility for it. Similarly, without a good information system in place, it is often impossible to measure individual performance validly.

5. *Include group and team performance in the evaluation.* Even in a system of individual pay for performance, it may be important to measure and reward group or team performance (Schuster, 1984; Von Glinow and Mohrman, 1989). One way to do this is simply to evaluate individuals on the basis of how much they contribute to the group. A more powerful alternative, however, is to evaluate team performance and base part or all of the merit awards on this evaluation. There are several ways to accomplish this. One option is to award separate amounts of money for team performance and individual performance. This is done in professional sports. Another alternative is to first evaluate the team's performance and then make that evaluation the starting point for each individual's evaluation. Within limits, individuals can be moved up or down based on their individual performance. The key to developing the right approach is determining how important and how measurable performance is at the individual and group levels of analysis.

6. *Consider special awards.* Most annual merit increase programs cannot effectively deal with major performance accomplishments. Normal merit budgets are typically not large enough to allow for large rewards, and the timing of annual increases is often wrong. Finally, in many cases the appraisal process for merit increases is not adequate to judge significant performance breakthroughs. What is needed is a separate, Nobel Prize-type award process. Many organizations have major awards for the R & D func-

tions. At IBM and Amoco, for example, these awards can exceed $100,000.

It is more difficult to give Nobel-type awards in areas other than R & D, but they can have quite an impact if good performance measurement is done. For example, American Express is trying to recognize its exceptional performers by given them "Great Performers" awards worth over $5,000.

Even small special awards can be motivational. For years supervisors at IBM have been able to give employees who do something special a small but immediate cash award or dinner for two. This has the obvious advantage of closely tying the reward to the performance and can be quite powerful if the supervisor does a good job of establishing and recognizing good performance.

To summarize, it may be more difficult to administer merit pay systems in the future. Organizations are becoming more complex, and the workforce is becoming more demanding. But in some cases it is also more important than ever that pay be tied to performance. There is no right answer for all organizations. Some organizations need to partially or completely abandon their merit pay plans. Others need to invest heavily in making their plans more effective through the use of bonuses and better communication processes.

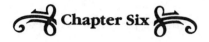 Chapter Six

Using Performance Appraisals to Drive Pay

The judging of one individual's performance by another is a regular, ongoing event in almost every human endeavor. On the surface it seems simple. One individual observes another performing a task and reaches a judgment about how adequately that task has been performed. In formal organizations, however, judging performance is substantially more complex than it is in most situations in which performance judgments are made. It is one thing for a fan at a sports event to observe and judge the performance of a player; it is quite another for a superior to observe and judge the performance of a subordinate. The fan may provide vocal feedback, but he or she has little reward power over the player and typically does not have an ongoing personal relationship with the player.

In an organizational setting the simple act of judging performance is complicated by the potential impact of an appraisal judgment on other events. The appraisal judgment can be and often is used to drive or at least influence a number of systems other than the pay system (Lawler and Mohrman, 1985). Indeed, it has often been said that performance appraisal judgments are at the very core of what the management of an organization is all about. They provide information that can be used for control purposes, planning purposes, and development purposes. As has already been stressed, without good appraisals it is usually impossible to relate pay to individual performance in a motivating way.

The objectives that I see stated for most performance appraisal systems reflect lofty goals. They talk about accomplishing multiple objectives: improving performance, improving motivation, clarifying the definition of a person's job, improving communication between the superior and the subordinate, helping individuals develop their skills and abilities, and helping individuals perceive a sense of the organization's overall direction and thrust. Unfortunately, the reality of performance appraisal systems is usually much less glorious than is suggested by these goals.

Problems with Appraisal Systems

Rarely is an organization satisfied with whatever performance appraisal system it has. The typical organization seems to revise its system at least every three or four years following an all-too-familiar pattern: A year is spent designing a new system. The changes that grow out of that time-consuming process are more cosmetic than real, however. Perhaps performance category labels are changed (the top category is changed from an A to a 7, for example) or the number of rating categories is changed. The first year under the new system is one of learning and testing, the second year sees increased dissatisfaction and demands for change, and the third and fourth years see work starting on a new system.

When asked why they are dissatisfied with their appraisal systems, organizations will typically list a host of very significant negative outcomes. For example, they point out that systems are often shot full of misleading data, including overly high ratings, erroneous reports by individuals concerning how well they have performed, unrealistic goals and performance objectives for individuals, and even a total failure to appraise the performance of some individuals. Small wonder that a whole consulting industry is based upon the revision, re-revision, and renewal of performance appraisal systems!

Because of the pressure that the appraisal system puts on superiors and subordinates, appraisals often lead to worsened superior-subordinate relationships. I have been in organizations where subordinates refused to speak to their bosses for weeks because of a difficult performance appraisal. Because appraisals are often done badly, instead of increasing motivation the appraisal system may lower it—and as a consequence lower performance. In addition, the system often creates dissatisfaction on the part of the person being appraised, and this in turn can lead to turnover.

For decades I have collected data on people's satisfaction with how their performance was appraised, and almost without exception the people being appraised have reported relatively low levels of satisfaction with the event. They complain that their concerns never get dealt with, that their boss does not listen to them, and that unfair pay actions result from the event (Mohrman, Resnick-West, and Lawler, 1989). Often what was intended to be a positive event ends up as a negative one.

An organization that is not careful can end up in a protracted court case because its performance appraisal system lacks the elements necessary to make it defensible in a court of law. Individuals can sue for unfair, discriminatory, and unlawful pay, promotion, or layoff actions that result from the outcome of the appraisal event. In California, lawsuits concerning firing increased at the rate of about 20 percent per year during the 1980s, with many settlements over $400,000. Many of these cases came about and were lost by companies because of their poor appraisal systems.

Finally, it is important to stress that performance appraisal systems have the potential to waste great amounts of valuable organizational time. Indeed, if everyone in the organization is to be appraised, good records maintained, and individuals trained, a significant amount of time needs to be spent on appraisal activities. If these activities are not carried out well, the potential for wasted time on the part of valuable employees is enormous. Performance appraisal involves all levels of management and staff, and thus it can waste the time of people from the top to the bottom of the organization. Managers in particular need to spend a lot of time managing the appraisal system, because they have multiple appraisals to do for their subordinates. They also need to be appraised by their boss or (in the case of matrix organizations) bosses.

Given the rate at which organizations seem to be abandoning their old performance appraisal systems and designing new ones, it seems safe to conclude that in most cases the systems fail to accomplish the lofty goals and objectives that are set for them. This, however, does not seem to discourage organizations from doing performance appraisals. Indeed, virtually every time there is a major need for increased productivity, organizations seem to renew their commitment to improving their performance appraisal system and doing a better job of paying for performance. A classic example of this was provided by General Motors in the late 1980s. As part of an effort to revitalize the organization, executives put in a new, "tough" appraisal system that forced managers to distinguish between good and poor performers. The system met with such resistance that it was abandoned within two years.

Why Appraisal Is Difficult

Because performance appraisal is so basic to paying for performance, we need to analyze in a little more detail why it seems to be such a difficult issue for organizations. Perhaps the major reason is that performance appraisal involves human behaviors and emotions. It is not the kind of act that can be completely programmed or controlled. Although it is tempting to think of it as a potentially objective event, performance appraisal is inherently a subjective, emotional process. One human being is asked to judge the performance of another in an area of performance that is often very important to both individuals. The person whose performance is being appraised is exposing his or her ego and risking negative feedback and a potential reduction of self-esteem. The person doing the appraisal is being asked to judge someone who may be a friend and who may react negatively to the judgment.

Appraisals are done by human beings, most of whom are not experts in giving and receiving feedback. Indeed, particularly in high-technology and knowledge-work organizations, many of them have their expertise in engineering and technical areas that stress the very antithesis of the kind of subjective measurement process inherent in performance appraisals. Technically trained managers asked to engage in this subjective process are often uncomfortable; they neither like the soft nature of the measures nor the emotional nature of the meetings. There is a tendency, therefore, for them to resist doing appraisals at all, and if the appraisals cannot be avoided, to get them over with as quickly as possible.

The tendency of supervisors to avoid doing appraisals was brought home to me in one of the first studies of appraisals that I did (Hall and Lawler, 1969). I interviewed a number of managers in an engineering organization, all of whom assured me that they regularly appraised their subordinates. When I interviewed their subordinates, however, I got a very different story: they talked of never having had an appraisal. My first thought was that someone must be lying, but in fact it was just that these two groups had different perceptions of reality. This became clear when I returned to the supervisors and asked them to describe how they had done the appraisals. Most described an occasion that was not clearly identified as an appraisal but during which they gave their subordinates some feedback. To them it was an appraisal; to their subordinates it was just another meeting.

In many respects performance appraisal is a test of power between two people. One person starts off with more power because of the superior-subordinate relationship, but this does not necessarily mean that the appraiser has *all* the power or that he or she will still have the preponderance of power after the event. Often the appraiser needs the individual being appraised as much as the reverse is true. Thus the appraiser may be hesitant to give too much negative feedback, and indeed may be trying to win favor with the appraisee just as the appraisee is trying to win favor with the appraiser. The power balance depends to a large extent upon the kind of skills that the person being appraised has, and how replaceable those skills are. In high-technology situations, often the person being appraised cannot easily be replaced and as a result has a considerable amount of power; he or she can effectively contest or ignore any negative judgments that are given by the boss.

In most cases there are simply no hard, objective measures available that would allow the appraisal to be based on objective data. Thus a judgment call is necessarily involved, the accuracy of which may or may not be accepted by the person being appraised. Acceptance of the judgment is partly a result of how the appraisal was performed and partly a result of the ongoing relationship between the appraiser and the appraisee.

Ultimately, a subjective judgment needs to be turned into an objective result. That is, the boss has to recommend whether a person should be promoted and/or get a pay raise and has to quantify the subordinate's score in terms of a rating scale; sometimes the appraiser even has to rank the individual in comparison to all the other individuals in that particular work area or work group. This latter feature of an appraisal system creates great stress, because it requires supervisors to assign a hard number or rating category that may have deep emotional significance for the person being appraised.

Time after time, when I have worked in organizations, I have found that ratings that to the casual observer seem to be quite acceptable are in fact unacceptable. For example, organizations often have a rating category such as "fully meets all job requirements." On the surface that phrase seems to indicate that the individual has performed the job well; it seems to be an acceptable rating. In many organizations, however, being rated in this category (or others like it) is seen as negative by most employees. Typically, this rating is the third category out of five in the rating system. Individuals so rated, with two groups ahead of them, tend to associate the category with the letter grade *C*, signifying average performance. Particularly in organizations that emphasize hiring the best, and that therefore end up hiring people who have good academic records, this category is simply unacceptable.

Finally, as was noted earlier, appraisals are used for many purposes by most organizations. It is precisely because of the connections between the performance appraisal system and other systems in an organization that performance appraisal is such a complex event. Indeed, it is the connections, or lack thereof, that often determine how effective the performance appraisal system will be and to what degree it can contribute to organizational effectiveness. These connections can produce a performance appraisal system that is more destructive than constructive and that will significantly harm the organization.

Because the performance appraisal system is tied into other systems, the appraiser and appraisee often end up with very different agendas for the performance appraisal meeting (Porter, Lawler, and Hackman, 1975). The superior typically has several organizationally mandated things that he or she has to accomplish during the appraisal, often giving these a high priority, emphasizing such things as getting a well-documented record of the subordinate's performance and giving the subordinate feedback about his performance during the last time period. Although the subordinate is typically interested in feedback about performance, of greater interest may be the implications of the performance appraisal for the individual's future rewards and career in the organization (Meyer,

Kay, and French, 1965). Ironically, career issues are usually near the top of the list of appraisal priorities for appraisees but low on the list for appraisers (Prince and Lawler, 1986).

Overall, the effectiveness of any appraisal event is influenced by the objectives that both parties bring to the event. The objectives in turn are at least partially a product of organizational decisions concerning what the performance appraisal system is expected to do, and how it is tied to other activities or systems in the organization.

Preconditions for Effective Performance Appraisal

A great deal has been written about the forms and procedures surrounding performance appraisal and how these can contribute to appraisal effectiveness. These issues will be dealt with later in the chapter, when we consider the design of performance appraisal systems. There are also situational factors that contribute to appraisal effectiveness, and it is to these that we now turn. It is extremely difficult to have an effective performance appraisal system when superior-subordinate relationships, job design, and organizational culture are not supportive of effective appraisal. Let us look at each one of these in turn and see how they shape the effectiveness of the performance appraisal system.

Job design is probably the most crucial determinant of whether performance appraisal can be done effectively. Unless jobs are designed in ways that allow individual performance to be measured, it is extremely difficult to do effective performance appraisal. One of the most common mistakes I see organizations make involves this point. They design work for *groups* and then ask supervisors to appraise the performance of *individuals*. Individual appraisal makes sense with such individual tasks as selling certain products, offering legal services, and producing simple products, but it does not fit selling complex computer systems, settling complex legal cases, or manufacturing many high-technology products (Schuster, 1984; Von Glinow and Mohrman, 1989). In the latter cases, *teams* of individuals need to perform well, and as a result good performance measures exist only at the team level.

Sports provide good examples here. Football does not allow

for good measurement at the individual level, particularly in the case of offensive linemen. Individual evaluation can be done, but the numbers are hard to defend because the performance of any individual is so strongly influenced by the performance of others. Something as simple as the success of a pass play is influenced by the performance of a number of individuals. The key measures look only at whether the quarterback completed the pass and which receiver caught it. Ignored are the blockers and the receivers who might have acted as effective decoys. The simple fact is that in football *teams* win and lose; thus it makes sense to measure and reward team performance. Quite the opposite is true in sports such as golf, tennis (except, of course, doubles), and track.

It is interesting to note that many of the job design characteristics that lead to effective performance appraisal are also associated with effective individual job enrichment (Hackman and Oldham, 1980). As research on individual job enrichment has shown, when jobs are designed such that people can do a whole piece of work, have responsibility for performing that task, and get feedback on the task, intrinsic motivation to perform is high. The same characteristics are also necessary for effective individual performance appraisal. Indeed, the feedback that comes to the individual and is key for intrinsic motivation is the same kind of data needed to appraise performance. In the absence of clear-cut individual responsibility for a whole piece of work, it is extremely difficult for the individual and for the supervisor to judge an individual's performance.

One option in situations where individual appraisals do not make sense is to do group appraisals. This is just what should be done in many high-tech and engineering situations. Work there is often assigned to teams with team goals. The logical approach to appraisal, therefore, is to measure team performance and to reward the individuals accordingly.

Effective performance appraisal also depends on open, effective communication between superior and subordinate (Mohrman, Resnick-West, and Lawler, 1989). In the absence of this kind of communication, it is virtually impossible to have effective performance appraisal. Supervisors need to gather information from subordinates in order to find out how well they have performed. In most cases individuals need to gather information from supervisors in order to understand what performance is expected of them and how their performance is being judged. Thus in the absence of good superior-subordinate relationships and effective communication, it is extremely difficult to have a performance appraisal system that reaches valid conclusions about subordinates' performance.

Performance appraisal is a time-consuming and difficult task to perform in an organization. It requires skills that many supervisors do not have and managerial behavior that is often difficult to demonstrate. The mere fact, for example, that negative feedback is sometimes required means that some supervisors will be quite uncomfortable conducting appraisals. Thus considerable support is needed for supervisors doing appraisals.

Because appraisal is difficult to do, an organizational culture that is strongly supportive of effective performance appraisal is required. The culture needs to be one in which doing performance appraisal well is valued, in which there are positive role models for effective performance appraisal, and in which the top management of the organization takes performance appraisal seriously. The right kind of attitude is shown in the following comment in an article written for the *Wall Street Journal* (Feb. 27, 1984) by Andy Grove, president of Intel: "At Intel, we estimate that a supervisor probably spends five to eight hours on each employee's review, about one-quarter to one-third of 1% of the supervisor's work year. If the effort expended contributes to an employee's performance even to a small extent over the course of a year, isn't that a highly worthwhile expenditure of a supervisor's time?

"We are paid to manage our organizations. To manage means to elicit better performance from members of our organization. We managers need to stop rationalizing, and to stiffen our resolve and do what we are paid to do."

In the absence of positive cultural conditions, it is extremely difficult to do performance appraisal well. Thus any consideration of whether pay should be tied to performance appraisal must consider the type of culture that the organization has and the degree to which the top of the organization will provide the necessary support and encouragement for doing performance appraisal effectively.

Appraisal System Connections

It is impossible to discuss performance appraisal effectiveness without considering the degree to which the appraisal system is connected to other systems. It is not simply a matter of understanding how the performance appraisal results influence such systems as the strategic planning process, the pay system, and the career planning process. This certainly requires understanding; but in order to understand the performance appraisal event it is also necessary to consider how the connections it has to other systems impact the performance appraisal event itself (Mohrman, Resnick-West, and Lawler, 1989).

A reciprocal influence process occurs in which the performance appraisal system influences the systems it is connected to while they in turn influence the nature of the performance appraisal event. Thus decisions about what to use performance appraisal for are not simply issues of how or whether performance appraisal can contribute to the effectiveness of the pay system or the career system. These decisions also raise issues of how the connections will influence the nature of the performance appraisal system and whether this influence will have a constructive or a destructive effect on the performance appraisal itself. The destructive effects may outweigh the advantages of connecting performance appraisal to a system that makes an appraisal more difficult to do well.

This point is particularly important in considering whether performance appraisal should be tied to pay. Any consideration of whether the pay system should be tied to the performance appraisal system must look at the positive and negative impacts on the pay system of tying it to performance appraisal results as well as the impact on the performance appraisal system of tying pay to it. Only when all these effects are considered is it possible to reach a sound conclusion about whether and how performance appraisals should be used to drive the pay system.

There is no single model of how to connect the performance appraisal system to the other systems of organization. Rather, the correct design must flow from other features of the organization. In essence, the kind of connections that are developed must be based upon the characteristics of the organization and must fit the particular situation in which they are developed. A diagnostic stance that considers the way the organization is designed, the capabilities of the members of the organization, and the type of work the organization does is particularly important when considering the connection between performance appraisal and pay. There is simply no right way to do things.

We will begin our discussion of how to connect pay to performance appraisal by considering the possible positive and negative effects of having the performance appraisal system drive the pay system. Then we will consider how and when pay and performance appraisal should be related.

The Impact of Performance Appraisal on Pay System Effectiveness. The reasons for relating pay to performance have already been mentioned but warrant repeating: individuals are motivated to perform more effectively, organizations develop performance-oriented cultures, and the attraction and retention rates of high performers are better. Overall, then, there are a number of positive advantages that can come out of effectively tying pay to performance appraisal results. There are, of course, other ways to attract and retain good performers, motivate individual performance, and create a performance-oriented culture, but it is hard to ignore the possible positive impact of performance-based pay.

If valid performance appraisal data are available, there are no readily apparent pay system negatives to relating pay to performance. The big "if" here concerns whether valid performance appraisal data can be obtained. If valid data are not available, tying pay to performance appraisal results can lead to the many negative consequences mentioned already.

The Impact of Pay on Performance Appraisal Effectiveness. Tying the performance appraisal system to pay can have positive and negative effects on the performance appraisal. On the positive side, research evidence suggests that when pay is discussed in the performance appraisal event, both the superior and the subordinate tend to take the appraisal more seriously and exchange better information about performance expectations and performance results (Prince and Lawler, 1986). The same research also suggests that individuals feel that pay and performance should be linked, and that indeed they should be discussed at the same time so that individuals have a chance to understand how the performance appraisal system affects their pay.

On the negative side, there is evidence that when pay and performance are discussed together, little attention is paid to long-term career development issues or to future performance concerns (Meyer, Kay, and French, 1965). Instead, the conversation focuses on past performance and on the impact of performance on pay. There may also be a tendency for the subordinate to withhold negative information about performance in order to look good during the performance appraisal. This can cloud the degree to which a valid performance discussion takes place; and if the appraisal data are used for planning purposes, such withholding of information can contribute to poor planning. In addition, when individuals feel that their performance appraisal results are going to be used for pay determination, they often set lower goals and are more conservative in their estimates of what they can accomplish. These lower goals often lead to lower motivation (Locke and Latham, 1984). They can also have a misleading effect on the planning process; individuals are in essence providing misinformation that will be relied on.

Perhaps the best way to summarize our discussion so far is to say that when appraisal and pay are connected, the pay system puts certain stresses on the performance appraisal system. These stresses are not necessarily negative, but they do need to be taken into account in the design of any performance appraisal system.

Substitutes for Performance Appraisal-Driven Pay

Sometimes other systems are available in organizations to do what can be accomplished by tying pay to performance appraisal. If adequate substitutes are available, the organization may want to put less emphasis on trying to relate pay and performance appraisal.

In the area of motivation there are adequate substitutes for driving individual pay by performance appraisal, particularly in high-participation work situations where work is designed for groups. In such situations the best measures of performance are often found at the group or organization level. As will be discussed in the next chapter, this creates the possibility of tying bonuses to group or organizational performance, which can be an adequate motivational substitute for individual performance appraisal–based pay. Admittedly, group bonuses do not tie pay directly to individual performance and therefore may not have as strong and direct an impact on individual motivation as individual bonuses do. Nevertheless, they can provide an adequate substitute in the area of motivation, particularly when combined with an employee-involvement management style and work designed for teams.

It is also possible that individuals in the organization can be motivated by social goals as they often are in voluntary organizations. If this is true, pay tied to individual performance may not be necessary. Indeed, it may be resented.

Another substitute for tying pay to individual performance is a good goal-setting process between superior and subordinate. It has been shown that goal setting can often be motivating even when pay is not affected by goal accomplishment (Locke and Latham, 1984).

Making the Decision

How should an organization decide whether pay should be tied to performance appraisal results? No formula exists that will allow this decision to be made in a highly programmed way. Indeed, it is unlikely that there ever will be one. The situation is simply too complex. It requires tough judgment calls. There is a natural inclination for organizations to choose to relate pay to performance appraisal data because of the important positive results that can come out of the connection. Quickly reaching the conclusion that this connection is desirable, however, is often a significant error. Too many organizations like the idea so much that they adopt it—only to find out that they do not want to do or cannot do what it takes to make the appraisal-pay union effective. In other words, they like the illusion but not the reality.

As I stressed earlier, the potential downside of tying pay to performance appraisals can far outweigh the positives. Even if performance appraisal is done as well as possible, tying pay to the results may have some negative effects: it can still lead to less open communication and more conservative goal setting. If there is little budget available for pay increases, the net effect of tying pay to performance will be an insignificant difference between the pay of good performers and the pay of poor performers. Pay should be tied to performance appraisal results only when most of the favorable conditions for tying pay to performance appraisal exist. In the absence of a strongly supportive culture, good job design, and open superior-subordinate relationships, it is not advisable to relate pay to performance appraisal results. Without the right conditions, not only will the pay system be rendered ineffective but the appraisal system itself will be likely to collapse under the stress.

The favorable conditions do not necessarily all have to exist in advance of performance appraisal implementation, but they do have to exist after the appraisal system is put in place. Because creating these conditions may involve major organizational change, firms would do well to initiate change before the performance appraisal system is put into place. Sometimes the performance appraisal system can help move the organization in the right direction, but assuming this will happen is a high-risk strategy.

An interesting example of an organization using its performance appraisal system to help change its management style is provided by Amoco Corporation. As part of a move to a more participative management style, a new performance management system was introduced in 1989. According to the letter that introduced the system, "Amoco Performance Management is different because it was designed to be highly *participative*—meaning that supervisors and employees will work together during each performance cycle. This emphasis on mutuality is the most significant difference between Amoco Performance Management and the performance appraisal system in place today. Amoco Performance Management introduces a change in our philosophy and management style that will result in higher levels of performance Corporate wide. It means more satisfaction for both you and your supervisor—because you will know, in advance, what is expected throughout the year. Most important: it represents a greater emphasis on employee involvement and participation, both now and in the future."

Overall, then, the warning is clear: do not be seduced by the potential advantages of tying pay to performance appraisal results.

These advantages are available only if *good* performance appraisal can be done, and this is by no means an easy thing to accomplish. Each organization needs a realistic assessment to determine whether favorable conditions exist (or can be reasonably expected to exist). In my consulting work I often use a combination of attitude surveys, observations, and interviews to determine whether the right conditions exist or can be created. All too often organizations fail to gather data on the potential of having an effective performance appraisal system; they simply install one. Not doing an assessment is equivalent to entering unexplored territory without a map—something that only the foolish or extremely risk-oriented explorer does!

Designing the Performance Appraisal System

The design of an effective performance appraisal system for driving pay begins with identification of the appropriate time period for the performance appraisal. As the work of Elliot Jacques (1961) emphasizes, each job has a "time span of discretion." These can vary from a few minutes to years, because jobs differ that much in how long it takes for performance to show up in measurable results. The organization that picks too short a cycle runs the risk of emphasizing short-term performance and making measurement difficult or impossible. The organization that picks too long a time period runs the risk of having employees lose sight of the connection between pay and performance and thus forfeiting the motivational potential of the performance appraisal.

Organizations typically pick an annual performance appraisal cycle; everyone gets appraised once a year. At the lower levels of an organization this is probably too infrequent an appraisal cycle, given that the performance of people in these jobs is typically evident on a much shorter-term basis. Indeed, at this level individuals have often left the job or the organization before the appraisal is due. At the top level, on the other hand, an annual cycle is too short: in that time period individuals in upper management do not have a chance to demonstrate their performance effectiveness. At the high levels a cycle of two years or more is often appropriate.

Once the cycle for individuals has been identified, the key

issues involve sequencing the events during the performance period. The best sequence starts with an appraiser-appraisee agreement on specific goals, measures, and the impact on pay of accomplishing these goals. In short, a performance contract needs to be established before the performance period begins. It must include measures of performance and specification of how performance will impact pay. It is particularly crucial that this discussion be a two-way one and that both the superior and subordinate feel that they have impacted the ultimate contract. If the subordinate does not see the goals as legitimate and does not understand their relationship to pay, much of the motivational impact of the process will be lost.

Although it seems obvious that agreement on performance goals and rewards should be reached before the appraisal starts, it often is not. In some cases it is delayed or not done at all. In one company I studied, agreement on goals was not done until year-end. At that time individuals were asked to list their accomplishments. In this system, conflicts often arose between appraisers and appraisees over whether appraisees were doing the right thing, because there was no preagreement.

There is one possible exception to the need for preagreements. In fast-changing environments and in some high-technology R & D situations, it is neither possible nor desirable to set specific performance objectives. Often good performance is recognizable only when it has occurred; it cannot be specified in advance. Still, in these situations general agreement about what performance areas will be looked at can usually be reached, so that the final appraisal discussion is not a completely unguided event.

Many systems do part but not all of this process. That is, they agree upon measures of performance, but they do not discuss the issue of pay. This is understandable—talking about pay can be difficult—but if pay is going to be an effective motivator, it is crucial that this kind of contracting exist. If it does not, the individual will be unlikely to believe that a clear relationship exists between pay and performance.

Potentially quite important can be a midcourse review of the goals, objectives, and performance of the individual. If situational changes make the initial goals unrealistic after the formulation, they need to be adjusted to fit current conditions; otherwise, the motivational impact of the system will be lost. Goals that cannot be reached are not motivating, nor are goals that have already been reached. In addition, sometimes ongoing feedback can help the individual correct existing performance problems and accomplish goals that otherwise would not have been accomplished.

At least two discussions are needed at the end of the performance period. The first is to provide the individual an opportunity to present his or her perception of performance during the period. Research clearly shows that this step is important in helping the individual perceive the performance appraisal process as a fair and reasonable one (Lawler, Mohrman, and Resnick, 1984). When it is omitted, individuals feel that their performance was appraised without adequate input and that as a result the appraisal is invalid.

We saw what happens when this opportunity is not provided in a study I did with colleagues for General Electric several years ago. Some parts of the company required supervisors to review appraisals with higher-level managers before discussing them with the individuals being appraised. At first glance this made sense, because it provided a test of the accuracy of the appraiser's rating. The problem was that it "locked in" the appraisal rating so that by the time the person being appraised got a chance to comment, the appraiser was no longer open to influence. Indeed, we found supervisors who admitted to subordinates that there was an error but refused to change the rating: "It would be embarrassing to admit to my boss that I was wrong." Often this was followed by the promise, "I'll make it up to you next year."

A second meeting should be held after the superior has had a chance to incorporate the employee's perceptions about performance into a written appraisal. At this meeting the final performance appraisal of the individual is discussed, and the pay action is specified. It is important that this pay action follow closely upon the final appraisal in order that a clear connection be seen between pay and performance.

Two common organizational practices concerning timing work against establishing a clear pay-for-performance relationship. One is the practice of varying the frequency of raises as a function of performance. Typically, good performers get raises more frequently than poor performers. When this practice is combined with an annual performance appraisal cycle, it has the effect of separating the performance appraisal sessions from the pay actions. For poor performers, it can mean a long wait for the next appraisal before they can be recognized for improved performance.

A second practice involves scheduling appraisals throughout the year rather than doing all appraisals at the same time. This is typically done to avoid overloading the appraisers. It accomplishes this, but it puts appraisal out of phase with the normal performance measurement cycle of the organization. (The financial system, for example, typically operates on a year-end basis.) This makes it more difficult to set goals and to compare the performance of individuals, because they are appraised on different results. Finally, it can lead to a timing effect in the favorableness of ratings. In some companies I have studied, there seems to be a tendency for supervisors to give high ratings early in the year and then to get tougher at the end. I have heard managers explain to individuals being appraised at the end of the year that the high ratings had been "used up" earlier in the year.

Appraisal Forms

The form used in performance appraisal is only one of several determinants of how effective the system is. Indeed, the form may be one of the least important factors. No type of form is vastly superior to others, but whatever form is used needs to do two things.

First, the form should focus on *observable* behavior and results. Forms that ask for ratings of such traits as attitude, cooperativeness, and reliability should never be used. They are not legally defensible, and they usually produce poor feedback and defensiveness on the part of the person being appraised. The term *reliability*, for example, is vague. In addition, it is emotionally loaded; few people like to be told that they are unreliable. It is also hard to agree on what changes will lead to a higher rating of reliability. Most traits can be converted into behaviors; if they cannot, they should be dropped. For example, *reliability* can be converted into "meets deadlines" and "has good attendance record." Attendance and performance against deadlines can be measured and are therefore good bases for appraisal.

Second, the appraisal form should give a quantitative score that can be translated into a pay action. A common error among organizations is to use an approach that asks appraisers to make judgments that are more precise than can be supported by a subjective performance appraisal process. For example, many organizations ask appraisers to rank their subordinates in terms of overall job performance. In a large work area supervisors may have to rank their subordinates from 1 to up to 25, 30, or more. In addition to the problem of telling someone that he or she is ranked 30 out of 30, this asks raters to make judgments that go beyond their mental ability to see differences among individuals. Research suggests that, at most, people can discriminate among five to seven different levels of performance. Thus many of the differences that are reported (for example, the difference between the person ranked 10 and the person ranked 12) are not defensible; they are the result of chance.

Different problems are caused by systems that ask raters to distribute their ratings using a forced-distribution format. This usually calls for a certain percentage of the ratings to fall into particular rating categories. For example, supervisors may be told to rate 5 percent of their subordinates as 1, 15 percent as 2, 30 percent as 3, 30 percent as 4, 15 percent as 5, and 5 percent as 6. This kind of approach assumes that the organization knows the correct distribution in advance—a doubtful assumption. A normal distribution is usually assumed, even though the people being rated are not a random sample of the population. Usually, in fact, they are carefully selected and trained to perform the job. In addition, the number of individuals being rated is far too small to render a normal distribution.

In many cases the forced-distribution approach asks appraisers to make difficult or even impossible judgments. For example, it may ask them to put 50 percent of the people above average and 50 percent below average. This assures that 50 percent will get a negative message, and it asks supervisors to divide the large middle group of individuals who typically are doing their job acceptably into an above- and a below-average group. In most situations this is impossible to do accurately, and as a result it is best to simply treat those employees as one large group.

The forced-distribution approach also has the disadvantage of letting supervisors "disown" the ratings. Time after time I have heard supervisors tell their subordinates that they had to rate them low because they had to put *someone* in the bottom category! This only serves to destroy the credibility of the entire system, of course, and it emphasizes the competitive nature of any forced-distribution or ranking system. When individuals are compared for rating purposes, it is hard to argue that cooperation and teamwork are valued and rewarded. The real message is that you must do better than others in order to be rated highly. In contrast, when individuals are rated against goals and job standards, they are competing against themselves, not each other.

I often suggest to organizations that people simply be rated as either outstanding, fully competent, or unsatisfactory—fully expecting that 80 percent of the people will be rated in the middle category. This does not give very precise performance information, but it may provide all that is needed and all that can be validly provided. Most appraisers can accurately identify their top performers and those who are failing. They get into trouble when they try to differentiate further. Although identifying only three groups does not allow many different levels of merit treatment, good performers can still be rewarded well and money can still be withheld from poor performers. Using only three categories also helps avoid the dreaded labeling problem by making it okay to be in the middle category. As I have noted, in systems where there are two categories above the middle category, the middle category is typically seen as equaling a *C* grade and therefore as negative. In many cases this means that *most* people get an upsetting, negative message from the system. This is acceptable if the organization needs a jolt, but it is not desirable if things are going well.

Conoco Inc. provides a good example of a company in which some divisions decided to go to a three-category system. As indicated by the following letter that introduced the system to employees, its approach was designed to reduce competition and assess individuals against present objectives: "The fundamental changes in appraisals are: There will be no peer comparisons. Performance will be measured against goals or job expectations, not peers. There will be no forced performance curves or balanced curves. Employee performance will be distributed without rules on how many employees should be in any performance category. There will be three performance categories instead of five." (Recently, Conoco Inc. has adopted a four-category system that is consistent across the entire company.)

I often find it useful to have appraisers at the same level of management meet to consider each other's ratings and address the issue of ratings inflation. There needs to be some downward pressure on ratings; otherwise they tend to drift up. In the U.S. military they have drifted up so high that over 95 percent of all officers are rated in the top category! Meetings in which appraisers have to defend their ratings can create a downward pressure, as can "suggested" or "guided" distributions, which provide some norms about what should be common practice. I much prefer these to forced distributions and rankings. I do not support systems that ask for *no* rating or summary judgment of performance, however. The absence of a rating avoids the labeling problem, but it is a cop-out if a pay action is to result from the appraisal judgment. It simply transfers the quantification of the appraisal from the performance rating to the pay-raise recommendation.

One interesting possibility is to allow each superior-subordinate pair to pick a form that they feel best fits their situation. In this approach the responsibility of the system designers is to provide forms that are acceptable to the organization and, if necessary, to help the superior and subordinate pick the best one. This choice process can be quite effective, because it helps each pair feel committed to the way the appraisal is done and to the form that fits their situation. I have seen this approach work rather well in one division of GE.

This and other methods of employee participation can help ensure organizational acceptance of the appraisal process. Nowhere is the participative design of reward system practices more important than in the case of performance appraisal. This is an area in which task forces can contribute a great deal of knowledge about the organization and in which their involvement in the design process can help ensure acceptance of the final design (Mohrman, Resnick-West, and Lawler, 1989).

Career Discussion

So far our discussion of the ideal appraisal process has not included a consideration of career and long-term personal development. This is intentional because it is assumed that career issues will be handled in a separate session and on a somewhat different time cycle. As was mentioned earlier, research evidence shows that career development is best handled in a separate system because the discussion of past performance and pay tends to drive consideration of career issues out of the appraisal event. Career discussions need not be annual; many individuals do not feel the need for that frequent a discussion of their career. In addition, if is often best left up to individuals to indicate when they would like to have such a discussion. Having individuals initiate discussion helps to reinforce the idea that a person's career is the responsibility of the individual, not of the organization.

Finally, it often turns out that the best person to do the career appraisal is not a person's immediate supervisor. Often the supervisor does not have a good overview of the career options available and thus may need help from higher levels of management or from the human resources department. Separating career development from pay discussions makes it easier to get these other individuals involved.

Chapter Seven

Paying for Organizational Performance

Bonus payments based on the performance of an organization are an old and potentially quite effective way to improve organizational performance. Proponents argue that such bonuses can improve motivation, build a work culture in which people are committed to and care about the organization's effectiveness, and adjust the labor costs of an organization to its ability to pay. There is no question that a number of organizations have been able to accomplish just these outcomes as a result of paying bonuses on the basis of organizational performance.

There are a number of well-publicized examples of companies successfully using bonus payments. One of the oldest and best-known cases is that of Lincoln Electric, a Cleveland-based manufacturer of welding equipment that has maintained a virtual stranglehold on a piece of the welding market despite significant foreign competition (Lincoln, 1951). Important keys to Lincoln's success are its profit-sharing plan, which relates bonus payments to corporate profits, and various pay-for-performance systems that reward individuals and small groups for their performance. This combination of pay-for-performance plans has allowed Lincoln Electric to have the highest pay rate in its industry while operating very successfully, a clear win-win situation.

Another successful example is provided by the Herman Miller Company, a rapidly growing and highly profitable furniture manufacturer that is frequently rated by *Fortune* magazine as one of the ten best-managed U.S. corporations. It has had a gainsharing plan and a strong emphasis on participative management for decades—a combination that appears to deserve much of the credit for the company's success.

Another interesting example is provided by the Motorola Corporation. At the beginning of the 1970s Motorola recognized the potential power of paying the members of organizational units, such as departments and project teams, based on the success of their work areas. Over the next ten years Motorola installed plans that related bonuses to the success of work units. These plans are credited by the organization with helping it compete in a variety of high-technology businesses. In essence, they helped Motorola convert from a struggling consumer electronics company to a successful worldwide competitor in high-technology electronics and defense contracting. Motorola has also often been recognized as one of the ten best-managed companies in the United States in recent years.

Finally, a more recent example is provided by the success of such new companies as Nucor Steel, Chaparral Steel, and AFG Industries. These three companies are particularly interesting because they operate in old industries—steel in the case of Nucor and Chaparral and glass in the case of AFG. They have been successful, while the traditional steel and glass companies have virtually given up on these industries. All three of these companies have done a number of things right, but one important feature of their management systems is bonus payments based on performance. In the case of Nucor this has led to productivity frequently estimated to be twice as high as that of traditional steel mills and to relatively high pay for employees. Pay at Nucor is made up of relatively low base wages, team-productivity bonuses, and a profit-sharing plan that is funded by 10 percent of pretax company earnings. Freed from the constraints of traditional work rules and motivated by incentive pay, Nucor is both paying well and making a profit.

AFG has been a star in the glass industry. Coming from nowhere, it is now the second-largest plate-glass maker in the United States. It too relies on bonus plans driven by plant productivity and on corporate-wide profit sharing.

There are literally thousands of approaches to paying for organizational performance, and there are many complex organizational issues that must be dealt with if a plan is to be successful. The good news is that decades of research have pointed out a number of things that must be done if plans are to be successful, so designing a plan does not have to be an unguided trip. Other organizations can do what Lincoln Electric, Herman Miller, Motorola, Nucor, Chaparral, and AFG have done.

Historically, there have been two major approaches to paying for organizational performance. In the oldest, profit sharing, bonuses are based on the profitability of the organization. This is undoubtedly the most widely accepted approach around the world, and as will be discussed later, it has important advantages (as well as major limitations). Less well known but increasingly popular is gainsharing, which differs from profit sharing in two respects. First, it combines a bonus plan with a participative approach to management; second, it typically measures controllable costs or units of output, not profits, in calculating a bonus. Employee ownership is a third (but somewhat less direct) way to relate pay to organizational performance. We will first consider what is known about gainsharing and profit sharing and then consider employee ownership. Once we have done this we will be in a position to consider what an organization should do if it wants to base pay on organizational performance.

Gainsharing

Gainsharing has been around since the 1930s. It has been successfully applied by hundreds, perhaps even thousands, of organizations (Frost, Wakeley, and Ruh, 1974; Lawler, 1988). Both employees and companies have profited from gainsharing—companies in the form of reduced costs and employees in the form of bonus payments and improved job satisfaction. The original and best-known gainsharing plan is the Scanlon Plan. Others include Improshare and the Rucker Plan. In addition to these plans, many companies have their own custom-designed gainsharing plans.

In the typical gainsharing plan, financial gains in organizational performance are shared on a formula basis with all employees in a single plant or company location. A historical base period of performance is established as a basis for determining whether gains have occurred; hence the name "gainsharing." Typically, only controllable costs are measured in computing the gain. Unless a major change takes place in the organization's product or technology, the historical base stays the same during the entire history of the plan; thus performance is always compared to the time period before the gainsharing plan. When performance is better than it was in the base period, a bonus pool is funded. When it falls short, no funding occurs. In the typical plan about half of the bonus pool is paid out to the employees; the rest is kept by the company. Payments are typically made on a monthly basis, with all employees getting the same percentage of their base pay.

No one has an accurate estimate of how many gainsharing plans there are in the United States and Europe. There are certainly at least 1,000, and there seems to be little doubt that their popularity has increased tremendously in the last ten years. Two surveys provide some interesting data on the use of gainsharing. The most recent survey covered the *Fortune* 1,000. It found that 26 percent of the organizations use gainsharing somewhere but that most use it in only a few locations (Lawler, Ledford, and Mohrman, 1989). Another survey found that gainsharing plans are used by 13 percent of a larger, more diverse sample and claimed that the use is growing rapidly (O'Dell, 1987). The White House Conference on Productivity, the U.S. General Accounting Office, and the President's Task Force on Industrial Competitiveness have all endorsed gainsharing.

In the 1950s and 1960s gainsharing was used primarily in small manufacturing organizations. Much has been written in the United States about the success of gainsharing in two companies that were early adopters, Herman Miller and Donnelly Mirrors. During the 1970s an interesting and important trend developed. Large companies such as General Electric, Motorola, TRW, Dana, 3M, and Firestone began installing gainsharing plans in some of their manufacturing plants. This trend of implementing gainsharing in specific units of large corporations is continuing, and it is resulting in the adoption of many more gainsharing plans. Dana, for example, now has most of its employees covered by gainsharing, while Rockwell, Amoco, and Mead have joined the list of companies installing gainsharing.

Gainsharing has also moved beyond the factory environment. Most of the early plans were in manufacturing locations, at least partly because of the relative ease of measuring factory output. During the 1980s, however, gainsharing has been adopted by a number of service organizations. Some Holiday Inns have gainsharing plans based on revenue and quality of service, for example, and similar plans have been tried by Taco Bell and other restaurant chains. Xerox has used gainsharing in its service organization, and Lincoln National Life Insurance has many of its claims processors on gainsharing plans.

Gainsharing plans have also been adopted by high-technology companies in order to encourage employees to be cost-effective and to do high-quality work. For example, Honeywell and TRW both have plans covering pieces of their defense contracting businesses. These plans are particularly interesting because in some cases they distribute the gains on a tripartite model: the customer gets a refund on the contract if it is completed for less than the bid price, and the employees and company share the rest of the savings between them. Overall, gainsharing has expanded from an approach used by a few small manufacturing companies to an approach that is used by a wide variety of businesses.

Why has there been an increase in the popularity of gainsharing? I believe the most important reason is that gainsharing plans are more than just incentive plans; they are an organizational development technology. To be specific, they are based on a participative approach to management and are often used as a way to install or reinforce other participative management practices. Thus they are in tune with two increasingly popular management trends: pay for performance and employee involvement.

My personal experiences with gainsharing have always been in situations where management has wanted to reinforce or institute a high-involvement approach to management. In my first experience I was invited to assess whether gainsharing would be a good fit in the Gaines dog-food plant in Topeka, Kansas—one of the pioneering participatively managed manufacturing plants in the United States.

When I began working with Gaines in the early 1970s, the plant had already established a considerable reputation for its effectiveness and its high-involvement approach to management (Lawler, 1978). Plant managers were concerned, however, because performance improvements were slowing down; they felt that they needed an additional productivity boost. They also wanted to be sure that whatever they did with pay would reinforce their strong commitment to participative management and to equitable treatment of all employees.

An analysis of the situation strongly suggested that a gainsharing plan would both produce performance improvements and support the well-established participative management system at the plant. We immediately ran into a major obstacle, however. Although local management was enthusiastic, corporate resistance at the parent company, General Foods, quickly surfaced. The corporation commissioned a task force to determine how well the plant was working and whether a gainsharing plan would be appropriate. After a year the task force concluded that the plant *was* well suited for gainsharing. It was already about 40 percent more cost-effective than other General Foods plants, and thus any performance improvement would warrant bonuses and be a true win-win situation.

About the time the work of the task force was completed, however, General Foods became so disenchanted with the local management team that it decided to replace them with a new group of managers. This personnel shift effectively killed the movement toward gainsharing. Needless to say, I was disappointed at not being able to put in a gainsharing plan. The Gaines plant represented, in my mind, an ideal opportunity to see whether a gainsharing plan could bring additional performance and rewards to a plant that was already operating in a highly effective participative mode.

A few years later I had the chance to actually put in a gainsharing plan in a similar plant, one operated by Butler Manufacturing (Bullock and Bullock, 1982). As I predicted, the plan paid off handsomely there, even though the plant was already operating effectively when the plan was installed. In the years since my initial explorations of gainsharing, I have helped install other plans and am convinced that they can reinforce an existing high-involvement system and even move the system ahead to higher levels of involvement and performance. The key to success lies in combining an effective participative system with an appropriate gainsharing formula.

The Participative System

From the beginning Joe Scanlon, the creator of the Scanlon Plan, emphasized that gainsharing fits a participative management style.

In many cases a participative system is needed in order for the plan to work, and in *all* cases it is needed in order for the full potential of the plan to be realized. In the absence of a change in employee behavior, there is no reason to expect a payout from the kind of formula that is typically developed in gainsharing plans. A payout requires an improvement in organizational performance, and that improvement requires more effective behavior on the part of individual employees.

Some improvement may be gained simply from the motivation that is tapped through tying pay to performance. This is particularly true in small organizations whose work is not highly skilled or interdependent; in those firms employee efforts often can directly influence organizational performance. In other situations, however, there are several reasons why a gainsharing plan without a participative system will not produce an appreciable improvement in performance.

First, in the absence of participative management the motivational impact of the plan may not be large, because most gainsharing plans aggregate a number of people together. As a result, the plans do little to improve the perceived relationship between individual performance and pay. This is particularly true in traditionally managed organizations, because there individual employees can influence only a few of the factors that determine organizational performance. The formula used is also relevant here. Some plans use very simple formulas that focus on the relationship between labor input and productivity (for example, the Improshare plan), while others use a comprehensive set of cost measures (for example, the Rucker Plan). Simple labor-based plans are more likely to affect motivation, because with them—even in a traditionally managed organization—employees may see a relationship between their efforts and their bonuses. Despite their attractiveness, however, simple plans are not always best from an organizational effectiveness point of view (as will be discussed later).

Second, in many cases simple effort and good intentions on the part of employees are not enough to improve the operating results. What is needed is a combination of people working harder, working more effectively together, sharing their ideas, and working smarter. This often requires a formal participative system that converts the motivation to improve performance into changes in the operating procedures of an organization. In the absence of new systems to accomplish these changes, they rarely occur.

In traditional gainsharing plans such as the Scanlon Plan, the key participative approach is a formal suggestion system. In addition to the shop-floor committees that review the written suggestions, there is often also a higher-level review committee that looks over those recommendations that involve several parts of the organization and/or large expenditures. This system of committees is one way of trying to ensure that new ideas will be seriously considered and, where appropriate, implemented.

Suggestion systems are a limited form of participation, however. They fall far short of the kind of participation that is practiced in the Gaines and Butler plants mentioned earlier. In them, and in other high-involvement plants, employees hire, fire, set production schedules, and determine work methods. In these plants individuals throughout the organization make decisions that influence more than just productivity; thus they can be motivated by measures of plant profit, operating costs, and other financial measures. They can be motivated precisely because they can influence these measures, and thus a line of sight exists.

Research Results

The most important thing we know about gainsharing plans is that they work. The following are some of the common results that have been found in research studies of gainsharing plans (Lawler, 1988):

- Coordination, teamwork, and sharing of knowledge are enhanced at lower levels.
- Social needs are recognized and met via participation and mutually reinforcing group behavior.
- Attention is focused on cost savings, not just quantity of production.
- Acceptance of change due to technology, market, and new methods is greater, because higher efficiency leads to bonuses.
- Attitudinal change occurs among workers, who demand more efficient management and better planning.

- Employees try to reduce overtime and to work smarter.
- Employees produce ideas as well as effort.
- When unions are present, more flexible administration of union-management relations occurs.
- When unions support gainsharing they are strengthened, because a better work situation and higher pay result.
- Unorganized locations tend to remain nonunion.

As can be seen above, gainsharing plans typically produce a number of positive results. In fact, research supporting this point has been around for decades. We know somewhat less about the frequency with which these plans work, but there is evidence to suggest that they work about 75 percent of the time (Bullock and Lawler, 1984; U.S. General Accounting Office, 1981; Schuster, 1983).

Quite a bit is also known about how to structure gainsharing plans. There are a number of books and articles that describe in some detail how to put together formulas, how to introduce plans, and how to manage the process side of plan development. As a result, there is quite a bit of how-to knowledge circulating. This is particularly true with respect to the Scanlon Plan (Graham-Moore and Ross, 1983). Indeed, careful reading of the literature on this plan can enable organizations to develop and install gainsharing without the help of a consultant. However, in my experience most plans *are* installed by consultants. Once a company has had some successful experiences with gainsharing, however, it may stop using outside experts and proceed on its own.

The research evidence also shows that certain situational factors favor gainsharing plans. They include the following:

- *Organizational Size.* The success of any gainsharing plan is based on employees' seeing a relationship between what they do and their pay. As organizations get larger, this relationship is harder to see. Thus most successful gainsharing plans cover fewer than 500 employees.
- *Performance Measurement.* In some organizations—especially those characterized by rapid technological and market changes—good performance measures and a reasonable perfor-

mance history simply do not exist and cannot be established. When this is true, gainsharing formulas are difficult to develop.

- *Measurement Complexity.* Often performance can be measured only in very complex ways. The truer this is of a given organization, the more difficult it is to make a plan work, because there is no clear, easily understood connection between an individual's behavior and rewards.
- *Worker Characteristics.* Successful gainsharing depends on the desire of employees to participate and earn more money. Admittedly, most employees have these goals, but not all do. Unless a substantial majority of the employees want the benefits the plan offers, it cannot succeed.
- *Communication.* For gainsharing to work, employees must understand and trust it enough to believe that their pay will increase if they perform better. For this belief to exist, a great deal of open communication and education are needed. If an organization does not have these already, they must be started if the plan is to succeed.
- *Management Attitudes.* Unless managers are favorable to the idea of participation, gainsharing will not fit the management style of the organization. In organizations where gainsharing has been tried simply as an incentive plan, without regard to management style, it has often failed.
- *Supervisory Skills.* Gainsharing requires supervisors to change. They are forced to deal with many suggestions, and their competence is tested and questioned in new ways. Unless supervisors are prepared for and accept these changes, the plan can fail. This point goes along with the general point that management must be prepared to manage in a different way.

As this list demonstrates, gainsharing does not fit every situation. Because manufacturing situations often have most of these favorable conditions, it is easy to see why for so long the installation of gainsharing plans was limited to them. However, although a great deal remains to be learned about how plans should be designed for service and knowledge-work environments, it appears that they can work in these settings as well. Indeed, gainsharing may prove to be very effective in service organizations, because their labor costs are crucial and performance is easily controlled by the people doing the work. Evidence to support this view is provided by Xerox and Taco Bell, which have successful gainsharing plans in their service operations. As will be discussed next, as long as some basic design features can be built into a plan, there is reason to believe that gainsharing can work in any organization.

Critical Gainsharing Elements

The design of a gainsharing plan for any organization is part science and part art. Because there are so many different gainsharing plans around, it is easy to lose track of the major elements that make for a successful gainsharing plan. Perhaps the key issue in gainsharing design is that of fit: the gainsharing formula and participative management features need to fit each other and the situation. Given the variety of situations in which gainsharing plans have been tried, it is appropriate that a wide variety of plans have been developed. Different situations require different designs; different designs require different practices. There are, however, some general elements that are needed in all plans if they are to be successful. Let us turn to a consideration of each of the elements and look at how they can be achieved.

A Credible, Trusted Development Process. Gainsharing plans vary widely in how they are developed. In some cases a knowledgeable expert comes with an already developed plan and convinces the organization that it will work. Probably the majority of the plans have been installed in this manner. The Improshare Plan, for example, is typically installed this way. It relies on an expert who comes equipped with a standard formula. The expert adapts the formula and then asks the employees to vote on whether they want the plan.

In other cases representative task forces are created within the organization. They investigate different plans and ultimately end up making a recommendation for their particular situation. They may even take responsibility for developing a custom formula that fits their situation. All the plans I have installed have followed this approach.

There is no right set of practices, but unless the practices lead employees to believe in the plan, gainsharing has little chance of success. Plans depend on the belief of employees that if they perform better, they will be paid more. Initially, this requires a leap of faith, because there is no payment until there is performance improvement.

There is no question that in some cases an outside expert can effectively install a plan. In my experience, however, a participative development process that utilizes a task force is more likely to lead to a high level of plan acceptance and trust. As will be discussed in more detail in Chapter Twelve, using a task force typically results in a much slower development process, however. On the positive side, once an organization has gone through this type of self-design process, it is usually in a position to operate and maintain the plan without the help of a consultant.

Understandable, Influenceable Bonuses. If a gainsharing plan is going to increase motivation, employees must have a line of sight and influence to the bonus. In short, they must be able to see how through their behavior they can influence the size of the bonus. Achieving this, particularly in a complex organization, is not simple. It is a matter of education, communication, participative management practices, and an appropriate measurement approach to determine the size of the bonus.

Typically, in gainsharing plans a formula is used to calculate the size of the bonus. This has the obvious advantage of being much more objective than the alternative, which is a discretionary decision about how much the bonus will be. We cannot rule out judgment as a possible vehicle for deciding the bonus, however. There are situations that, because of rapid change or complexity, do not lend themselves to a formula. If a valid, trusted decision process can be developed, it is still possible to have an effective plan in the absence of a formula. In some cases, for example, committees have been successfully used to make bonus decisions, while in others a trusted top manager has made them based on preset objectives or goals.

Any discussion of formula raises the question of what to measure. Some advocates of gainsharing push strongly for simple plans, operating on the principle that it is best to keep *any* plan simple. Time after time I have heard advocates of this approach use the saying, "Keep it simple, stupid," to convince companies that a simple plan is best. In this spirit some plans simply measure the units of output per labor hour. These plans are effective if labor costs are the key issue and if the business is a simple one. In most cases, however, ignoring other costs (such as the cost of materials and supplies) can be quite dangerous and counterproductive. Similarly, ignoring quality and customer satisfaction can be dangerous.

Time after time I have seen gainsharing plans cause problems because employees have reduced measured costs at the expense of unmeasured costs. A common situation is one in which labor costs go down (people work faster), but material and supply costs go up (people are less careful in their use of consumables). Just this happened when Donnelly Mirrors initially introduced a Scanlon Plan, which covered only labor costs. The employees who ran the diamond-grinding wheels quickly discovered that they could increase labor productivity by running their machines faster and discarding diamond wheels when they started to wear out. Labor costs went down but supply costs went up—the net result being higher costs (diamond-grinding wheels are expensive). In many cases gainsharing formulas need to include multiple costs precisely because employees control multiple costs, and this means complexity. In these situations it is stupid to keep a plan simple, because you will get simple performance in a situation that needs complexity. Complex situations also call for high levels of employee involvement. Involvement can make the complex understandable and the remote influenceable.

Every bonus plan must have a standard that triggers payment. Many profit-sharing plans use a financial break-even point or a certain return on investment. As was noted earlier, gainsharing plans typically use a historical performance level. There are a number of advantages to using historical performance; foremost is its credibility. Employees know that it can be achieved and understand where it came from. It is not an "arbitrary" number based on some economic concept such as return on investment; nor is it an estimate by someone of what performance should be. It is often desirable from an organization's point of view because improvement over it represents real improvement in organizational performance, and it is thus possible to argue that any bonuses are self-funding. (Without improvement there are no bonuses.) It is not, however, the only correct basis for a standard.

In organizations that have had a dramatic change in products or technology, history may not be a relevant basis for setting the standard. For them, some other, more subjective approach (such as a committee decision) may be required. Similarly, in organizations that are on a learning curve, historical performance may be too easy to achieve. Projections of the learning curve may be used instead, but they are risky. Typically, I recommend against gainsharing plans in such situations, because it is too difficult to establish a valid curve. Most plans I have seen based on this approach have failed, but a few have worked. The successful ones occurred where the technology was well understood and trust was high, allowing credible changes in the standard when necessary.

Finally, in situations where historical performance is very low, it may not make economic sense to use it as a permanent standard. Using extremely low performance as a standard might be too expensive if the company is a poor performer and needs to improve to just gain parity with its competitors. Paying bonuses for performance that gets the company only to a competent level may not solve the organization's problems, because labor costs go up along with performance. What can be used instead is either a moving standard or a cut in base wages. I have seen both of these work, but either option needs to be fully, carefully, and openly justified based on business needs.

Timely Bonuses. Gainsharing plans typically pay bonuses on a monthly basis. There is no magic in monthly payments, however. The important principle is that bonuses should be paid as soon after the performance as possible. In situations where the work process is simple, a month may be the right time period—or even too long. In other, more complex situations, however, a month may not be long enough for the organization to complete the production of the product or the delivery of a service. In this case, quarterly or even semiannual bonus payments may be appropriate.

Comprehensive Measures. In simple manufacturing situations, a simple formula is often quite appropriate. However, it can be dangerous in businesses that involve multiple controllable costs. Focusing on any one cost can lead employees to reduce it while increasing others. For example, plans that fail to focus on quality may find that it goes down while productivity increases. Focusing on quality is particularly important in service situations since it often is easy to cut costs by reducing service quality. In the long term this can of course be disastrous. Xerox includes measures of service quality in its gainsharing plan in order to avoid just this problem. Thus organizations need to zero in on *all* the controllable areas of performance. This may lead to a more complex plan; but as was noted earlier, it is much better to have a complex plan than one that fails to deal with the true complexity of the business. Simple plans are great for simple businesses, but complex plans are needed for complex business situations.

Involvement Opportunities. Employees need to be able to influence the measures used as the basis for calculating their bonuses. As has been stressed already, this has some direct implications for the kind of participative management models that fit different bonus formulas. If the bonus is based on labor costs only, the kind of suggestion program used in Scanlon companies is often quite appropriate. Through written suggestions employees can come up with work-method improvements that speed production and reduce labor costs. However, if the gainsharing formula is a complex, multiple-cost formula, other forms of employee involvement are needed so that employees can influence the payout. Employees need to be able to influence not just direct production decisions but also decisions involving costs of materials, supplies, inventory, and so forth. The use of work teams and task forces can allow employees to influence these major business decisions.

To repeat, there is no right formula for employee involvement; the key is fitting the employee involvement approach with the formula, which in turn needs to fit the business situation. Simple business situations can use simple formulas and basic approaches to employee involvement. More complex business situations require more complex gainsharing formulas and higher levels of employee involvement.

Maintenance. All gainsharing plans require maintenance. Businesses change, environments change, and formulas and involvement approaches need to change as a result. The keys to successful change are timeliness and credibility with employees. Typically, the change process is best handled by an ongoing task force composed of representatives from all levels in the organization. This group needs to regularly review the plan and recommend changes. It needs to be staffed by trusted, knowledgeable individuals who understand the business and are capable of making good decisions and communicating them to the rest of the workforce.

The alternative to an ongoing task force is an outside expert who comes in and updates the plan on a regular basis. This can work, but it has the disadvantage of making the organization dependent on an outsider, and it is possible that the outsider will not be as credible as an internal group.

Profit Sharing

Profit sharing is better known, older, and more widely practiced than gainsharing. Data indicate, for example, that at least one-third of all organizations in the United States have profit sharing. Among the *Fortune* 1,000 this number is higher, with about 15 percent of these large organizations covering all employees and as many as 60 percent covering some employees with a profit-sharing plan (Lawler, Ledford, and Mohrman, 1989; Metzger, 1964).

Some definitions of gainsharing include profit sharing as a form of gainsharing; however, profit sharing differs in two respects. It does not necessarily have a participative management component, and it does not use formulas that measure only increases in employee-controlled or productivity-related financial performance. Instead, profit sharing is usually based on a formula that measures the company's overall financial performance. Typically, after some base-level profit is achieved, a percentage of all additional profits is shared. Sometimes individual bonus amounts are based on a percentage of pay, sometimes all employees receive the same dollar amount, and sometimes organizational level influences payout size (with larger percentages usually given at higher levels). Less common is a fourth approach, which bases bonuses on individual performance. Because the first three measurement approaches are not related to individual performance, profit-sharing plans are typically much less effective than gainsharing plans in influencing motivation and in producing the kind of social and cultural outcomes that are associated with gainsharing. This is particularly true in large organizations, where the line of sight from individual performance to corporate profits is virtually nonexistent.

Some organizations have attacked the size problem by creating divisional profit-sharing plans. DuPont, for example, has done this for its Caribbean operations and for its fibers division, and Motorola has done it for some of its lines of business. In diversified companies this approach is probably superior to having a corporate-wide payment, but in most large companies the line of sight is still unlikely to be there. Unless the amount that individuals receive is based on their own performance, the advantages of having divisional profit-sharing plans are limited to the areas of culture, communication, and control of labor costs in a given business area. In the typical profit-sharing plan the line-of-sight problem is even further compounded; most firms (estimates suggest about 85 percent) defer profit-sharing bonuses by putting them into retirement plans (Weitzman, 1984; Metzger, 1964). This compounds the problem of tying rewards to present controllable performance to such an extent that profit sharing can have little if any impact on the motivation and behavior of most employees.

Some companies even further destroy the line of sight by making the payment of profit sharing totally discretionary. For example, Wells Fargo Bank has made profit-sharing payments irregularly, based on management discretion. In 1989 management decided that the bank had a good year and gave all employees a check for $500 and a coupon for $35 to be given (as was mentioned earlier) to the colleague who had been most helpful to them. There is little chance that this kind of program affects motivation because there is little chance that employees can influence whether or not a bonus is paid; it is a clear case of rewards that have no impact on motivation. They may have an impact on culture, but this impact may not be positive: discretionary profit sharing may create unrealized expectations about what will happen in the future. It may also reinforce the power of management and remind employees that they are dependent on management's "generosity."

Before we dismiss profit sharing as completely useless from an organizational effectiveness point of view, we need to stress that there is some evidence that it leads to better corporate performance. No exact numbers exist, but studies suggest that it may lead to a 2 percent or greater productivity improvement (Blinder, 1990; Weitzman, 1984). In addition, there are three things that even a deferred profit-sharing plan can accomplish in a large corporation.

First, there is potential symbolic and communication value in paying all employees based on organizational performance. It can effectively point out that everyone is part of the organization and that a cooperative effort is needed. Because corporate executives are often paid on the basis of profit sharing, it can also help to assure that there is an alignment between the rewards received by top management and those received by people throughout the organization. This can help avoid the all-too-common problem—one that often happens in such large corporations as AT&T and General Motors—of executives getting large bonuses while lower-level employees receive none. In 1985 General Motors, which appeared to have solved this problem by putting all employees on profit sharing, made the mistake of creating different plans for managers and union members. The plans treated the executives much better than they treated the unionized employees, further polarizing the relationship between labor and management.

Second, some companies, notably Hewlett-Packard, have effectively used their profit-sharing plans as vehicles for educating employees about the financial condition of the business. When employees are actually sharing in the profits, their involvement brings alive for them the issue of what profits mean and how they are calculated, and it can increase their interest in learning about profits and organizational effectiveness. Hewlett-Packard does a number of things to reinforce the communication value of its plan. It pays out semiannually, and the payment is always the subject of numerous meetings and discussions. In addition, employees are educated in the economics of the business.

Finally, perhaps the most important advantage that profit sharing offers is that it makes the labor costs of an organization variable, adjusting them to the organization's ability to pay (Weitzman, 1984). When profits go down, labor costs go down; thus labor costs, rather than being fixed, become at least in part variable. This is a particularly desirable feature for organizations that are in cyclical or seasonal business. In most U.S. companies changes in labor costs are handled through increases and decreases in the size of the workforce. This is a necessity when wages are high and fixed, because there is no other way to reduce labor costs to reflect the company's ability to pay. With profit sharing, it is possible to reduce costs significantly without reducing the number of employees or adopting work sharing. Most Japanese companies have used this approach to varying labor costs for decades. As is the case in Japan, profit sharing can allow an organization to make a much stronger commitment to employment stability and help it gain the advantages inherent in having a stable workforce.

A key issue in profit sharing is just how much of an individual's pay should be at risk through the profit-sharing plan. In Japan the figure is often a large percentage of the base pay—as much as 30 or 40 percent. This gives employers a significant cushion and helps make their guaranteed employment model work. This is probably too great an amount for most Western countries, but most companies can operate with 10 to 20 percent of total compensation dependent on profit sharing.

Employee Ownership

A number of pay plans exist that place some or all of the ownership of a company in the hands of employees. These include stock option plans, stock purchase plans, stock grant programs, and employee stock ownership plans (ESOP). There is little question that stock ownership plans are increasingly popular. According to one study, some eleven million employees in over 8,000 businesses now own at least 15 percent of the companies employing them (Blasi, 1988). It is difficult to generalize about the impact of ESOPs because they vary widely in how much ownership employees receive and what employees have to do to receive the stock; their impact is also likely to depend on the organizational situation.

Much of what has been said about the impact of profit-sharing and gainsharing plans is relevant to the impact of ownership. There is one important difference, however: stock ownership typically produces a weaker line of influence than do gainsharing and profit sharing, because ownership depends on the valuation that the financial markets put on companies—a factor difficult to control. Every time the employees begin to believe that there is a strong connection between the company's financial performance and stock prices, a large swing in stock prices can occur (who can forget October 1987?), making it appear that stock prices are uncontrollable.

In some situations there is reason to believe that ownership can have much the same impact as an effective gainsharing plan (Rosen, Klein, and Young, 1986). Research has shown that in a small organization in which participative management is practiced, employee ownership has a good chance of increasing organizational performance (Blinder, 1990). The key here is combining ownership with employee involvement so that a line of sight exists. In a large organization stock ownership can impact the culture positively by creating integration across the total organization—if, of course, all employees are included in the ownership plan.

A number of organizations have used employee ownership as a key part of a turnaround. Many of them, such as Wierton Steel, are small; others, such as Avis, are large. The one common factor is that they have combined employee ownership with participative management. When this combination exists, there is evidence that employee ownership can improve organizational performance (Conte and Tannenbaum, 1980).

A number of companies have stock ownership programs that are targeted at creating a culture of ownership and caring. America West Airlines requires all employees to invest 20 percent of their first year's salary in company stock. This program fits nicely with the airline's participative approach to management and its work-teams approach to organizational design. In 1989 American Express gave all employees stock, while PepsiCo gave its employees stock options. For years Digital has given stock options to a wide range of employees based upon their individual performance. Giving stock options and restricted stock is one way to build loyalty and to retain employees, because to exercise the options the employee has to remain a member of the organization.

Because the line-of-sight problem is so severe with stock, it is unlikely that the plans of American Express and PepsiCo will have any effect on motivation. That is not necessarily true of Digital's plan, however, because it is based on individual performance. A performance-based plan also can help to retain the best performers, because they are the ones with the most unexercised options.

Because of the tax laws in the United States, certain types of ESOPs can help organizations raise capital and finance themselves. They can also help put stock in "friendly" hands so that hostile takeovers are more difficult. Indeed, most ownership plans are probably installed precisely because of the tax, antitakeover, and financing advantages they offer (Blasi, 1988). Additionally, stock ownership can have a more positive impact on attraction and retention than does profit sharing. Particularly when deferred or not easily salable, ownership can help to lock someone into the organization both financially and psychologically.

Overall, then, there is reason to believe that ownership strategies can have a positive effect. Their usefulness, however, is likely to be highly situationally determined. For instance, in small organizations such strategies may make profit sharing and gainsharing unnecessary; and if combined with an appropriate approach to employee involvement, they can contribute substantially to employee motivation. In large organizations, on the other hand, they can be a useful supplement to other pay-for-performance systems. Because of line-of-sight problems, they have little impact on motivation in large organizations, although they can contribute to a positive culture and to organizational integration.

Designing an Effective Performance Pay System

Our analysis so far suggests that gainsharing, profit sharing, and employee ownership can be useful practices for most organizations. They ought not to be looked at as competing approaches, however, but as compatible approaches that accomplish different, important objectives.

Profit sharing can have the desirable effect of creating variable costs for an organization, thus allowing it to adjust its costs to its ability to pay. It can also affect the communication pattern and culture of an organization in ways that emphasize the performance of the total organization. Gainsharing, on the other hand, if correctly designed, can increase motivation and produce a culture in which people are committed to seeing their organizational unit operate effectively.

The effect of employee ownership will vary as a function of the size of the organization and of how extensive the ownership is. In small organizations with a high percentage of ownership, it can do a lot to motivate employees, impact culture, and help with attraction and retention. In large organizations its ability to impact motivation is limited. Like profit sharing, it can influence culture and help contribute to the employees' understanding of the business. If the stock is held in trust or paid on a delayed basis, it can help with retention. Finally, it can help to make an organization safe from unfriendly takeovers, because it gives the employees a vote in who will run the company.

The ideal combination for many large corporations would seem to be corporate-wide profit-sharing and stock ownership plans, with gainsharing plans in major operating plants or units. Just this type of model is starting to emerge in such U.S. corporations as Mead, Kodak, Dow Chemical, Xerox, Apple, and TRW. The combination of gainsharing and profit sharing addresses the need to motivate employees and the need to have variable costs.

Gainsharing tends to be based on subunits of the organization and on measures that do not include all the operating costs of the business. Thus the possibility exists for bonuses even when the organization is performing poorly. From a motivational point of view, this is desirable if the employees are performing well against the things that they are measured upon and can control. However, employees may erroneously feel that the organization is in good shape whenever they receive a bonus. The addition of a profit-sharing plan can help the organization call attention to the fact that the organization's performance is not satisfactory. It can also adjust labor costs according to the organization's ability to pay—something a gainsharing plan may not do.

Finally, employee ownership can tie employees and other stockholders together so that they do not have competing agendas. This is particularly important if senior management has stock options and other stock-based incentive plans. Unless stock is widely owned in the organization, these plans can separate the interests of top management from those of other employees.

The amount of profit-sharing and gainsharing money that is paid to individuals probably should not be the same at all levels in the organization. At the lower levels gainsharing should potentially produce larger payouts than the profit-sharing plan. (The emphasis here is on *potential;* the actual amount should be determined by performance.) The logic is that gainsharing is easier for low-level employees to relate to, and significant money must be involved for it to be motivating. At higher levels profit sharing should have the greatest payoff potential; indeed, at the top levels gainsharing may not exist at all.

Profit-sharing, gainsharing, and stock ownership plans can be combined with individual pay-for-performance plans. One approach is to use individual performance appraisals to decide how much of a gainsharing, profit-sharing, or stock payout an individual gets. This makes sense when the organizational situation makes a strong focus on individual performance appropriate. Another approach is to have a regularly budgeted individual bonus plan that operates independently of the profit-sharing and gainsharing plans. This fits best where more emphasis on team and group performance is appropriate.

Finally, when the dominant focus needs to be group performance, it may be appropriate to have *no* individual pay-for-performance plan but to rely on gainsharing, profit sharing, and ownership. These plans may not offer a clear line of sight, but they are likely to produce strong group norms that support good performance. With no individual rewards, it is clearly in everyone's best interest to have all individuals perform at their best; no one loses out because someone else gets a bigger reward for better individual performance.

A number of organizational conditions must be considered in

the design of pay systems based on organizational performance. The more interdependent the different units of an organization are, and the smaller the organization is, the more profit sharing should come into play. The logic here is that the more these are true, the easier (and more important) it is for employees to focus on organizational performance. At the other extreme, in a highly decentralized organization, stock ownership and corporate profit sharing may not make any sense except for top management. In this situation there is no need to integrate the organization and create the feeling of a single unit. Thus the best approach may be to base pay only on the performance of different business units.

Overall, the evidence is clear: basing pay on organizational performance can lead to a number of positive outcomes for both employees and organizations. However, it is not a quick fix or panacea for the ills of an organization. Careful design is critical, and in most cases a number of other changes are required if all the advantages of performance-based pay are to be realized. If a heavy commitment is made to gainsharing, profit sharing, and ownership, considerable education, communication, and power sharing need to occur in order for many of the potential advantages to be realized. In addition, as will be discussed later, organizations may need to work on employment stability guarantees and develop knowledge-based pay systems. In short, to be effective, paying for organizational performance must be more than a pay approach; it must be combined with a congruent management system.

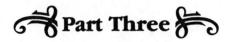

Part Three

Determining Base Pay

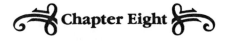

Paying the Job

Organizations hire individuals; but once individuals join most organizations, the amount they are paid is determined primarily by the type of job they do. Why this switch from the person to the job? There is no simple answer. Basing pay on a person's job is a well-established practice that has a long history in the United States. Research on it goes back over fifty years, and it reveals some clear advantages. But basing pay on a person's job is not the only way to operate. Some other countries—Japan, for instance—do not do it, and, as will be discussed in the next chapter, some U.S. companies are moving away from it.

Job-based pay typically rests upon the foundations of a job evaluation system. Frequently, this system takes a point-factor approach to evaluating jobs (Henderson, 1985). The arguments in favor of this approach are many and have a long history behind them. The Hay system, the product of a consulting firm by the same name, is probably the best-known approach to job evaluation, but there are many others (Rock, 1984; Hills, 1989). Every major compensation consulting firm has its own approach, as do many corporations. Installing and monitoring job evaluation systems is a major business in its own right. A good guess is that over 95 percent of the major U.S. corporations use some kind of point-factor approach. In addition to its use in the United States, job evaluation is being successfully sold by consulting firms in Europe and other parts of the world.

For those who are not familiar with the point-factor approach, a brief description is in order. It typically starts with a carefully written job description for every job being assessed. Job factors are then identified corporate-wide and given a relative weight. Typical plans include four job factors that differ substantially in their weight—that is, some carry the potential for earning more points than others. Commonly used factors include physical working conditions experienced, problem-solving ability needed, knowledge required, and accountability demanded. Usually a job evaluation committee then assesses jobs by comparing these factors against each job description and deciding how much of each factor every job contains. Points are then assigned to the jobs for each factor, resulting in a total point score for each job.

In the most complete job evaluation systems, every job in the company ends up with a score. Point totals can then be compared to salary-survey data that show how much other organizations pay for jobs with similar point totals. The point score is then translated into a salary level or pay grade. Thus, through a series of subjective decisions, an organization can translate the tasks that it asks individuals to perform into an "objective," quantified result and a pay level. This is often facilitated by some moderately complex mathematical manipulations of the data, which give the results an appearance of scientific objectivity.

Advantages of Job Evaluation-Based Pay

There a number of reasons why organizations adopt job evaluation-based pay. I would like to review them briefly and then turn to the problems this pay approach creates.

Perhaps the most important reason why organizations adopt job evaluation-based pay is that it facilitates making comparisons to what other organizations are paying. In other words, it facilitates market testing and therefore can help an organization assess whether it is paying more or less than its competitors and whether its labor costs are higher or lower than those of other organizations. Job evaluation can do this because it allows apples and oranges to be compared. That is, it allows jobs from one organization to be measured and scored on measures that are identical or at least comparable to those used in other organizations. Thus even though organizations have different ways of organizing and end up with different jobs, job evaluation can allow an organization to compare its jobs to those of another organization if the other organization uses a similar job evaluation system. This makes the market test for how well an organization is paying easier and provides data that allow an organization to position its pay rates relative to other organizations.

The more widely used job evaluation systems, such as the Hay system, make available to their clients an extensive set of market data. Because they are so dominant in the business, they receive data from most large business organizations within the United States, and within those organizations they have data on many jobs. Thus they can tell an organization how its pay rates compare to organizations in their own industry and in other industries, they can compare organizations on a geographical basis, and so forth. Organizations greatly value this feature of job evaluation plans, because accurate comparative pay data are critical to attracting and retaining the best performers and effectively managing labor costs.

Just as it is possible with the more sophisticated job evaluation systems to compare across companies, it is also possible to compare within organizations. Thus for organizations that desire high levels of internal equity or pay comparability, job evaluation is a useful tool; all the jobs in the organization can be paid according to a single system. An organization can pay people the same thing for comparable job duties, regardless of which division, nook, cranny, or far reach of the organization they are in. For many large organizations this is seen as an advantage, because they often have a commitment to internal equity, fairness, and comparability of pay, regardless of where people are in the organization.

Having internal equity is not just a "nice" thing to have; it does have some practical organizational outcomes. For example, it makes movement from one part of an organization to another much easier. With internal equity, moving from a lower-level job to a higher-level job should always lead to a higher pay rate. Without job evaluation, however, changing divisions or moving across major organizational boundaries (with different pay approaches) may lead not to a pay increase but to a pay decrease; thus movement may require major changes in the pay system or special treatment of individuals who move to higher-level jobs. With a good job evaluation system, on the other hand, a move to a "bigger" job will always result in a pay increase for the individual.

Job evaluation–based systems allow for centralized control of an organization's pay system and pay costs. It is not accidental that when consulting firms sell job evaluation to companies, they typically focus their sales effort on senior management. In their presentations to senior management, they stress that job evaluation can help ensure that no division or group is out of line (that is, paying too much), and that it gives the ability to audit any part of the organization for comparability and "equitable" pay rates.

Until the Jack Welch era began in the early 1980s, General Electric was a good example of a company with a centralized job evaluation–based approach to pay. It had a corporate-wide job evaluation system and a single set of company-wide pay grades. Jobs were paid according to how they were evaluated and put into the pay structure. This was supposed to guarantee that comparable jobs would be paid the same, regardless of where they were in the company.

The use of a single pay system also gave GE's corporate staff the ability to audit a division to see if it was properly paying people according to the company-wide structure. Thus it was possible for senior management to control the wage rates in the different operating units of this large, multibusiness corporation. It could, in effect, tell if an appliance plant in South Carolina or a nuclear energy facility in California was "overpaying" people relative to other parts of GE. All that the corporate staff had to do was look at a job description to see if the job was correctly evaluated and then determine what the evaluation score called for in terms of a pay rate. As was mentioned earlier, GE could then go to the outside market and compare what it paid that job to what other companies paid it. Although GE has abandoned its centralized system, other major companies, including IBM and Exxon, still use this approach.

A real advantage of using one of the commercially available job evaluation plans is that most are proven pieces of technology. That is, they have been used for so long that there are few mysteries; little R & D remains to be done. They represent an off-the-shelf, relatively easy-to-use approach to determining pay rates. In contrast, skill-based pay, which will be discussed in Chapter Nine, requires work on the methods, procedures, and formulas that are needed to support it.

Precisely because job evaluation is so well established, and in some cases is based on complex quantitative methods, it has the

appearance of objectivity. This can be important in helping convince people that it is a fair system. Of course, quantification does
not necessarily mean fairness, but for someone who is not terribly
sophisticated in quantitative methods, it certainly provides an aura
of science and objectivity.

In addition, there is no question that the idea of internal
equity has a strong appeal to many senior managers. They are attracted to it from a value perspective, and they like the idea that
people are paid the same regardless of where they work in the company. This takes one conflict out of the life of senior managers, who
are no longer faced with subordinates who argue that they (or their
people) would be paid more if they were in a different part of the
company or in a different business. If job evaluation systems work
correctly, senior management can say with some confidence that
individuals are paid the same regardless of where they are. Thus
senior management does not have to arbitrate disputes between one
part of an organization and another or worry about career movement that is driven by an individual's desire to get into "higher-
paying parts of the company."

In many respects, then, job evaluation can reduce the amount
of conflict that senior managers face, and in the short run it can
make their jobs easier. It also can give them more control. But as
we will see, job evaluation may lead to other problems, some of
which are very serious.

Disadvantages of Job Evaluation-Based Pay

Many of the specific criticisms of job evaluation rest on the argument that it is more than a way to pay employees; it is an approach
to management and a strategic business orientation. It makes a
number of assumptions about the way an organization is managed
and fits a particular style of management and a particular approach
to dealing with key business issues (Lawler, 1986a). It is for this
precise reason that it has significant limitations and that it is a poor
fit in many business situations.

Promotes Bureaucratic Management Style. The relationship between job evaluation and management style is often not obvious to

organizations when they first consider installing a job evaluation system. They may see only an objective, "fair" way to pay people, but job evaluation is more than this; it is an approach to thinking about work and people's relationship to their organization. Indeed, it was originally developed to be supportive of traditional bureaucratic management.

The first indication of the bureaucratic orientation of job evaluation is its starting point: the job description. Basic to the bureaucratic approach to management is the idea that an individual should have carefully prescribed activities to perform and should be held accountable for how well those activities are performed. Working from a tight job description facilitates performance appraisal and an evaluation of the worth of the individual's job to the organization. It emphasizes control and doing what the organization specifies. In this sense it is highly congruent with a top-down, control-oriented bureaucratic approach to management. Indeed, this is just the kind of management that was seen as the best style when job evaluation was originally developed in the early 1900s.

As I have already pointed out, our concepts of what makes for an effective management style are undergoing a rapid and dramatic change. The old management concepts have been found wanting in a number of respects. Essentially, they do not seem to fit the way organizations need to be managed if they are going to survive in the turbulent, competitive world economy of the 1990s (Peters, 1987). Briefly stated, the old management is too bureaucratic and rigid, and it does not use people effectively enough to be competitive. What is needed, in many cases, is a management approach that focuses on people doing what is right rather than what is prescribed, developing and using new skills, focusing on customer-client relationships, and generally being involved in the management of the business.

Implicitly Specifies What Not To Do. Inherent in any job description is a message to individuals about what is *not* included in their responsibilities. Again, this fits well with the traditional management idea of holding people accountable for certain specified duties. It does not fit well, however, with an orientation that says an individual should jump in and do what is right in the situation rather than what is called for by the job description. Admittedly, this implicit message is only one small part of the problem with the evaluation approach, but it *is* a problem. Sometimes the limiting effect of job descriptions is carried to an extreme, with employees refusing to do things that are not in their job description.

The productivity costs of this nonperformance are well documented, and the difficulties of changing job descriptions are many, particularly where unions are involved (Grayson and O'Dell, 1988). What often happens when organizations want to more effectively utilize their people is that individuals demand a pay increase. They have bought into the value system that says you are worth what you do; therefore, if you are asked to do more things by an organization, you obviously should have your job reevaluated and upgraded. It is problems like this combined with the constant changes that many organizations need to make that suggest that the whole idea of a job may be obsolete.

Reinforces Hierarchy. Traditional bureaucratic management depends on a steep, well-reinforced hierarchy for its effectiveness. The hierarchy provides the coordination and control needed when most individuals are not committed to the organization and do not understand its strategy or operations. Orders and directions are provided from higher levels, and effectiveness depends on lower-level employees doing what they are told. Job evaluation fits this quite well, because it measures jobs in terms of their hierarchical power, control, and responsibilities.

Many job evaluation points are typically assigned to factors concerned with level of responsibility and number of reporting relationships. As a result, job evaluation scores clearly say to everyone in the organization who has the most responsible job, the next most responsible, and so on. They even have the capability of differentiating among people who are at the same management level and have the same titles. In some respects they play the same role as the ranks (for example, *general* and *private*) do in the military. This has some obvious advantages when jobs are being priced and when a clearly defined hierarchy is needed, but it may also have some severe negative consequences.

Job evaluation can create unnecessary and undesirable pecking orders and power relationships in the organization. In several organizations that I have studied, installation of a job evaluation system led groups that were previously relatively egalitarian and cooperative to become much more hierarchical and power-oriented. In knowledge work and high-technology work there is good evidence that the last thing that is needed is a rigid hierarchical structure (Von Glinow and Mohrman, 1989). Indeed, often the key to success is utilizing the technical knowledge and innovations that come from the bottom of the organization (Lawler, 1986b). This utilization needs to be supported by an organizational culture in which individuals are respected and rewarded for their expertise and ideas, not for the "value" of the job they hold.

Depersonalizes Value Orientation. Job evaluation is based on the principle that people are worth what they do. In many cases this may not be the most desirable cultural value to communicate in an organization. It tends to depersonalize people, equating them with a set of duties rather than with who they are and what they can do. It tends to deemphasize paying people for the skills that they have and for the performance that they demonstrate. In today's rapidly changing, highly competitive environment, a message that says grow, develop, and perform well seems to be more on target than one that says you will be rewarded for outgrowing your job and getting promoted. In organizations whose key assets are its human resources, a system that focuses on people rather than on jobs would seem to be a better fit.

Fosters Internal Focus. Competitive benchmarking—that is, a focus on what other companies are doing in the marketplace—is becoming an increasingly important part of many companies' strategy for business success (Peters, 1987). As Xerox and other companies have shown, this approach can motivate change and provide valuable feedback. In the ideal case, pay rates should be part of this external comparison process. Indeed, some companies now try to target their salary levels to how they perform in comparison to their competitors. Job evaluation, on the other hand, tends to focus on the internal pay relationships among jobs; it purports to provide a common metric (based on points) that is comparable across all jobs in the organization. The following quote from a company document describing the firm's pay equity approach states the issue very clearly: "The approach is to pay what is felt to be right internally with an eye towards the external market to make sure we are reasonably in line with what others are paying." Clearly, the emphasis is more on internal comparisons than it is on the external market.

Thus, at a time when employees should be focusing on the competition, they often end up focusing internally—on how other individuals are paid and on how they can improve their relative pay position. This takes them away from the key business issues, which are external competitive comparisons, and tends to lead to a ratcheting up of internal pay rates. Job evaluation makes it possible for individuals to look across the organization and determine how their job "should" stack up in terms of pay. The natural tendency is to find a job that is relatively highly paid and use it as the benchmark that drives the internal pay structure. This is a virtually inevitable consequence of individuals' being able to compare their jobs with other jobs on a common metric, and it leads to higher and higher pay levels. Indeed, the greatest problem with job evaluation may well be the high salary costs it produces. This is particularly likely to be true in organizations that operate in a number of businesses, some of which have different pay rates for what is essentially the same work. Almost always the organization ends up paying everyone whatever is paid by the highest-paying business it is in.

Impairs Strategic Orientation. Pay levels can be an important strategic factor, helping to reinforce the excellence of an organization in a particular function or area. If, for example, there is a competitive advantage in being the best at production, compensation can help by providing higher levels of pay and better incentives to production people. High-technology organizations often feel that they can gain a competitive advantage by hiring the best technical people. To accomplish this they may need to pay them at a high market rate, but because they are not trying to gain an advantage through excellence in other areas, they may be able to compensate by having relatively lower salary costs in such functions as marketing and personnel management.

A good example of the need to pay at different levels for certain functions and types of work is provided by the banking industry. For decades large banks have operated with job evaluation–driven pay systems. Recently, as they have tried to diversify into investment banking and other new businesses, job evaluation has caused them a great deal of difficulty. Many of the new businesses require higher pay rates than the banks' job evaluation systems call for. Some banks have responded by paying the rates called for by the job evaluation system and as a result have suffered high turnover in areas such as investment banking (because the pay rates in other kinds of firms doing this work are so much higher). A few have abandoned job evaluation and simply paid market rates. This has allowed them to maintain the existing pay levels in their traditional banking areas and to pay higher wages in other activities.

It is often to an organization's advantage to have particular units and particular businesses focus on their strategic pay issues independent of what is occurring in other parts of the organization. A company in multiple businesses can target compensation levels and practices to those multiple businesses. This has the potential advantage of aligning costs more closely with the competitors' costs and causing people to focus more on the competitive environment.

Company-wide job evaluation systems, rather than aiding strategic compensation management, often end up as a hindrance. They make it less politically acceptable to target certain functions and/or certain business units for different levels of compensation. The natural tendency in job evaluation systems is to encourage internal equity and therefore to shift the focus from external business equity and strategic advantage.

Obviously, an internal orientation can be overcome for pay purposes if organizations are willing to translate the same points into different dollar amounts either in different businesses or in different functional areas. This is often politically difficult to do, however, because the company-wide job evaluation system highlights the fact that this "inequity" is occurring.

Discourages Organizational Change. Today organizations operate in a world that is characterized by a rapid rate of change and by the need to quickly and easily adapt to change. If anything, the job evaluation approach discourages organizations from changing. It does this in several ways. First, by the amount of work it takes to create a job description and do a job evaluation, it generates a high investment in the status quo. Organizational change and reorganization become major workload issues in this system. It is no small task to rewrite all the job descriptions and reevaluate all jobs when a major reorganization occurs.

A major factor in any change is the potential effect the change may have on the pay of individuals. Most major organizational changes involve a reassignment of responsibilities and accountabilities. If the job evaluation approach is used, a reassignment of responsibilities means that some people get increased pay and other people lose. This sets up a competition among individuals for job duties and responsibilities that lead to high job evaluation scores, and it often results in a strong resistance to much-needed change. In short, job evaluation systems often end up as servants of the status quo rather than as stimulants for needed organizational change.

Encourages Point Grabbing. After organizations have had job evaluation systems for a while, individuals become quite sophisticated in how to get jobs evaluated highly. They realize that creatively written job descriptions and inflated job duties can lead to increases in pay. Thus considerable time and effort may be spent by individuals on rewriting job descriptions so that they will be scored more highly.

Job evaluation can also lead individuals to grab or develop added responsibilities in order to get more points. The responsibilities added can include extra budget and more subordinates—items that add to the cost of doing business. In a rather direct (although unintended) way, point-factor systems reward individuals for creating overhead and higher costs, because these lead to more highly evaluated jobs. This is exactly the opposite direction from the one in which most organizations are trying to move: toward low overhead, leaner and flatter organizations, and careful expense control.

Erodes Honesty/Credibility. Because enhancing job descriptions can lead to higher pay levels, there is a real danger that job evaluation systems will encourage and reward dishonesty. It is all too easy to learn that the way to "beat" the job evaluation system is to write overly flamboyant and inclusive job descriptions. This kind of corporate misinformation can be destructive of the long-term credibility of the organization. Evidence that this goes on is provided by the fact that most job evaluation systems have an internal audit or a desk audit activity to catch supervisors who are lying about their duties and those of their subordinates.

In some ways this is not a fault of the system so much as it is a fault of the individual managers, but there are features of the system that tend to encourage this kind of misreporting—most notably, the tying of pay levels to the job description itself. This provides a powerful incentive to inflate job descriptions. Many organizations I have studied have admitted that they feel most of their job descriptions are inflated by from 20 to 50 percent. This is often clearly evidenced by the steady upward movement of jobs over a period of years. In some systems this results in few if any jobs being left in the lowest pay grades.

Over time, the writing of inflated job descriptions can become standard operating procedure in an organization. This can have three important negative consequences. First, job evaluation inflation can occur, and as a result the organization simply ends up paying everyone too much. No data exist on how common a problem inflation is, but my guess is that it is very common. In some extreme cases organizations find that the only cure for inflation is to start over again with a new job evaluation system. Second, it can contribute to an organizational culture in which it is okay to provide misinformation to the personnel department. Finally, it can lead to an adversarial relationship between the compensation department and the rest of the organization. Conflict occurs when the compensation group tries to correct the inflation problem or simply maintain the integrity of the system by doing audits of job descriptions and job evaluations.

Inflates Pay System Operating Costs. A job evaluation system is expensive to develop and administer. It usually requires a rather extensive internal compensation staff as well as external consulting help. Indeed, when one looks at the amount of external support needed to maintain job evaluation systems, it is easy to see why many consulting firms are so enthusiastic about their use. Organizations typically pay for the installation of systems and for ongoing audits, market data, and even administrative help. Putting the system in is the razor for consulting firms; servicing it is the blades.

Inside the organization there is usually the need for a rather large staff to administer the system. After all, thousands of job descriptions may need to be written and maintained, job evaluation committees need to meet, people need to be trained in job evaluation technologies, and jobs need to be priced. As was mentioned earlier, system maintenance can also take the time of all employees; not only do they need to provide job descriptions, but they typically serve on job evaluation committees. In short, job evaluation is a tremendous producer of records and bureaucratic overhead.

I had the chance to observe what happened when one large organization installed a new job evaluation system. During the almost three years it took to develop the system, work on the system dominated the agenda of the human resources department. Other much-needed work was put aside. Hundreds of line managers spent incalculable hours in job evaluation committee meetings, and (of course) a compensation consulting firm had a number of individuals assigned to the project. The total cost? No one knows—but assuredly in the millions. The stakes were high, given the payroll expenditures of this multi-billion-dollar company, but I still find myself doubting that the effort was worth it.

Fails to Encourage Skill Development. In job evaluation systems that assign a heavy weight to factors concerned with level of responsibility and reporting relationships, the idea of hierarchy and upward career moves are strongly reinforced. Point-factor systems create an internal wage structure in which the major way for individuals to increase their compensation is to be promoted. Promotion is the surest way to increase the value of one's job, and therefore one's pay.

A hierarchical approach to pay makes considerable sense in organizations that are looking for the best and the brightest to move up the hierarchy. It encourages individuals to develop managerial skills, because those skills lead to higher rewards. It strongly reinforces a "linear career orientation," in which people see their career as onward and upward, and fits well with traditional top-down, control-oriented management (Lawler, 1986b). In traditionally managed organizations it is highly desirable to have most if not all individuals striving for upward mobility and to assure that the best and the brightest end up in the top management positions. These are the critical positions in the organization, and thus staffing them well can lead to a competitive advantage.

The importance of senior management was clearly recognized by AT&T during its day as a regulated monopoly. The organization did a number of things to ensure that it had a large number of well-qualified senior managers available: it offered extensive management development programs, opened assessment centers to determine who the high-potential managers were, and adopted a very hierarchical pay system that encouraged the best and the brightest to try to get to the top. In a system in which the top makes most of the important decisions, guiding the rest of the organization through numerous policy guidelines and measures, the top is exactly where the best and brightest should be.

The situation is quite different, however, in knowledge work and high-technology work. To be successful in those areas, organizations need individuals who achieve technical excellence. They also need individuals who are willing to make horizontal career moves in order to develop a broad-based understanding of the organization that will allow them to operate as integrators and effective problem solvers.

Technical specialization and horizontal career orientations are clearly not reinforced by the typical job evaluation approach. Individuals in knowledge and high-technology careers can look forward to static and potentially even declining compensation if their organization uses a point-factor approach. This can be disastrous for the organization that needs technical excellence to compete effectively, because it drives the best technical people into managerial roles, where they may not be successful. In addition, it does nothing to encourage those who stay in technical jobs to develop their technical skills.

One additional point is relevant here. As organizations become flatter and leaner, there is considerably less opportunity to move up the hierarchy. This raises further questions about the desirability of a pay system that strongly rewards people for upward mobility. If upward mobility is less available, perhaps it is not as important to motivate people to try to achieve it. Indeed, it may be counterproductive to strongly motivate this kind of behavior, because in flat organizations it will produce large numbers of frustrated, disillusioned, dead-ended individuals.

Makes Promotion Too Important. Inherent in the job evaluation approach is the idea that promotion warrants a significant pay increase—not because a person is necessarily more valuable or skilled or has accomplished anything worthwhile but because of the additional job responsibilities that result. One of the best pieces of evidence that a job evaluation system has become dysfunctional concerns promotion. When employees considering a new job think first and foremost about job evaluation points rather than about learning and skill development, it is good evidence that the organization has a bad case of bureaucratic "gridlock."

In many organizations, whether a job change is considered to be an upward move or not is dictated by the number of additional job evaluation points that the new job involves. If people learn to look for a certain number of additional points before making a career move, an organization can become relatively inflexible in its career paths. If this calculation becomes too strong a part of an organization's culture, certain desirable moves get ruled out simply because they are not worth enough additional points.

The following beliefs are typical of those that develop in job evaluation–driven pay systems. "I realize the new position they are offering is very different from my previous work, and would open up a whole new realm of experiences for me. But it is a lateral move in terms of levels. I'm concerned it wouldn't look good on my record. Perhaps I'm better off waiting for another level increase. . . . A pay level increase is the best indicator of personal growth and professional progress in this company. I've been told it's more important from a career standpoint to go for the level rather than the developmental value. The thing in any move is for the change to be seen as successful you have to move *up* a level."

Rewards Wrong Behavior. It is possible to challenge the logic of giving someone a pay increase simply because he or she moves to a higher-level job. For example, an alternative approach is to wait until the person has demonstrated the ability to do the new job before giving any additional money. Giving a person money simply for taking on new responsibilities is a non-performance-contingent reward practice. As a result of it, many organizations end up spending a great deal of their pay dollars to reinforce job changes rather than outstanding performance or needed skill growth. Is it any wonder that individuals often spend more time worrying about what their next job will be than worrying about how well they are performing their present job or about how to improve their skills?

Other Uses and Misuses. In many organizations the points developed by a point-factor job evaluation approach end up getting used for a number of nonpay purposes. These include who gets parking spaces and other perquisites, who gets included in meetings, and who gets communications. In short, a whole host of positives get attached to achieving higher and higher point totals. The problem with using job evaluations in these ways stems from the fact that the system was not designed to be a multipurpose evaluation of who should engage in a wide variety of organizational activities and get a wide variety of organizational perquisites and benefits.

Using job evaluation results broadly has two decidedly negative effects. First, it makes them even more important to individuals than they might be if only pay were contingent upon them. This would not be a problem if they were always objective and correct, but they are an inherently subjective form of evaluation and, as was noted eralier, subject to some manipulation and error (Risher, 1989). Second, their use for other purposes is often inappropriate simply because they do not necessarily measure and represent the factors that ought to be considered when such things as memo circulation and meeting attendance are being decided. They get used, however, because they are there, they are quantitative, and they seem to be objective. It is perhaps unfair to criticize job evaluation because it is used in ways that it was not intended to be used. Nevertheless, it does get used in these often dysfunctional ways.

Job Evaluation: Some Final Thoughts

My criticisms of the job evaluation approach highlight the fact that it is more than just a pay system; it is a way of thinking about work and organizing people. It reinforces a particular value system and a particular orientation to management. The decision to adopt job evaluation should therefore not be taken lightly. Once it is installed, it can be a terribly captivating and dominating part of an organization's corporate culture. It is not unfair to say that in some cases organizations end up managing in ways that are designed to make their job evaluation system work! For example, an organization's job evaluation system may end up influencing the kind of businesses it goes into, the kind of reorganizations that it makes, and the kind of career moves that it encourages. This is a classic example of means-ends reversal. I think we would all agree that the pay system should be designed to help the organization be effective and should not prevent it from doing the things it needs to do to be effective.

It may sound as if I am ready to conclude that a job evaluation system never makes sense. Not so. For certain situations it still represents the best alternative. It is the best approach if high levels of internal equity and centralized control of compensation are needed for organizational effectiveness, for example. These factors are often important in large centralized corporations that operate in a single business. As I mentioned, the old AT&T is a classic example. Internal equity was important there because it allowed for the easy movement of individuals and helped to integrate a geographically diverse organization. Centralized control of salary costs was important because many of the large functions (for example, manufacturing) had no profit responsibility, and there was no market or competitive pressure to keep wages down. Having a centralized compensation group was a way to keep wage costs down as well as to keep wages comparable across the organization.

Although there are situations where point-factor job evaluation is appropriate, in most organizations that want to use job-based pay it is not the best alternative. My preference is to simply take all or virtually all jobs to the market individually. This solves some of the problems with the point-factor approach. It can help to focus the organization externally and may produce more competitive overall compensation costs. It can also allow an organization to pay at higher levels in certain functions and to be more strategically driven.

Not all of the problems with job evaluation are solved by taking jobs to the market, however. Any form of job evaluation requires job descriptions, and thus some of the bureaucratic flavor of the point-factor approach is present. Pricing jobs in the market is unlikely to reduce the tendency to write inflated job descriptions and the resistance to change that are present in so many job evaluation systems. And it may increase the workload for the compensation staff, because pricing jobs in the external market means greater effort in the salary-survey arena. It may also mean less precise pricing of jobs, because of the difficulty of matching them to jobs in other organizations. Finally, it is unlikely to change the hierarchical nature of an organization's pay system, because the market is hierarchical.

Overall, comparing whole jobs to the market will lead to a pay system that looks like those in other organizations—that is, job-based and hierarchical—but the resulting system should be more market-oriented.

A very different alternative to job evaluation-based pay is skill-based pay. As will be discussed in the next chapter, this approach is currently used for production employees in high-involvement plants, as well as for technical and knowledge workers in many organizations. As will be shown, it has the potential for much wider application.

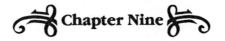

Paying the Person

Paying people according to their value in the market, the alternative to job-based pay, leads to a focus on people and on what the market pays. In many respects this alternative makes a great deal of sense. After all, it is people who move from job to job and from company to company, it is people who develop skills, and it is people who are the important organizational assets. Paying people based on their value reflects these factors, while paying them for the job they hold may not. Indeed, organizations that rely on job-based pay run a risk of either overpaying or underpaying employees. Overpayment is likely when employees are still learning the job, and underpayment is likely in the case of the experienced individual who has worked in a number of different jobs or has developed great skill in a critically important area.

A person-based pay system can do more than simply pay people what they are worth. For example, it can help an organization to actively manage the skill-acquisition process by directly motivating individuals to learn specific skills. In the typical job-based system this happens indirectly, with higher pay offered for some jobs than for others. Thus individuals are rewarded for learning the skills that lead to higher-paying jobs. Once individuals are offered higher-paying jobs, they are typically rewarded for taking them before they demonstrate that they can do them, however. They get a large promotion reward, but little of their pay depends on how they perform once they take the job. The alternative is to reward individuals for mastering job skills.

The most common approach to paying the person is knowledge- or skill-based pay. The most recent estimate of the popularity of this approach suggests that as many as 40 percent of large companies use it, but they use it for only a small percentage of their workforce (Lawler, Ledford, and Mohrman, 1989). As was mentioned earlier, it is frequently used in new high-involvement plants (Lawler, 1978; Tosi and Tosi, 1986). Other approaches to person-based pay include paying individuals according to their family situation, their age, their years of experience, and their seniority with the organization. Although these approaches are used in some countries where they fit the culture, they will not be discussed here. Our focus will be on skill-based pay because of the potential it has to make fundamental changes in the way pay is managed in industrialized countries.

The Nature of Skill-Based Pay

The design of skill-based pay systems first requires the identification of those tasks that need to be performed in the organization. Next, the skills that are needed to perform the tasks need to be identified, and tests or measures must be developed to determine whether an individual has learned the skills. Once this has been done, skills need to be "priced" so that pay rates can be determined. The next step involves identifying the number and kind of skills that each individual can learn. This is a key decision, because it determines how skill-based pay will affect skill development. The opportunity to learn skills needs to fit the management style, organizational practices, and organizational strategy. Finally employees need to be told what skills they will be encouraged to learn given their position in the organization. Individuals are typically paid only for those skills that they currently can and are willing to perform.

Skill-based pay is easiest to describe in the case of a production work group in a manufacturing plant. Typically, it is relatively easy to identify all the tasks that a production group needs to do, and it is possible to specify what constitutes skill acquisition. When skill-based pay is in place, individuals are usually told that they can learn all of the skills needed to do the work of their group and that they will be paid more as they learn more of these skills. Thus employees earn pay increases at a rate commensurate with their ability to acquire new skills. The typical pay progression in such a work group starts with an entry rate that represents the going rate for unskilled labor. Each skill is then given a value. Sometimes all are given the same value (for example, $.50 an hour in additional pay) and sometimes they are given values that are based on how hard they are to learn or how greatly they are valued in the local labor market.

Although most skill-based pay plans I have seen give individuals pay increases when they learn a new skill, a somewhat different approach is used by Volvo in Sweden and by one American company I worked with. These firms give every employee in a work area an increase when the employees in that area collectively prove that they can operate without a supervisor. Obviously, this provides a powerful motivation for groups to make their supervisor unnecessary. I have also seen organizations give one-time lump-sum payments rather than pay increases to employees for learning skills. This can work well in a situation where wages are already high, but in most cases I think a progression system is best.

Many of the systems currently operating in plants use peer-group assessment of skills, but there is no reason why this particular approach has to be part of a skill-based system. Skill-based pay merely requires *some* test of skill acquisition. Depending upon the situation, this test can take the form of a supervisor's judgment, written questions and answers, or peer-group appraisal, to mention some of the more obvious possibilities.

In manufacturing plants most individuals learn tasks that are considered "horizontal" to the tasks they otherwise would perform. That is, they learn jobs up- and downstream in the production process. Horizontal plans usually contain a requirement that employees learn a certain minimum number of skills in order to continue to be a member of the organization (in most of the plans that I have seen, that minimum is four or more) and that they be willing and able to perform, when asked, any skill that they are paid for.

In addition to paying for horizontal learning, many plans pay for depth of skills in a particular area. In the case of maintenance employees, for example, different levels of skill can usually be identified in any specialty, and individuals are paid more for achieving higher skill levels. An emphasis on depth skills is a particularly good strategy when an organization needs to emphasize technology leadership or when it operates in high-technology businesses because it encourages individuals to develop high levels of skill.

Some plans also reward individuals for learning skills that are normally possessed by managers and staff professionals. These upwardly vertical skills may include inventory control, quality control, scheduling, and team leadership. One Digital plant rewards economic skills and knowledge of the business and the corporation. Encouraging the learning of vertical skills has particularly important implications for management style. Having production employees learn these skills makes sense only if the organization allows work teams or individuals a significant degree of autonomy and self-management (Hackman and Oldham, 1980). Allowing autonomy without ensuring that some team members have these skills is as foolish as training employees in them and then managing in a traditional, top-down way that does not use the skills.

In some skill-based pay plans, individuals are asked to learn all the jobs in a plant. The Shell Canada chemical plant in Sarnia, Ontario, is an example of this approach. Individuals reach top pay only when they have accomplished this level of competency—an amount of learning that can take eight or more years. This approach fits particularly well with a high-involvement management style, because it helps develop highly skilled employees who can manage themselves and participate in a number of decisions.

The idea of paying for skills is not quite so easily and straightforwardly applied to nonproduction work. Skill-based pay for managers and professionals in an organization can take several forms. Managers and higher-level professionals can be paid for learning skills that are horizontal just as a production worker can. For example, a personnel manager can learn accounting. Managers can also, however learn skills that are lower than theirs in an organization—that is, downwardly vertical skills. Examples here would include manufacturing production skills, typing skills, customer service skills and so on. They can also be paid for learning upwardly vertical skills, such as higher-level management skills. Finally, they can be paid for learning the skills that are needed to perform their job in greater depth. An accountant, for example, can learn more about the tax code.

The development of a skill-based pay system for managerial

and professional employees in an organization involves a number of interesting and difficult decisions about which skills it is desirable for people to learn. The organization must determine what mix of vertical skills, horizontal skills, and depth skills it wants its higher-level employees to learn.

In the case of many high-technology and R & D employees, it is obvious that depth skills should be rewarded. Because being at the forefront of technology is essential to the success of a high-technology organization, skill depth is often a critical competitive factor. In these organizations, therefore, it is usually to everyone's advantage to have at least some employees who develop a real depth of skill in particular technical areas.

Earlier I mentioned that any skill-based pay system needs to rely on measures of skill acquisition or competency. These can be difficult to develop in the case of managerial and professional work. Sometimes the only way to assess advanced skills is after the fact— that is, to evaluate the person's work over an extended period of time.

Skill-based pay systems can price skills in the marketplace. Just as with job-based pay, an organization can go to the market and assess how much people with similar skills are paid. This method of determining the pay for particular skills can be tricky, however, if there are no other organizations in the market with this approach to pay. Often no other organization exists that has employees with the same mix of skills. Nevertheless, there is nothing in the concept of skill-based pay that in any way contradicts the principle of paying market rates.

Skill-based systems can—but need not—include the idea of paying for individual performance. They are, in a sense, neutral on the point of whether individuals should receive more pay depending upon how well they perform a particular skill. They deal with the issue of whether someone can perform the job, while pay for performance focuses on how *well* someone performs the job over a period of time.

It is quite possible to do performance appraisals for individuals, assessing how well they perform each of the skills for which they are being paid, and to base pay changes on these assessments. In this respect, skill-based pay is identical to job-based pay; it allows organizations to vary the amount of total compensation that an individual receives according to the individual's performance. An important difference remains, however. In skill-based pay the starting point for pay is determined by the mix and depth of an individual's skills rather than the particular job to which the person is assigned.

In summary, the concept of skill-based pay simply says that individuals are paid for the number, kind, and depth of skills that they develop and utilize. These skills may be horizontal, depth, or vertical skills. As we shall see, the kind of skill development an organization decides to reward needs to be a function of both the purpose that it hopes the skill-based system will serve and its business strategy.

The Incidence of Skill-Based Pay

Several estimates exist of the actual adoption of skill-based pay plans. A 1987 study by O'Dell found that 5 percent of the 1,598 companies surveyed reported having a skill-based system (O'Dell, 1987). Most of these reported that the plans were recently installed. Higher use was found by a study of New York and American stock exchange companies; 8 percent of these companies reported using skill-based pay plans (Gupta, Schweizer, and Jenkins, 1987). A study I did with Susan Mohrman and Gerry Ledford found that 40 percent of the *Fortune* 1,000 service and manufacturing organizations have skill-based pay plans somewhere in their organization (Lawler, Ledford, and Mohrman, 1989). Most of these companies indicated that they use skill-based pay for only a small part of their workforce, however. Part of the reason that our study found greater use of skill-based pay probably lies in the different definitions of skill-based pay used by it and the earlier studies. The latter limited their definition to pay for the number of jobs a person can do and related skill-based pay to the team concept, while our study gave a more general definition that included any approach that focused on a person's skills.

Technical "ladders" probably represent the most widespread and long-standing use of skill-based pay in organizations today. These ladders pay individuals for the depth of skill they have in a

particular technical specialty. Although they are used by many organizations, they are most commonly found in the R & D
department of large organizations and in apprenticeship systems for
the skilled trades. Technical ladders are also found in such diverse
organizations as universities (where they are used for the payment
of faculty) and corporate law departments (where they are used to
recognize the development of legal skills).

The technical ladder, which has been around a long time, is
not often identified as a form of skill-based pay. Rather, it is usually
treated as part of a job-based pay system; different job descriptions
are written for different positions on the technical ladder. Nevertheless, in most cases it is in fact a form of skill-based pay—one that
is based on depth skills rather than horizontal or vertical skills.
Until recently, in many R & D pay systems age was used as a measure of skill. It was assumed that individuals who had more work
experience were more skilled. Currently, most pay systems do not
consider age, largely because to do so is now illegal. Instead, they
focus on years of professional experience, paying individuals more
as they gain experience. Pay increases are particularly large during
an individual's first few years in the profession. In many cases no
direct tests of skill acquisition are made, however, so there is a real
danger that the organization is rewarding individuals for surviving
rather than for improving their skills.

Since 1970 many skill-based pay plans have been installed in
new high-involvement manufacturing plants (Lawler, 1978, 1986b).
Estimates of exactly how many high-involvement plants have skill-
based pay vary from 200 upward. I have helped install skill-based
plans in new plants built by Johnson & Johnson, General Electric,
Honeywell, Eaton, Digital, and TRW. Other companies that have
used skill-based pay include Procter & Gamble, Mead, General
Foods, Northern Telecom, General Motors, Motorola, and ARCO.
Skill-based pay is typically used to pay production workers (sometimes called "associates," "technicians," or "team members") in
such high-involvement plants but typically is not used for managerial and other employees. Thus the typical high-involvement plant
has both a skill-based and a traditional job-based pay system.

Procter & Gamble is probably the leading installer of skill-
based pay systems. It started putting high-involvement plants in

place in the late 1960s and by the 1980s had at least twenty plants in which the production employees were on skill-based pay plans. As is true with most organizations, the original installations of skill-based pay were in new plants. Recently, however, Procter & Gamble has installed skill-based pay in older manufacturing facilities, as have a number of other organizations. Despite Procter & Gamble's widespread use of skill-based pay, it (like many other companies) has not used skill-based pay at the managerial level.

Effectiveness of Skill-Based Pay

The critical questions concerning any management practice involve its effectiveness. In the case of skill-based pay the obvious question is, How does it compare in effectiveness with job-based pay? This is not an easy question to answer. First, there is a real paucity of data on how effective skill-based pay systems are. Second, it is often difficult to separate the impact of a pay system from that of other organizational practices. Pay is such an integral part of the overall management system in many organizations that it is difficult to tease out the effects of the pay system from the effects of other things. It is also possible that the advantages of skill-based pay may differ from situation to situation and from person to person; for example, skill-based pay is likely to have a different impact on managers than on technical workers. Finally, skill-based pay has been tried in only a limited number of situations. Thus the effects of many different forms of skill-based pay and their applicability to different types of organizations are as yet untested.

Despite the lack of experience with skill-based pay, it is possible to identify some of the gains and losses that come from its use. Certainly enough research is available on high-involvement plants to discuss with some confidence the effects of skill-based pay there.

Advantages of Skill-Based Pay

The most obvious advantage of skill-based pay in a production situation is flexibility. When individuals can perform multiple tasks, organizations gain tremendous flexibility in utilizing their workforce. There are a number of conditions that can make this flexibility extremely desirable. These include filling jobs after turn-over and covering for employees who are absent, who are being trained, and who are in meetings. In addition, if the organization's products frequently change or if other things, such as parts short-ages, cause an irregular work flow, it can be desirable to have a highly trained workforce that can smoothly adapt to changes in the production or service process. This advantage is likely to become increasingly important in the future because of the tendency for products to have shorter life cycles, the increasing demand for pro-duct customization, and the need to respond quickly to market changes.

I had an experience that brought home to me the importance of an organization's ability to rapidly change its technology and products. As part of some work I did with Johnson & Johnson, Doug Jenkins and I designed a skill-based pay system for a plant that makes Tylenol. As a result of the Tylenol poisoning tragedy, Johnson & Johnson decided to completely redo its packaging of Tylenol to add greater safety. The skill-based plant quickly in-stalled the new technology needed and got back into production. Not so with its sister plant, which was a traditional, job-based seniority-driven plant. Seniority rights and traditional pay grades got in the way of people's flexibility in adapting to the new tech-nology. In addition, the traditional plant, unlike the skill-based plant, did not have a history of providing training, valuing per-sonal growth, and encouraging employees to do new things. Thus the transition to new packaging equipment was a major challenge for it.

Flexibility can also be important if there is a need for most employees to be working at a particular stage in the production process. For example, in manufacturing situations it is not uncom-mon to face parts shortages or a need to rework products. If every-body can do all portions of the assembly process, all employees can work in problem areas or focus on solving the problem. If only a few individuals can work on each particular phase of the produc-tion process, production is bottlenecked or the product shipment is held up until the relevant individuals can correct the problem or install the missing part. Skill-based pay can also help make just-in-time manufacturing systems work effectively. Just-in-time manufacturing can lead to temporary parts shortages, and these are more easily handled when skill-based pay is used because individuals can be shifted to the work that can be done.

Traditionally, organizations have recognized the need to have some multiply skilled individuals. Most companies that use assembly lines, for example, have utility workers who are trained to do multiple assembly tasks. Usually they are limited to a small percentage of the workforce, however. There is an important difference between having a few utility people and having a horizontal skill-based pay plan: with skill-based pay, all individuals are flexible and can work at many points in the production or service process. This, of course, means that there is a much greater degree of flexibility in a skill-based pay system.

Overall, the flexibility that comes from skill-based pay may lead to slightly leaner staffing among production employees. Because multiple individuals can fill in, the organization does not need to have as many extra employees to cover for absenteeism and activities that take people away from direct production. In addition, sometimes employees discover that some jobs can be eliminated, because two people can do the work of three or because people can do some of their own maintenance or material handling, thus eliminating the need for support workers.

Not all employees like skill-based pay, but the evidence is growing that many do because it gives them more control over their pay and frequently leads to higher pay. Skill-based pay can also lead to lower turnover and possibly less absenteeism. Individuals who are paid more because they know more are unlikely to find jobs in other companies that are as attractive. Part of the reason for this is that most other organizations are not arranged in ways that utilize flexible employees, so these multiskilled employees are simply not worth a higher pay rate elsewhere.

As was mentioned earlier, many of the flexibility advantages inherent in a skill-based pay system can be gained by simply having a significant portion of the workforce cross-trained as utility workers. Flexibility does not require a full-blown skill-based pay plan that rewards individuals for vertical and self-management skills. Thus the advantages of skill-based pay must extend beyond simple flexibility to make an extensive skill-based system worth-while.

When combined with a participative approach to management, skill-based pay can produce benefits other than those that stem from having a flexible workforce (Lawler, 1986b; Walton, 1980). This seems to be particularly true when the system includes the acquisition of upwardly vertical skills by nonmanagement employees. When employees learn both horizontal and vertical skills, they gain an entirely different perspective on the organization's operations, the way in which it is managed, and the information system that supports it. This allows them to do a number of things that they could not do in the absence of this breadth of understanding and perspective.

First, it allows employees to solve systemic problems more effectively. Their broader perspective helps employees to be more innovative in improving operations. Thus they are more effective in quality circles and other problem-solving arenas (Lawler and Mohrman, 1985, 1987).

All too often I have seen quality circles and problem-solving groups flounder because no one in the group had an overview of how the entire production or service process operates. Typically each individual knows a piece; but in the absence of someone who understands the whole, a total understanding is impossible. Similarly, when multiply skilled employees who know the entire production process are working on a particular phase of production, they are often more effective in solving problems and in making operating decisions. They are not limited to the perspective that comes from doing just one step in the process. Too often I have seen employees comes up with ideas for improvement that look great from their perspective but are unusable because of roadblocks elsewhere in the organization. Because they were not aware of what went on outside their limited area of work, the employees simply could not anticipate the problems.

Second, employees often gain a greater sense of commitment to seeing that the organization operates effectively when they have an overview of the entire operation. Feedback about such things as quality and production rates becomes more meaningful to them, and thus their intrinsic motivation to perform increases (Lawler,

1973). This can result in improved performance and better operating results for the organization, because, among other things, it increases the motivation to do high-quality work.

Third, skill-based pay is an important reinforcer of a participative culture. It is a concrete way that organizations can back up their commitment to participative management and to such statements as, "People are our most important asset." It delivers a tangible reward to individuals for doing just what the organization says it believes they can do: grow, learn, and develop. Because of this, organizations that have skill-based pay typically have cultures that value human development and are optimistic about the capability and potential of the people who work there. This effect, although sometimes difficult to quantify, is nevertheless a very real and important advantage of skill-based pay.

Finally, and perhaps most important, when employees are broadly knowledgeable about the operations of an organization, the potential exists for them to be more self-managing. That is, they are in a better position to control their own behavior, to coordinate with others, and ultimately to participate in self-managing groups and teams that operate a particular part of the organization. They can communicate more effectively with individuals doing other parts of the production or service process because they understand what the others are doing. This, in turn, can lead to better decision making while individuals are doing their work. Because they know what others are doing, they can discuss problems and often come up with good "fixes." This is particularly likely and important when the production process is highly interdependent.

In many chemical, energy, and food production situations, what is done at one step in the process needs to take into account what is done at all others. Coordination and problem solving can be achieved either by managers acting as coordinators and controllers or by knowledgeable employees talking to other knowledgeable employees. To the degree that skill-based pay aids in self-management, tremendous savings are possible. It can lead to fewer levels of management and can also reduce the number of staff and support personnel. I have seen plants in which the first level of supervisors has a ratio of one manager to every hundred employees and plants where no managers are needed to operate the plant during the evening shifts.

Most skill-based high-involvement plants I have seen operate with only three levels: plant manager, area supervisors, and technicians. The savings from reductions in management levels can be quite large. It was large enough in one company that Gerry Ledford and I worked with that it made the difference between building and not building a new plant. Traditional cost numbers for the plant made it seem a poor investment; but when a leaner management structure was assumed, the return on building the plant reached an acceptable level. It was therefore built and is now operating successfully. The plant produces a product that is a big winner for the company—a winner that might never have been produced if some new thinking about how to manage had not been tried.

Reduced management overhead is particularly likely when upwardly vertical skills are emphasized so that individuals learn management and staff support skills. Not only is there no need in these cases for people to waste valuable time waiting for a specialist to come solve a problem; there may be no need for the staff specialist at all, because the individuals can do the problem solving themselves. In some cases employees can also take on the responsibilities for operating some of the systems that typically are run by staff groups. For example, they can do some of the administrative work normally done by the personnel department and they can do their own quality control. The effect can be a reduction in the need for staff.

In summary, the advantages of skill-based pay are of two types. First, there are those that stem simply from horizontal flexibility. These include leaner staffing; fewer problems with absenteeism, turnover, and work disruptions; and the ability of many employees to help with and adjust to glitches in the production process. Although these are important advantages, they are not always significant enough to justify the cost of an extensive skill-based pay system.

The second kind of advantage comes about when skill-based pay includes vertical skills and is combined with a management style that pushes information, knowledge, and decision making to the lower levels. In this situation it is possible for an organization to operate with fewer people, to do better problem solving, and to have a more motivated and committed workforce. This comes about because individuals have the knowledge and skills to become self-managing. Self-management in turn triggers intrinsic motivation, which encourages individuals to do a high-quality job and to be concerned about production results. The savings potential in these situations is often very large and usually easily justifies installation of a skilled-based system.

Disadvantages of Skill-Based Pay

There are some disadvantages to skill-based pay that need to be considered. Probably the most obvious has to do with the high pay rates that it tends to produce. The very nature of the system encourages individuals to become more valuable to the organization and as a result to be paid more. Typically, nonmanagement employees are paid more than they would be under a more traditional pay system—one that limits their growth, development, and therefore value. Although skill-based pay systems typically have higher average hourly wages than do non-skill-based pay systems, this does not mean that total wage costs have to be higher. If the organization can make better use of its people, total costs can be significantly lower.

Skill-based pay systems are designed so that everyone has the opportunity to learn multiple skills. This requires a large investment in training, which is expensive: the time of trainers is expensive, as is the loss of production time that results from people learning new skills. The time of trainers is often not a significant problem, because much of the training in skill-based pay plans is peer training and is done as a normal part of the job. The more serious problem is that individuals are constantly learning new jobs, and thus there are production losses and problems due to inexperienced people doing the work. Because individuals are always trying to learn new skills, there is a constant need to make trade-offs between production and skill acquisition. Indeed, the worst-case scenario for an organization is frightening: many people know how to do every job, but at any point in time all jobs are being done by individuals who do not know how to perform them at a high level of competence.

Skill assessment can also be a problem with skill-based pay systems. In many respects the problem here is no different than it is with the performance appraisal part of a traditional pay system. However, it is a more frequent problem, because individuals have to be assessed on multiple skills. This can lead to assessing individuals several times a year—whenever they feel they have learned new skills. Thus it is particularly important in a skill-based pay system to have good assessment procedures in place.

Usually the individuals who work with someone have the best idea how well the person can perform (Kane and Lawler, 1978). In skill-based systems where co-workers do the training this is especially true. This suggests using peer groups to do the skill assessment. The problem with peer evaluation is that peers are sometimes unwilling to do the type of hard evaluation that is needed to make sure that individuals have adequately learned skills. I have seen a number of organizations in which the skill assessment component of a skill-based pay system has failed simply because the decision process in the peer group was poor. On the other hand, I have seen many in which assessment has worked well—better even than the best performance appraisal system I have seen in traditionally managed organizations.

An engine plant I worked with provides a good illustration of how peer assessment can go wrong. In many respects the plant was just like others in which I have seen skill-based pay work well: participative, performance-oriented, team-based, and organized around small business units. Teams produced parts for the engine and fed them to a final assembly team. When I asked managers if this plant had skill-based pay, they said yes. When I asked how the pay system worked, they said that each year employees got an increase if they knew more. A check of the records showed that over 95 percent of the employees got a raise every year. I then asked if individuals were adding both horizontal and vertical skills. They responded that some individuals tended to pick a job and stay on it while others rotated. In some cases, they acknowledged, employees wanting to change were blocked by those who did not want to change jobs. In effect, some individuals were getting one year's experience over and over again and being rewarded for it because they claimed that their skills were growing. Clearly, this was a skill-based pay system that was not working. A little further investigation revealed why.

When the plant was opened, a number of key things were not done: no skill blocks were identified, no tests or standards were developed to define what constituted acceptable levels of skill mastery, and team members were neither trained in how to do assessments nor were they told that this was one of their responsibilities. Every successful skill-based plan I have seen has done these things. They are the necessary conditions for success. In addition, a skilled team leader is usually needed to make skill-based pay work. This leader helps the group with the initial assessments and challenges the group if it is not doing the assessments well.

Skill-based pay also makes market comparisons a bit more difficult. As was mentioned earlier, it is difficult to go to the market and get a pay rate for a skill, particularly when that skill is being looked at in the context of someone who has several other skills and will be performing that skill only part of the time. Thus in many cases the pay rates developed for individuals have to be an estimate of what it takes to attract, retain, and satisfy somebody with a particular skill mix. One way to think of this is as setting pay rates at a replacement-cost level. This requires shifting the salary-survey process from looking at what others are paying for jobs to looking at what they are paying to hire particular kinds of individuals.

Skill-based pay systems have a problem that occurs with maturity. Even in the most ambitious skill-based pay system, individuals can "top out"—that is, they can learn all the skills that the program calls for them to learn. This can lead to discontent for individuals who have become accustomed to learning, growing, and receiving higher pay. Such employees are better off than they would be in the typical pay system, but they may nevertheless be unhappy about topping out. This is not a serious problem, however, because the individuals end up so much better off in terms of pay and skills than they would be in a traditional pay system. It is a small grumble when compared to the grumbles produced by job-based systems.

There is a certain level of administrative complexity that accompanies skill-based pay systems. Keeping track of exactly who is qualified on all the different jobs and of the different pay rates certainly requires some administrative support. Developing and keeping track of all the skill tests that are needed in skill-based systems also require time and effort. In addition, because individuals can move into a new skill and master it at almost any time, pay changes occur throughout the year, and thus pay administration is not a simple matter of changing peoples' pay once a year based on merit or seniority.

The desire of individuals to move from job to job can be counterproductive if it means that they are unwilling to stay and produce in the job that they have just mastered. For this very reason, many organizations with skill-based pay have required a payback period—a period of time during which an individual has to perform the job that has just been mastered in order to pay back the organization for the investment it has made in his or her learning how to do the job.

It can be hard for an individual to remain current in a large set of skills. Thus, although an individual may be paid for having multiple skills, he or she may not be able to perform all of them as well as when originally learned. Most skill-based pay systems require that individuals regularly perform skills in order to be paid for them. This is a good principle, but it can get lost in an organization's desire to get production out and to operate effectively. It is all too easy to forget the importance of rotating people to be sure that they still have skills when there is a need for them to do some other task.

Finally, there can be sticky issues when technological and organizational changes occur. Major technological changes can mean that certain skills are no longer needed. What happens to the individuals whose pay was based on those obsolete skills? Often these transitions are handled by guaranteeing individuals the old pay rates for a year or so after a major change and then paying them based upon the new skills. Skill-based pay can thereby have the positive effect of emphasizing to people that learning is not something that stops in an organization and of motivating them to learn new skills when their work changes.

Major organizational changes can create the need for a total revision in a skill-based system. Not only can certain skills become obsolete, but combinations of skills that at one time made sense may no longer. Thus individuals can find that their skills no longer fit the way work is organized. The result is that the organization may have to make extensive revisions in its skill-based pay plan and individuals may have to learn a number of new skills. The same thing is likely to be true if the organization has a job-based system— that is, new job descriptions need to be written and individuals need to learn new jobs—but with skill-based pay there is often more retraining and system revision needed.

Where Skill-Based Pay Is Applicable

Now that the advantages and disadvantages of skill-based pay have been considered, it is possible to talk in more depth about where skill-based pay is likely to be effective. Not surprisingly, it seems to be ideally suited to exactly the place where it has been used the most: new high-involvement plants. It fits particularly well with a participative management style because it can encourage individuals to learn just those skills that are required to make participative management work. In addition, it can create an organizational culture that supports learning and puts pressure on the organization to train employees.

There are some obvious reasons why skill-based pay is relatively easy to install in a plant start-up. In new situations there is no job ownership to overcome on the part of established workers who have progressed to the most desirable jobs and want to hold on to them. In addition, skill-based pay reinforces just what a new organization needs at start-up: learning.

Many established organizations are trying to make the move from a traditional to a more participative form of management. Skill-based pay seems to be highly applicable here as well. It can be an incentive for veteran employees to acquire new skills and to allow others to learn their old skills. The reason, of course, is that both the veteran and the less-experienced employee can now earn higher pay. A veteran's refusal to let others learn becomes a negative both for the veteran and for the person who would like to learn the skills.

Problems can arise in moving to skill-based pay if it is difficult to offer longer-term, highly paid employees more to learn additional skills. I know of no easy solution to this problem. One possibility that I mentioned earlier is to make one-time payments for skill acquisition. Some organizations have used another alternative: a red-circle-rate approach in which the higher-paid employees are guaranteed their existing pay rate for a period of time but then have to learn new skills or take a drop in pay. This approach is not always happily accepted by higher-paid employees, but it can be successful. One GE plant I worked with simply cut employees' pay back when it started its skill-based pay plan. This had the desirable effect of immediately motivating everyone to learn new skills. It did not produce a major employee uprising, because the business was failing and the employees knew that if they did not do something, the plant would be shut down. Short of this kind of desperate situation, however, it is probably not advisable to start a skill-based pay plan with a pay cut!

Some plants have used a simplified pay-grade structure as a way of changing traditional work settings. In this approach a few generic job descriptions (for example, production technician) and pay rates are established, and individuals are simply told that they are expected to do anything that needs to be done in their work area. Several unionized General Motors and TRW plants have adopted this approach, as have the new Japanese-managed U.S. auto plants of Honda, Toyota, and Nissan. In the auto plants individuals are put into teams, all paid the same, and told to learn all the skills needed to operate their part of the assembly line. This approach simplifies the pay system but removes much of the direct incentive for learning new skills. In some cases this incentive problem has been solved by adding several pay steps, so that individuals can be rewarded for learning new skills.

In several respects there may be more to gain from using skill-based pay in existing situations than in new situations. It can provide a reason for change that encourages high-seniority employees to become more flexible and to learn new skills. In new situations, on the other hand, pay rewards (although desirable) are often not needed to get employees to conceive of their jobs broadly and to learn multiple skills; nor do new employees have any bad habits to unlearn.

The nature of the workplace technology plays a major role in determining the applicability of skill-based pay and the kind of advantages it offers. Two especially relevant aspects of technology are the level of coordination and the level of employee skill and flexibility that are required. Skill-based pay is most applicable in those situations where organizational performance depends upon good coordination and teamwork among individuals. It is not surprising that skill-based pay has been particularly successful in process-production plants in the chemical, food, and paper industries. In these operations the level of effectiveness depends on the degree to which employees maintain high levels of coordination and teamwork, continually engage in diagnosis and problem solving, and understand the "big picture."

Organizations with more traditional batch or mass-production technologies (for example, those producing cars and electronics) benefit most from the employee flexibility associated with skill-based pay. The ability of employees to cover for absenteeism and turnover, their ability to shift tasks when production bottlenecks arise, their ability to set up and make repairs on their machinery, and their adaptability to shifts in product mix or the production process are often important to the effectiveness of these organizations. Horizontal skill-based pay can help address these issues even in the absence of a participative management culture. If the culture is or is becoming participative, vertical skill-based pay may have additional benefits.

Although skill-based pay has rarely been attempted in non-manufacturing organizations, it is potentially applicable in many of these organizations as well. If a high level of coordination and teamwork and/or a high level of employee skill and flexibility is needed, skill-based pay may be particularly advantageous. For example, some banks have developed skill-based pay systems for branch employees as a way of improving customer service. Tellers become skilled enough to respond effectively to customer inquiries about the rapidly growing mix of products offered by these organizations. Skill-based pay also allows personnel to be moved throughout the work day in response to shifting patterns of customer traffic.

Another service-industry example of skill-based pay is the airline industry, where skill-based pay can be used to encourage employees to work where they are needed. There is a great advantage to having flexibility in this business because the workload demands are so variable. At some times more counter people are needed, at others more baggage handlers are needed, and at others more flight service personnel are needed.

In situations where tasks are highly independent, it is not clear that horizontally oriented skill-based pay always pays off. For example, insurance sales people often operate very independently. It is not clear that training them to do other parts of the insurance process will necessarily make them better salespeople, although it might improve their relationship with the home office and the people doing the support work. In any case, theirs is clearly a much different situation from that of a person operating a work station in a manufacturing plant or in an office "paper factory." In these latter examples, knowing what happens in the total work flow has the advantage of making employees better problem solvers, increasing their ability to coordinate their activities without supervision, and helping them to make better operating decisions. Thus it is not surprising that insurance companies such as Shenandoah Life use skill-based pay in office settings.

Although I do not often see advantages in skill-based pay when work is independent, I recently found a successful example. A trucking firm developed a plan that rewarded its mechanics for being able to do all truck maintenance activities. Even though the mechanics worked alone, it paid off for the company, because it gave the organization tremendous flexibility in assigning work to mechanics. Trucks rarely had to wait for the "right" mechanic to be available. This meant less downtime for trucks—a critical performance factor, because trucks make money only when they are on the road.

Where Skill-Based Pay Is Questionable

The one area in which a major question remains about the utilization and effectiveness of skill-based pay is managerial and staff support work. So far, there are virtually no applications of skill-based pay to this type of work; although I know of several large corporations that are heading toward using skill-based pay on a corporate-wide basis. It can be argued that in high involvement organizations it is important to put all employees on skill-based pay in order to put everyone on the same footing and create a homogenous culture. However, the problems in applying skill-based pay to managerial and staff work are significant.

First, there are a number of difficult issues concerning what skills to pay for. These issues include whether to pay for downwardly vertical skills and how much cross-training makes sense for managers and staff specialists. Skill assessment is often more difficult in this area and thus can make implementation more difficult. Finally, changing just one unit of an organization to skill-based pay can put the managers out of step with the organization's standard career and pay tracks. I have run into this problem several times when I have tried to install skill-based pay for single-plant management groups. Local managers liked the concept but resisted going off the corporate plan. They saw their careers as being with the company not with the plant; so they were afraid that if they were paid differently and learned different things than their peers elsewhere, it would harm their careers. This suggests that putting in skill-based systems for managers is best done on an organization-wide basis.

Applying skill-based pay to managerial work could have the desirable effect of eliminating pay increases for promotions. Instead, increases would begin once a person demonstrated that he or she has mastered a new set of skills. Thus the power of a large promotion increase would not simply encourage people to take a new job they probably would have taken anyway; it would encourage people to learn the skills associated with a new job. If this leads to individuals turning down promotions because they do not result in an immediate pay increase, it is probably best for all concerned that they did not take the job. I would rather see someone take a job, particularly a managerial job, because of the nature of the work than because it results in a pay increase. Too often, good technical people become poor managers because they cannot turn down the lure of an instant pay increase.

One population trend may encourage organizations to use skill-based pay for managerial employees. There is going to be an increasingly large number of individuals in the age groups that typically occupy management positions. However, organizations are trying to reduce the number of managerial employees by becoming flatter and leaner. Thus there is a direct conflict between an increasing number of people who are aspiring to upward mobility and the decreasing availability of managerial jobs. Unless something changes, this means that many individuals will be in dead-end jobs with no pay progression or learning opportunities for much of their adult life. For example, one organization I worked with recently concluded that under their present policies, over 80 percent of their managers will receive no more promotions!

Skill-based pay represents one potential approach to ameliorating this problem. Individuals could be paid for horizontal learning as well as for vertical learning if skill-based pay were in place. This would have the effect of raising their wages and giving them an opportunity to continue to grow and develop. Thus skill-based pay could help make careers more satisfying for individuals and could serve to legitimate the idea that a good career move can be horizontal as well as vertical.

Because of the way the reward structures are set up in most large U.S. corporations, the only legitimate career move for many individuals is upward. The reward system rather clearly says that this is the only kind of mobility that is valued. This makes sense if management wants a large number of people striving for the fewer and fewer positions in upper management and developing skills that only a few of them will ever get the opportunity to utilize. It does not make sense, however, if the concept of management is a more participative one in which a large number of individuals are developing a broad understanding of how the organization operates and developing multiple skills so that they can become more self-managing.

Skill-based pay for managers makes particular sense if an organization is operating with a matrix or networking approach to organizational structure (Galbraith, 1973; Miles and Snow, 1986). These approaches work best when the individuals in them have had experience in a variety of functions and business areas, because this allows them to understand the position of others when they are dealing with the complexities of a matrix structure or negotiating a deal with a supplier. Skill-based pay is a way to make this type of training happen.

The use of technical ladders to encourage the development of depth skills increasingly makes sense. Technical ladders are a well-established practice in many organizations already, and they fit well with the major trends that are occurring. The growth of high-technology work and knowledge work means that more and more individuals should be paid on a technical ladder basis.

One key to making technical ladders successful concerns how much pay progression they offer. All too often they offer little progression, and as a result they do not encourage the most talented individuals to pursue technical careers. If they are to be effective, they must offer titles and pay levels that approach those associated with senior management positions. Motorola provides a good example of just this approach. Individual contributors doing staff and technical work there can become vice-presidents (there are over 250) and be paid accordingly. This fits Motorola's strategy of being a technology leader in products and management systems.

New Approaches to Skill-Based Pay

If skill-based pay is to be widely used in organizations, approaches need to be developed that solve the administrative complexity problems associated with it and that effectively tie it into the external pay market. Let us look at the issue of administrative complexity first.

One promising approach here may be to install skill-based pay in combination with a computerized personnel management system. If the computerized system includes a skill component and an approach to certifying skills, it should be easy to use the skill component to handle the logistics of keeping track of individual skill and pay rates.

Wider adoption of skill-based pay may be aided by going to simpler forms of it. As was mentioned, the early plans priced each skill and then added up the points or cents for the skills to get to a pay rate. This is effective in production jobs but may not fit managerial jobs. What may make more sense for managerial jobs is a kind of technical ladder that starts by placing individuals at one of a very few management levels in the organization. For example, there might be a first-level or supervisory pay rate, a unit manager rate, and a few others. The level of pay for each management level would be determined by what the market pays someone to join an organization at that level of management. Individuals could progress from the base rate by learning additional skills of whatever type fit the situation. Both horizontal and vertical learning (both upward and downward) would be okay. Each individual would be asked to establish a learning plan and get this approved by his or her manager. Pay could be managed through a three- or four-level approach so that individuals could move up as they learned new skills.

A system somewhat like this is being used by 3M for its new-venture managers. It focuses on depth skills by rewarding managers for getting better and better at managing new ventures. The system was developed because 3M kept losing its best start-up managers; they took promotions as the only way they could advance. This was obviously not desirable in an organization that prides itself on starting new businesses.

Simpler systems could also help in those situations where rapid change is taking place. As was mentioned, change can be more disruptive of skill-based systems than of job-based systems. Both approaches have rigidity built into them. Overall, however, in most situations the skill-based organization is likely to be more flexible. Why? Because skill-based pay systems tend to produce organizations with cultures that value learning, growth, change, and individuals who are not overly protective of their "turf."

Increasing the vertical learning opportunities for employees is one way to solve the topping-out problem—a problem that in many respects is artificially created by management systems that assume that only a limited amount of vertical skill is desirable. If learning vertical skills is encouraged, topping out ceases to be a problem. One qualification is necessary here, however: extensive vertical skill training is likely to make sense only where an advanced form of participative management is practiced, because without it the skills are likely to be underutilized.

It is possible to imagine a situation in which the skills in an organizational unit would be available for learning by all employees. This could create a situation where production employees would in fact become indistinguishable from managerial employees. It could also create a situation in which somebody doing a production task would be among the highest-paid employees in the organization. At first glance this seems a bit radical, but if that person had the most knowledge about plant operations, he or she could in fact deserve the highest pay. There remains the issue of whether doing production work would be the best utilization of this person's time, of course, but it is possible that it might be in certain situations—particularly if doing production work helps that employee understand the organization's overall operation and condition or if it leads to important insights about how production can be improved.

The future of skill-based pay appears to be quite bright. It fits a participative management style, and this approach is increasingly popular in the United States. It also fits well in organizations in which work is highly interdependent and cooperative and/or is rapidly changing. These types of organization are increasingly common in the United States as work becomes more high-technology-oriented and service-oriented. Finally, it fits rather well with knowledge-based work, particularly when it takes the form of a technical ladder, and this type of work is also increasing in the United States.

Part Four

Administering Pay Systems

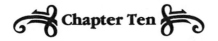

Chapter Ten

Setting Total Compensation Levels

The total compensation that an individual receives is made up of all the material rewards that the organization provides. The most obvious of these are cash and fringe benefits, but the rewards that an individual receives rarely stop there; many organizations also offer a large number of perquisites. This is particularly true at the executive level, where as many as fifty different kinds of perquisites are offered, ranging from air travel on corporate jets to memberships in country clubs and other social clubs (Ellig, 1982; Gomez-Mejia and Welbourne, 1988; Finkelstein and Hambrick, 1988; O'Reilly, Main, and Crystal, 1988). At other levels in the organization, perquisites may include participation in social events, discounts on company products, and (in the case of university faculty) reduced prices for athletic events.

The cost is obvious when cash compensation is given; it is not always obvious, particularly to employees, just how much benefits and perquisites cost. In most large U.S. organizations during the 1980s benefits equaled about 40 percent of cash compensation, and their cost was rising (McCaffrey, 1989). Thus benefits are clearly a significant cost for organizations. I know of no good number on the cost of perquisites, but they are undoubtedly also a significant cost for most companies. I make this point to stress that in looking at total compensation, organizations cannot stop at cash and benefits. To understand the behavioral impact of the organization's reward system, it is important to look at the *total* material reward received by employees.

Impact of Total Compensation Levels

The most obvious impact of the total compensation level received by employees is on attraction and retention. Simply stated, organizations that have high levels of compensation have lower turnover rates and larger numbers of individuals applying to work for them. All the data on employee decision making about where to work show that the level of rewards received is an important influence on people's decisions about which organization they work for (Mobley, Hand, Meglino, and Griffeth, 1979). Money and benefits are important, and those organizations that offer more attract a larger number of people.

The impact of the total compensation level does not end with the attraction and retention of employees, however. As was mentioned earlier, total compensation can affect other features of an organization. For example, the culture of an organization can be affected when it makes a very public point of paying high levels of compensation in order to attract the best and the brightest. Organizations that have high pay often point out that because they are high payers they are very selective, and tolerate only the best performance from their employees. This can result in an elitist culture in which high-performance expectations are the norm and individuals feel that they are fortunate to work for the organization. Once individuals believe that their organization is the best payer, they are much less likely to look for other job opportunities. If it is clear that the organization is consistently the best payer, why bother to spend the energy looking elsewhere?

In the computer industry at least two organizations have adopted a high-compensation stance quite successfully. Both Apple and Hewlett-Packard claim to be top payers, and they have used this claim very skillfully to develop an internal culture of excellence and to foster the perception that they are great places to work.

Total compensation levels also have a direct impact on the cost of an organization's doing business. In order to achieve a high market position, organizations must spend more on pay than their competitors do. This may be offset by cost savings in such areas as recruiting, training, and productivity, but high total compensation levels always have a direct negative impact on an organization's labor costs. Similarly, low compensation levels represent a potential savings to an organization.

Total compensation levels can impact the structure of an organization if certain groups are singled out for special treatment of one kind or another. This sometimes occurs when organizations decide that they need to pay individuals in a particular function or division more because of its strategic importance. I have seen this done with engineers in technology firms and professors in universities, for instance. Wherever I have seen it done, it has tended to make that group feel special—differentiated from the rest of the organization but aligned with each other—and to produce feelings of internal inequity on the part of others. Thus integration and differentiation are affected by policies that target particular groups of employees for special treatment with respect to levels of total compensation.

Finally, total compensations levels can affect performance—if it is in fact seen that they are related to performance. The motivational key is the perceived relationship to performance. Simply paying everyone high levels of total compensation will not motivate high performance. As was noted earlier, individuals quickly adapt to higher levels of pay, deciding that they deserve the money; thus high pay alone does not motivate performance. Moving certain individuals or groups toward high total compensation because of their outstanding performance can in fact be a motivator of performance, but only if individuals see the pay-for-performance relationship. Similarly, moving a total organization toward a high market position can motivate performance if that move is contingent on performance, as it might be in the case of a profit-sharing plan or other variable compensation plan.

Factors Involved in Setting Total Compensation Levels

There is no one correct level at which to set total compensation. Let me illustrate this by comparing two companies in the same business, IBM and Digital Equipment Corporation. They compete head to head in the computer business and both emphasize setting compensation in comparison to other computer companies, but they differ in the level that they try to achieve. As was noted earlier, IBM emphasizes being one of the top payers, if not *the* top payer, in the computer industry. This has a number of advantages, including low turnover, long lists of job applicants, an internal culture of excellence, and a perceived people orientation.

There are, of course, costs to this pay strategy. Aside from the additional payroll costs, there is a danger that an important part of the relationship between employees and IBM may be based on the financial advantages of working for IBM. So long as these financial advantages are there, there is little problem, of course; but if the situation were to change—that is, if IBM were no longer an outstanding payer—the company would run the risk of losing a number of employees. In addition, it always runs the risk of losing individuals whom other organizations are willing to "buy."

Digital's approach is different. The company prefers to pay at levels that are about average for the computer industry, arguing that this not only gives Digital a labor-cost advantage but ensures that people who come to work there will do so for other than purely economic reasons. Digital emphasizes that it wants a culture based on people's enjoyment of the firm's management style and its particular form of organizational life. Because Digital does not "buy" people into the organization, managers claim that they run little risk of losing people simply because pay may fall below the market for a while or because some other company offers more money. Indeed, they hope that they can develop a strong bond to the company based on things other than financial attraction. I have often heard Digital employees say that if all people want is the top pay rate, they probably should work for IBM or Hewlett-Packard, because they will never get it at Digital. On the other hand, employees say at Digital they will have more fun, more freedom, and a chance to participate in a different kind of culture.

The obvious financial advantage to Digital of this stance is that it can lead to lower salary costs. The danger is that it will lead to an inability to compete for certain individuals needed to make the business successful and that the organization will lose people if the nonfinancial reasons people go to work there decrease. Digital talks about providing an above-average quality of work life to compensate for average pay, but this can be hard to deliver. It requires that executives constantly monitor and deliver on the idea of above-average nonfinancial rewards.

A somewhat different approach to total compensation is taken by a successful aerospace company that targets its pay to the fiftieth percentile. In many respects this policy has worked well for them. Turnover is low because this organization operates in a city with a high quality of life and few competing firms. Thus once it hires people, it rarely loses them. It does sometimes have a problem attracting the best college graduates from other parts of the country, however. In many cases new graduates are not willing to trade salary dollars for a life-style they have not experienced. Finally, there is the risk that this strategy can attract too many individuals for whom work is not the central life interest—in other words, employees who may focus their efforts on enjoying the quality of life rather than on doing their job.

It seems that most major corporations say that they will be above-market payers. This simply cannot be; there is no way that 80 percent or more of the companies can pay above-market wages. The statistics simply do not work out, and with the extensive salary-survey data available it is usually easy to see who has not lived up to their commitments. Companies that lag can play catch-up by aggressively raising wages the next year, of course, and many do. Given the competition to be a good payer, it is hardly surprising that wage increases sometimes seem out of control on a national level and that some firms end up paying their way out of a cost-competitive position.

There are times when organizations may have to pay, or may decide to pay, well below what the market pays. This is a strategy fraught with risks. It can cause significant problems in recruiting and retaining the best and the brightest individuals. It can also lead to an internal culture of low esteem and to feelings that the organization in general is second best and lacks the resources to do a first-rate job. This strategy makes sense when the only viable approach is to keep labor costs at as low a level as possible and when human performance is not a major determinant of organizational performance. It is also important that a plentiful labor supply exist so that individuals can be easily replaced as they leave for more lucrative jobs.

A low-wage strategy is particularly likely to be effective in situations where the work is so simple and repetitive that even the least talented individuals can do it effectively with a minimum amount of training. Retail stores that pay minimum wage in order to reduce labor costs are able to cope with high turnover because training costs are minimal and, until recently, it has been easy to replace their departed employees. The biggest challenge for them, as for any low-paying organization, is finding new employees to replace those who have moved on to better-paying jobs in other kinds of work. Another challenge is providing a satisfactory level of customer service, given that they are employers of last resort, and only temporary at that.

Using Pay Comparisons in Setting Compensation. Critical to any total compensation policy is the decision about the comparison base for determining compensation levels. This is one of the most complex issues in the area of total compensation, because there are any number of comparisons that can be chosen. This choice is inexorably intertwined with decisions concerning how high or low the compensation levels should be relative to the market. Let me briefly review some possible types of comparisons and then look at some of the reasons that an organization might choose one over the other.

One of the most obvious comparisons is pay rates in other parts of the same organization. As was noted earlier, this is a natural focus for people, because it is both visible and relevant to the kinds of internal career moves that individuals make.

A second comparison for most individuals is the local job market. Here the comparison is essentially a geographical one. It too is quite obvious: information about the local market appears in the local want-ads and is revealed in conversations with friends. Next-door neighbors, for example, just happen to mention what they are paid by their organization, or they make home improvements indicating that they are well paid. For many individuals, the local market is the key market comparison (Adams, 1965; Goodman, 1974; Fay, 1989). If they are going to leave their current employer, it will be for another job locally.

Somewhat removed from the local scene, but very important to certain types of employees, is the national labor market. For people in the professions and senior management, this is a relevant and important comparison. Often these people are mobile beyond their local community, and thus what is being paid elsewhere is important in determining whether they will change jobs. In addition, if they are in professional associations, as is often true of lawyers, accountants, and engineers, they see considerable data about what people are paid to do their kind of work elsewhere in the United States. Thus they are quite aware of how their organization's pay compares to that of organizations in other parts of the country.

Often the most important comparisons from an organization's point of view are to industry competitors. These comparisons are important because they determine an organization's cost competitiveness. If an organization has significantly higher or significantly lower labor costs, it can end up with either a competitive disadvantage or advantage. Often this comparison is not as apparent to individual employees, because their movement patterns are not necessarily governed by the type of business that the organization is in. Their commitment may be to their profession—accounting, for example—rather than to work that is located in only one industry, or it may be to a particular community or region.

Certain special kinds of work and skills exist only in a particular industry. For example, engineers who do semiconductor design are likely to look for work only in other semiconductor companies, because their skills are specific to the kind of work that is done in that industry. Similarly, other professionals in organizations may develop skills that are industry-specific. When industry-specific skills exist, the key comparison for individuals is often to other companies within their particular industry rather than to industry in general.

Finally, there is the issue of international competition and the degree to which offshore competitors form a realistic pay comparison. Historically, in the United States at least, international comparisons have been ignored. As a result, in most areas U.S. employees have been paid much more than their foreign competitors. Often this has put U.S. companies at a competitive disadvantage in global markets. In some instances this has changed, however; other countries (for example, Japan and West Germany) have equal or higher labor costs for certain production employees.

International comparisons often interest only senior management because of their concern for the competitive position of the company. Most employees are not in a position to move internationally and are not knowledgeable about international pay rates.

Technical and managerial employees are the people in an organization who are the most mobile internationally. These employees do sometimes move across national boundaries for new jobs; and indeed, people from other nations are recruited to engineering and managerial jobs in the United States, because these jobs offer higher pay.

In the auto, glass, and steel industries, however, senior management has often called the attention of workers to international comparisons and has tried to influence union wage settlements by making these comparisons. This has had some impact, but they are difficult comparisons to support in most cases. In addition, U.S. management often finds itself in the rather awkward position of arguing for the relevance of international comparisons when they are in union negotiations, while they themselves are very highly paid relative to foreign competitors. In the United States the senior executive in a large corporation is typically paid at least fifty times more than the lowest-paid employee in the same corporation. No exact numbers exist for other countries, but estimates suggest that the top-to-bottom ratio is about nine to one in Japan and perhaps fifteen or sixteen to one in Europe. Overall, a good guess is that during the 1980s typical U.S. senior executives made at least twice as much as their counterparts in most other countries.

Complicated as they are, there is no question that international comparisons have to become much more relevant for an increasing number of organizations. As businesses become increasingly global, organizations cannot afford to ignore the wage levels of their international competitors. The simple fact of the matter is that many products and services are cost-competitive, and as a result companies can gain an important competitive advantage if their labor costs are significantly lower than the competition's. Additionally, the day may come when more individuals become mobile across national boundaries; then international competition will be strong for technical and management people. Some kinds of work are already very mobile. They can easily be moved across borders, where the best wage rates exist.

Given the wide array of possible pay comparisons, how can an organization decide what or who to use as a comparison? Unfortunately, there is no easy answer to this question. In many cases the right comparison for one group of employees may not be the right comparison for another. In addition, the kind of comparisons that make sense depend very much on the type of business an organization is in, the type of competitors it faces, and the type of internal culture and management style it wishes to adopt. For example, a low- to middle-priced restaurant probably needs to worry only about local comparisons. One that is at the higher end of the market, however, may need to make national or even international comparisons for some of its employees. In today's business environment highly sought-after chefs are international in their scope, and thus even a local restaurant may need to pay international rates for a chef if it wants to compete at the top end of the market. On the other hand, that same restaurant may not need to compete internationally or even nationally for many of its other employees.

I have seen many different strategies successfully used. The typical strategy is to simply look where individuals are hired from and lost to and set the comparisons based on those labor markets. For the typical organization, this means most unskilled employees end up being compared to the local labor market while managerial and technical people end up being compared to the national market. As a general rule this is a good strategy, but it is not the right approach for all organizations. Different industries tend to pay different wage rates; for example, aerospace companies and oil companies tend to pay better than many service organizations and low-capital manufacturing operations. It is rarely realistic or advisable for organizations to compare themselves to a national market made up of industries that are higher paying than their own.

Because of the differences among industries and the desirability of focusing attention on the competition, a strong case can be made for basing pay comparisons predominantly on business competitors. This is not always the best strategy, but it is typically superior to simply basing pay on national or local labor markets. The fact of the matter is that most organizations do not compete for either labor or profits in a broad national market. They compete with a group of organizations that are in the same business that they are in. Ignoring this can lead to potentially serious cost problems.

All too often I have seen organizations in relatively low-paying industries emphasize paying on a national labor market basis. Some worsen the problem by making the comparison to their idea of the best national companies—that is, they compare themselves to the IBMs, the Hewlett-Packards, and the Exxons. Doing this can "justify" top pay for managers and technical people; and it can be very ego satisfying, because it means playing with the big names of U.S. business. However, it also can price an organization out of a number of businesses. A dramatic example of this problem has occurred over the years in the chemical business. As energy companies such as Mobil, Arco, and Exxon have taken over or developed chemical operations, they have paid oil industry wages to managers and technical people in their chemical operations. In many cases this has made their chemical operations noncompetitive, because chemical companies—particularly independent ones— have paid historically lower wages than energy companies. This problem has been even more severe when energy companies have gone into such unrelated businesses as office products, land development, and department stores.

Paying industry wages can sometimes produce interesting conflicts in local markets. For example, some large companies that believe in paying industry wages at all locations can end up in communities where they are far and away the best payer. In some respects they are "wasting" money; they are spending more in the particular local labor market than they need to spend to attract and retain the best people. They continue this policy simply because it produces a sense of internal consistency and fairness and supports their policy of easy movement of people from one location to another. The alternative, of course, is to have a policy that says an organization is the best payer in that particular market and ignores the national data.

A more intriguing situation is that in which employees are paid industry wages in a market where average local wages are in fact higher. This is obviously the more difficult situation to manage, but my experience says that it can be done if the organization emphasizes its policy from the beginning and provides regular and frequent updates explaining the policy and how it is being implemented. Of course, even a well-administered program will not attract and retain everyone the organization wants if other alternatives are available. However, it can prevent some of the negative reactions that are associated with what are seen to be unreasonably low pay rates.

One defense contractor that Gerry Ledford and I studied opened a munitions plant in the high-wage part of the Midwest. The host city was dominated by unionized auto plants and steel operations. It was clear that the organization could not compete for new business if it paid the prevailing wage rate in the community. Thus from the beginning it told employees that pay rates would be based on industry standards and that the emphasis would be on making the organization competitive so that it could win new contracts and stay in business. Because of high local unemployment, the organization was able to attract a good workforce and has successfully operated for a number of years with wages below the local market. It has not been easy—the organization has lost some good people to better-paying jobs—but overall the policy has worked, because the employees see the business rationale for what is being done and do not resent it. One indication of this is that they have stayed nonunion despite organizing efforts.

One final, important point needs to be made about pay comparisons. Just as organizations compare wage rates to set total compensation levels, employees compare wage rates to "test" their compensation. To a degree, organizations can influence the kind of pay comparisons that their own employees make. If organizations provide employees with data on their pay system, are clear about the comparisons that they are making, and have a definitive policy that specifies who they are going to compare employees' pay to, they can help shape the perceptions of employees about how fairly they are paid. In Chapter Three I described a company that opened two plants, one in the South and one in the North, and announced very different pay comparisons in each. By outlining clear policies, the organization was able to influence what employees focused on in comparing their pay—the local market in the case of the southern plants, union wages in the case of the northern plant.

Overall, then, organizational policies, core principles, data-gathering and -disseminating activities, and communication practices can influence the kind of comparisons that employees make. Admittedly, organizations are not in total control here, because employees base their comparisons on the professional groups they identify with, what happens to their neighbors, and a whole host of other factors. In many cases individuals seem to pick whatever comparison makes their present pay look bad and justifies their being paid more! This follows directly from the often-repeated point that pay is important to individuals and they want more of it. Football players justify their demands for higher salaries by comparing their relatively low salaries with those of baseball players, English professors justify their demands by talking about the higher salaries of business school professors, and teachers compare their salaries with those of administrators. In short, in case after case there is a tendency for individuals to choose unfavorable comparisons.

What an organization *is* in control of, however, is the comparisons that *it* chooses to make. Similarly, as was mentioned earlier, it is in control of how it calibrates its pay to the markets that it chooses. So far I have argued that for most organizations the best approach is probably to base pay in comparison to business competitors at the management level, while at the nonmanagement level the local-market comparison is preferred for most organizations. (However, comparing to business competitors is frequently a good alternative at the nonmanagement level as well.) Although many organizations relate pay to national markets more than to their business competitors, I would once again like to emphasize that this can be a dangerous policy: it can make an organization noncompetitive in its labor costs.

Finally, I have argued against internal comparisons as a basis for setting wages in most situations. The reasons for this are simple and business-based. Internal comparisons run the great risk of producing pay rates that are not competitive and they focus the attention of individuals away from where it should be: on their competitors. As will be discussed later in this chapter, they also make it difficult for a firm to gain strategic advantage by adopting a higher market position for individuals with critical skills or by paying higher wages in some lines of business.

Determining Market Position on the Basis of Performance. An interesting alternative to compensation policies that simply target a particular position in the market is one that takes organizational performance into account in targeting a market position. That is, instead of the organization's saying, "We will pay top dollar," or "We will pay average market rates," the organization says, "Our pay position will be determined by our business performance." Implementing such a policy requires the use of variable compensation, typically in the form of incentive pay or profit sharing. This can allow the organization to vary its market position for individuals according to how the overall organization performs.

On the surface, varying market position with performance is an attractive policy because, among other things, it has the effect of reducing an organization's compensation costs when business performance is down. And because it varies total compensation with performance, it may also have the effect of making total compensation a motivator for some individuals. It can also help to retain people in good times, because it leads to high pay rates when an industry is doing well. There are some risks with this policy, however.

Perhaps the most obvious risk is that an organization will fall upon hard times and lose its key individuals because its market position for pay falls dramatically. This is particularly likely to happen if an organization's performance is significantly worse than that of its competitors. It is not as likely to happen if the drop in organizational performance is the result of an economic downturn, in which case all organizations will suffer and the competition may not be hiring. It is important to lock individuals in during industry upturns, however, because it is during the good times that other organizations want to hire experienced employees.

I studied an appliance manufacturer that gained a real attraction and retention advantage by using performance-based pay. It had a sales commission plan, while its major competitor used a merit-based salary plan. The appliance industry is a cyclical one, so there are definite advantages to any pay system that varies costs, but in this case the advantage of variable pay went beyond cost variability. In good times the variable pay company could attract salespeople from the merit pay company because it paid more. Yet it did not lose them when the market was down, even though pay was low, because there were no competing job offers. Some managers of the company with the commission-based pay plan argued that they ended up with a different type of employee—one who was

more risk-oriented, less bureaucratic, and more entrepreneurial—
although I could not prove it.

TRW introduced an interesting approach to executive compensation in the mid 1980s. It stated that as a matter of policy
corporate compensation at the executive level would reflect corporate performance, as measured on a number of economic indicators
against a group of ninety-nine comparison companies. When TRW
outperformed those comparison companies, executive compensation would rise to a level reflecting that comparative performance.

The interesting thing about this approach is that it looked
only at *comparative* economic performance, ignoring absolute performance. This meant that TRW could pay out handsome bonuses
in an economic downturn so long as it outperformed its competitors, and it could pay out poor bonuses even when the company set
records for profitability and economic return. The latter would
happen, of course, if TRW performed well—but not as well as
industry competitors.

From a motivational perspective, this plan is an ideal pay-
for-performance plan because it rewards individuals according to
how well the organization performs relative to the environment in
which it operates. Relative performance is more under the control
of the organization than unadjusted economic performance would
be. The plan runs the risk of losing key individuals in times when
the economy is strong, however. If, for example, TRW were to
underperform its competitors in a strong economy, it would expose
itself to losing its key people. They undoubtedly would have opportunities to move elsewhere at substantial pay increases, because
TRW's compensation level would be targeted at a below-market
rate.

It is hard to argue against the practice of determining individuals' market position by their individual performance. Outstanding performers tend to have a higher market value and to
attract more offers than poor performers. This is particularly true
when they are in visible positions and/or positions where performance is easily measured. Thus organizations need to be sure that
at least the best performers are at or above the market. On the other
hand, organizations may be able to afford to have poor performers
below the market, given that losing them is not a great loss and

other organizations may not be willing to pay more for their services anyway. Indeed paying low performers below market wages can be an effective way to remove them from the organization. This situation often occurs in retail firms such as Nordstrom that have salespeople on commission. Thus paying for individual performance can have the effect of attracting and retaining the right individuals if it leads to high market positioning for good performers and low market positioning for poor performers.

In summary, then, there are considerable advantages to having market positions reflect organizational and individual performance. This can often be successfully achieved with a combination of individual pay-for-performance plans and organizational pay-for-performance plans. The overriding caution for those moving to this kind of strategy, however, is this: it can lead to the loss of valuable employees if a wrong set of circumstances occurs. It can also lead to attraction and retention problems for certain individuals. People who want to be guaranteed a high market position, for example, may well shy away from an organization that makes market position dependent upon performance. This may not be a problem, of course—for example, in an organization that wants an entrepreneurial, risk-oriented type of culture and individuals. Indeed, it may help to sort out job applicants who want to be entrepreneurial and work in a risk-oriented environment.

Varying Market Position by Organizational Level. I have already pointed out that different levels in an organization sometimes need different pay comparisons. For example, it may make sense to compare executives to national or international markets and production workers to local markets. What I have not yet addressed is whether it makes sense to have a policy that systematically positions individuals from different levels in the organization at different levels relative to their market. That is, does it make sense to pay executives well above market while paying production employees well below market, or vice versa? The right answer to this question rests primarily on the criticalness of people at different levels in the organization—that is, the degree to which particular positions in the organization offer an opportunity for competitive advantage in the marketplace. If a position offers an opportunity for competitive advantage, given the technology and the management style of the organization, it may well make sense to pay people in that position somewhat more relative to market than their co-workers.

This can be a risky strategy, of course, because it affects not only the attraction and retention of people but also the culture and career development patterns of the organization. Particularly if the organization tilts toward paying executives higher in the market than others, this strategy can lead to a culture of elitism and separatism for the senior people. In essence, they can become completely differentiated from the rest of the organization and lose their credibility with the people they are trying to manage. United Airlines suffered this problem in 1988, when the board paid the CEO, who was asking the pilots for wage and work-rule concessions, a bonus of $5.8 million. The head of the pilots' union, angered by the CEO's high pay, would not agree to a new contract, and eventually the pilots engaged in a work slowdown.

Perhaps the most important determinant of whether different market positions should be targeted for different management levels is the issue of management style. As was mentioned earlier, a more traditional management style rests upon the view that senior managers are the critical people in the organization. They have the power, the information, and (one hopes) the expertise to make the organization effective. They are expected to set direction, while people lower in the operation are typically in implementation roles. Thus it is typical and usually appropriate to pay senior executives well when a top-down management style is used. Given all that is asked of these executives, it is critical that the best and the brightest get to the top of the organization and that pay plans encourage them to do their best and stay with the organization. (In Chapter Fifteen we will discuss whether this practice has gone too far, given the multi-million-dollar compensation levels of many senior executives.)

Just the opposite situation exists in more participatively managed organizations. There the emphasis is on locating power, information, knowledge, and rewards at lower levels, and as a result the criticalness of the lower levels is much greater. People there do often handle make-or-break decisions for the organization, and they are expected to develop many more skills and capabilities than employees in traditional organizations. It makes sense, therefore, that they have a relatively high market position compared to people working in traditional organizations.

As was noted in the previous chapter, a high market position typically results with skill-based pay; and although skill-based pay can raise costs for an organization, that may not be a disadvantage. Indeed, it can be an advantage, because it retains people in whom the organization has invested considerable resources and training. In effect, skill-based pay creates individuals who are uniquely valuable to the organizations they work for, because no other organization is designed to use exactly those skill combinations. Thus it is unlikely that individuals will leave a skill-based system; not only are they well paid relative to the market, but they have skills that are of lesser value to other organizations.

An interesting issue is whether managers and executives in highly participative organizations should have *lower* pay relative to the labor market than their top-down counterparts. Because they have less formal power, should they be paid relatively less than individuals heading traditional top-down organizations? One company that thinks so is Ben and Jerry's Homemade, Incorporated, which has a policy that calls for high pay at the nonmanagement level and a five to one ratio from the top to the bottom. Herman Miller is another: it has a twenty to one ratio. In some cases this approach is probably valid, but in others it encounters problems. For example, the skills that are required to run a participative organization are perhaps even scarcer than those required to run a top-down organization, because few managers are trained and developed to be participative managers. Thus, although a participative management style may not call for high levels of compensation for executives, the labor market may force organizations to pay high levels of compensation in order to attract individuals who can lead participative organizations.

It is probably safe to conclude that participative organizations should not, as a matter of policy, pay compensation amounts to senior managers that are higher in the market than those they pay lower-level employees. If senior managers in participative organizations are to be highly paid, the correct policy is probably to have this come about as the result of variable pay based on organizational performance. High pay for *all* based on the success of the organization is much more consistent with employee involvement and participative management than is simply paying senior managers high wages because of their position.

An interesting subquestion is whether pay should be handled differently for different levels in the hierarchy during especially hard times. When a company encounters a period of poor financial performance, wage reductions are often in order—but whose wages should be reduced? Again, management style is key. In the case of an involvement-oriented organization the answer is obvious: everyone's. This is the only answer that is consistent with the idea that everyone is important and responsible. Just this approach has been taken by a number of firms, including Hewlett-Packard and Control Data. In 1989 Control Data cut the pay of its executives by 4.5 percent while cutting the pay of other employees somewhat less. During one downturn Hewlett-Packard had all employees and managers working a reduced work week.

The appropriate response in a traditionally managed firm would seem to call for executives to suffer the major loss for poor firm performance. They are the ones who made the key decisions after all. In Japan CEOs often resign when their firms make a major error, while in the United States executive compensation levels sometimes do drop dramatically when firm performance is poor, particularly when stock options and bonuses are a key part of the executive compensation package. Sometimes, however, executives do not seem to suffer at all. Instead, other employees are laid off and asked to take pay cuts while executive stock options are repriced and bonus plans changed to make them pay out.

Varying Market Position by Organizational Function. Just as it is possible to argue that different management levels in an organization might logically have different market positions, it was argued in our earlier discussion of job-based pay that different functions in the organization could have different market positions. Again, the issue is the criticalness of each function to the success of the business. If a few functions are particularly critical to the organization because of the kind of business it is in, paying people more in those functions makes strategic sense. For example, technology-based organizations often depend on technology leadership for their success. Thus it may well make sense for them to pay engineers and scientists above the market for their skills while paying sales and marketing people at the market.

Although such a policy may produce undue competitiveness among the functions, it can be very supportive of certain business strategies. In essence, it puts compensation dollars into attracting individuals to those functions whose quality of performance is particularly vital to the success of the business. Replacement costs may also come into play here; sometimes it is simply a lot more expensive to replace a scientist or an engineer than it is to replace a marketing person or a secretary.

If the decision is made to pay a certain function above others, it is desirable, as was noted earlier, to avoid a point-factor job evaluation approach. All it would do is highlight the internal "inequity." A superior approach is to take whole jobs to the market and then price them according to a differential pricing strategy.

Varying Market Position by Line of Business. Many large corporations that operate several businesses may decide to pay certain businesses better than others either in terms of the market or in terms of internal job evaluation comparisons. Both of these approaches make a great deal of sense for the multibusiness conglomerate. In such an organization it makes no sense to worry about internal equity comparisons and internal pay rates among unrelated business units. An example of an organization that has recognized this and changed dramatically in response is General Electric.

General Electric is in a wide range of businesses. It makes major appliances, plastics, and jet engines and has become a major participant in the financial services business. As was noted earlier, for a long time the organization had a policy of paying equally across the total corporation. In other words, it emphasized that people were employed by GE and paid GE rates rather than rates based on the aircraft engine market or the plastics market. Its single job evaluation system and single set of pay rates had the effect of making career movement easy and created a homogeneous culture within General Electric. The downside was clear, however: the policy eliminated local control and local ownership of pay programs, and pay rates in many parts of the firm did not fit the competitive market.

When Jack Welch became CEO of GE in 1981, he decided to change the pay strategy of the organization radically. He decentralized it to different lines of business and told each to develop pay structures and pay rates that made sense in their particular situation. This made the movement of people somewhat more difficult, and it perhaps decreased the unified GE culture. But it also built local ownership and commitment and allowed the individual businesses to target pay rates and forms of compensation to the competitive situation they faced. It is hard for me to argue with what was done at General Electric. Admittedly, people may be better paid in one part of GE than another, but as long as such differences are strategy- and market-driven, I think they are defensible and desirable.

It is much better to have a pay approach that is decentralized to business units than to have a single, company-wide structure that limits the ability of different business units to compete and perform effectively. Perhaps the greatest risk in the decentralized strategy is that some parts of the organization will get out of control and pay wages that are simply too high. If different job evaluation approaches are used in different units, this inflation may not be easily detected by a corporate group. Out-of-control wages usually happen only in decentralized units that do not have profit responsibility. Units do need some pressure on them to keep labor costs down, but this does not have to come from a corporate-wide job evaluation program or from pay comparison standards; it can come from a desire to have a profitable unit.

Quite a different situation exists in single-business companies, of course—firms such as IBM, Digital, and American Airlines. They gain little advantage from allowing different parts of the organization to go their own way in the area of compensation. Indeed, there are a number of disadvantages that can occur, including undesirable movement of people and a breakdown of a single corporate culture into subcultures. Subcultures can lead to competition among parts of the business that need to cooperate with each other, and as a result they can be quite dysfunctional.

The Right Strategy

More than most features of a pay system we have discussed, total compensation policy and practice need to be driven by an organization's business strategy. Throughout this discussion I have stressed that setting total compensation levels needs to be done in the context of a business strategy. The comparisons used in setting total compensation levels must be driven by the kind of business an organization is in and the kind of management style it decides to adopt. The actual position of total compensation also needs to be driven by business strategy. These are not decisions to be made casually by an organization. Making them correctly takes considerable time, thought, and (after they are made) good communication and management. Clearly, making them well can provide an organization with a competitive advantage and can align the pay system of the organization strategically in a way that is important for the overall effectiveness of the organization.

Chapter Eleven

Determining the Total Compensation Mix

The amount of total compensation an organization pays is one determinant of how individuals respond to their pay. A second important determinant concerns the makeup of the total compensation package. There are literally hundreds, perhaps thousands of different forms that compensation can take, ranging all the way from cash and cashlike vehicles such as stock and stock options, through perquisites such as parking spaces, executive dining rooms, and child-care facilities. Because there are so many forms of compensation, there is a great deal of flexibility in the total compensation mix that organizations can provide to their employees. They can, for example, provide large amounts of incentive compensation or very low amounts; they can provide extensive fringe-benefit coverage or none.

No one approach to mix is right for all organizations. The key to what is right for a particular organization can usually be found in the kind of management style the organization wishes to operate with and the kind of people it wishes to attract and retain. These factors are important because the total compensation mix can have a strong impact on motivation, attraction and retention, and the organization's structure, culture, and costs. Let us look at each of these in turn to see how each can be influenced by the total compensation mix that an organization offers.

Potential Impact of the Compensation Mix

As has been repeatedly stressed, for a pay system to affect motivation a significant portion of the pay package has to be performance-based. This means that individuals have to have a significant amount of their pay at risk in any particular time period. No studies have shown exactly how much pay has to be involved for employees to be motivated by a change in pay, but as I mentioned earlier, a good guess is that at least 5 percent of cash compensation needs to be at risk in any one pay period for it to make any difference at all (Varadarajan and Futrell, 1984; Giles and Barrett, 1971). For pay to be a *significant* motivator, however, the amount that should be at risk is probably closer to 10 to 20 percent, depending upon a person's situation and the organizational conditions that apply.

Whether the performance compensation depends upon organizational performance or individual performance determines whether the individual will be concerned primarily with individual performance or organizational performance. However, because individual performance is directly controllable, a smaller amount of individually determined risk compensation can be motivating. Organizational or group performance is harder to influence; thus it may take a larger amount of at-risk compensation to affect motivation. In short, in low-control situations people need large stakes, while in high-control situations they can be influenced by smaller amounts.

The attraction and retention of employees is also strongly influenced by the compensation mix an organization offers, because the different forms of compensation vary in their attractiveness to individuals. Extensive benefits, for example, may be highly attractive to an individual with a large family and a spouse at home, while most benefits may be only minimally attractive to a single employee newly in the labor market. Similarly, at-risk compensation may appeal to some individuals but not to others; some are willing to give up the opportunity to make considerable additional money in order to get security, while others much prefer the combination of risk and potential gain.

Finally, some individuals prefer the kind of perquisites and status symbols that are given out by organizations. While some individuals may not care whether their desk is wood or metal, whether their carpet is thick or thin, or whether they have a corner office or no office, others are very concerned about these issues. Thus the compensation mix that an organization puts together, along with the total compensation offered, is an important driver of who will be attracted and retained by the organization.

The issues we have already discussed—how much compensation is at risk, how much is put into fringe benefits, and how much is devoted to perquisites—are strong drivers of the culture of an organization. For example, organizations that offer many perquisites, particularly ones that are dependent upon organizational level, tend to develop hierarchical cultures with strong status-oriented pecking orders. On the other hand, organizations that have a considerable amount of compensation at risk tend to have a more entrepreneurial spirit.

In subtle (and not-so-subtle) ways the total compensation mix of an organization can serve to reinforce or even develop particular features of an organization's structure. For example, strongly tying reception of certain perquisites to organizational level very much reinforces the hierarchical nature of the organization. The common practice of increasing office size, furniture quality, and view as one goes up the organizational hierarchy is a good example of a compensation practice that reinforces the hierarchy and the desirability of upward mobility.

In another vein, putting large amounts of compensation at risk for the executive level but none for anyone else clearly tends to set executives off from other members of the organization. In a not-so-subtle way it says that they are the ones really responsible for organizational performance, while others are there more as a support cast than as major participants in the business.

Finally, the kinds of compensation an organization chooses to offer can very much influence its cost of doing business in two respects. First, compensation mix influences the cost effectiveness of the reward system; second, it influences cost flexibility. In the case of cost effectiveness, the key issue is the attractiveness of the rewards that are offered. A reward not valued by members of an organization has no real benefit, but it adds costs to the organization. Thus an organization that wants to be particularly effective in spending its compensation dollars needs to match the components of the total compensation package to the needs and desires of its employees. Failure to do this almost guarantees that money will be wasted.

Cost flexibility can be critical to an organization that periodically needs to reduce its labor costs. Historically, as was mentioned earlier, labor-cost reduction has been handled by layoffs. There are alternative means, however. For example, organizations can place a significant percentage of pay at risk and thereby bring down total compensation costs without having to lay people off. In many cases this is a much more cost-effective solution, because layoffs can be quite expensive and counterproductive in the long term.

Factors That Influence Compensation Mix

Now that we have seen why total compensation mix is an important factor, we can consider some organizational factors that might influence the desirability of various compensation mixes. We begin this discussion by looking at the role of performance, then at the potential role of organizational level, function, and line of business, and finally at the issue of whether individuals should design their own compensation mix.

Performance. There is little question that if an organization wants to develop a performance-oriented culture, it needs to have a significant portion of its compensation dependent upon one or more pay-for-performance systems. The actual percentage at risk may vary by management level (with the more senior levels having a higher percentage of risk than the lower levels), but *all* levels need to have some compensation at risk. In good times bonuses and other compensation at risk can be a relatively high percentage of an individual's total compensation package, while in times of poor organizational performance it can shrink to a very small (or even nonexistent) percentage.

The organizational advantages of compensation at risk are obvious: it increases the cost flexibility of the total compensation, it can help focus individuals on organizational performance, and it fosters an entrepreneurial, performance-oriented culture. The risk is that it will cause individuals to leave the organization when performance is poor. As was mentioned earlier, this is not a problem if an individual's low pay-for-performance payment is due to poor *individual* performance; in fact, that individual's departure is desirable and represents a real advantage of pay-for-performance systems. However if an individual whom the organization wants to keep resigns following a low payment that resulted from poor *or-*

ganizational performance, the risk has been realized. One way to handle this problem, of course, is to create a pay-for-performance system that allows the best performers to get significant pay-for-performance payments even when the organization as a whole is not performing well. This can keep key individuals' total compensation relatively high in the market even when organizational performance is poor.

Another policy that can help retain individuals in a high-pay-at-risk situation is guaranteeing job security—an interesting complement to a total compensation package that is made up of a considerable amount of at-risk compensation (Rosow and Zager, 1984). To many individuals, having guaranteed job security—the knowledge that even in poor times they will continue to be employed by the organization—may be as attractive or more attractive than having high compensation levels in good times but layoffs when there is a business downturn.

Profit-sharing plans, gainsharing plans, and individual bonus plans are all effective ways of varying the pay of individuals with performance. Decisions about how much of an individual's pay should depend on each of these kinds of plans need to be made carefully and with an eye toward organizational structure, culture, and motivation. As has been stressed, in order for any pay plan to be motivational, there must be some line of sight for an individual. Thus at lower and middle levels in an organization it may make sense to have pay based upon the performance of individuals or units.

At higher levels of management, however, the best approach may be to vary pay on the basis of the organization's performance. One widely applicable approach is to have multiple pay-for-performance systems in a organization, some covering all levels (for example, profit sharing), some covering just top management (for example, stock options and long-term incentives), and some covering just lower-level employees (for example, gainsharing). This pattern can lead to all levels in the organization having compensation at risk and to all people having at least part of their compensation under their control. However, as will be discussed a little later in this chapter, it can serve to differentiate the organization by hierarchical level.

Type of Organization. Different types of organizations require different compensation mixes. As has already been suggested, mature bureaucratic organizations typically depend upon stability, reliability, and a hierarchical type of management. This calls for a compensation package that is job-based, with little compensation at risk, and seniority-driven benefits that are designed to produce stability of employment. The opposite situation exists in a risk-oriented, entrepreneurial venture. There it makes sense to put a great deal of compensation at risk and to downplay the role of benefits and perquisites. As I mentioned earlier, Apple does just this; it has no retirement plan because it does not want to attract individuals who are security oriented.

Typically, entrepreneurial organizations are staffed with younger individuals who are not concerned with such things as retirement plans and hierarchically driven benefits. Thus it makes sense to stress compensation at risk—particularly compensation at risk based upon the performance of the organization—so that a high sense of integration is produced in the organization and people are strongly motivated to see the organization succeed. Stock options, stock ownership, and profit-sharing plans fit well in this type of organization.

There are other kinds of businesses in which it makes sense to have a high percentage of the total compensation package dependent upon organizational performance. Organizations in cyclical businesses need the variability of the compensation at risk to adjust their costs to their ability to pay. For example, oil companies and basic industry companies (such as auto, steel, and glass) tend to have business cycles that call for them to reduce their costs periodically.

Organizational Level. In a traditional organization management level is a strong determinant of the total amount of compensation an individual receives and the form that compensation takes. In nonmanagement jobs an individual is typically on an hourly pay rate with a benefit program that covers just this level. At the executive level multiple forms of compensation are usually at risk, so that individuals can potentially increase their base salary by several times. In addition, top individuals receive many perquisites and benefits. In short, level in the hierarchy is everything. Each step up the hierarchy brings a change in total compensation and mix.

The typical old-line plant, with its personnel divided into hourly and salaried employees, provides a good example of a hierarchical approach to pay. It often turns out that there are dozens of ways in which hourly employees are treated differently than those who are salaried, from the punching of timeclocks to the distribution of benefits. Most of those differences are in the direction of communicating to hourly employees that they are trusted less and valued less than their salaried co-workers. The salaried group is typically divided still further for reward system purposes. Managers are usually separated from salaried nonmanagers, and within management itself there are often divisions made. These differences are important, because they determine access to such perquisites as parking spaces and dining rooms.

A hierarchical approach is highly consistent with a management style in which information, knowledge, and power are centered at the top. It makes the top the most desirable place to be in the organization. The reward mix reinforces the fact that people at the top are in charge, that they are the ones responsible for the organization's destiny, and that they should be respected and listened to because of their hierarchical position in the organization.

A strongly hierarchical approach to total compensation mix clearly does not fit a participative organization—one in which people at all levels are expected to feel responsible for and be motivated by the success of the organization. Nor does a hierarchical approach make sense when hourly employees are asked to be partners in the business and are using complex technological skills to operate expensive equipment. In these organizations a person's job level should have virtually no role in determining compensation mix.

Such perquisites as executive dining facilities, reserved parking spaces, and other special treatment factors run directly counter to the idea of a cohesive, integrated organization in which all employees are focused on the success of the organization. They also run counter to the idea that power should move to expertise, knowledge, and information rather than to position. They make it hard for lower-level employees to influence decisions even when they have the expertise.

I can remember vividly one Ford manager telling me how hard it was to be heard and feel important when he went to visit Henry Ford in his executive offices at the top of the Ford world headquarters building in Dearborn. This manager may have had the expertise with respect to the decision that was going to be made, but by the time he went up in Henry Ford's private elevator, went through several levels of security, and entered an office that covered almost the entire top floor of the building, he was not feeling particularly powerful—nor was Mr. Ford particularly oriented toward listening to his input.

In contrast to the Ford Motor Company system is Digital Equipment Corporation. Digital executives have no reserved parking spaces, their offices are accessible and relatively modest by U.S corporate standards, and there are no special dining rooms or executive airplanes. The helicopter system that runs from plant to plant is open to all employees who have a business need to use it, and executives are not allowed to bump other employees simply because of an important meeting. The assumption is that if employees are on the helicopter for company business, it is as important that they get to their destination as it is that executives get to theirs.

Legendary within Digital are stories of the CEO, Ken Olsen, arriving late for meetings because he could not find a parking space. Yet when someone suggests that he get a reserved parking space for his next visit to a plant location, he always refuses because that would signify that his time is more important than someone else's and he does not want to send that message. Clearly, what Olsen is trying to produce is a culture in which people are heard and have influence according to their knowledge and expertise. Compensation strategies that differentiate individuals by level clearly work against this kind of culture. They indicate that some people are more important (and generally that they have more authority) simply because they have a hierarchically superior position in the organization.

Some Japanese organizations (Honda, for example) go Digital one better: they eliminate offices entirely. All employees sit in large, open office areas. One American company, Mars, does this as well. In notable contrast is the office policy of one high-technology company I studied. Executives proclaimed that they wanted the firm to be a technology leader, but some of their policies worked against this. A particularly clear example was a policy that said only managers could have offices; thus leading engineers and scientists were prevented from having their own offices unless they took management jobs.

A hierarchical approach to perquisites can also work against a culture in which senior managers are in touch with the actual culture and operations of the organization. Perquisites such as special entrances and private dining rooms effectively prevent senior managers from experiencing the organization as it actually operates and shield them from coming in contact with most of the employees of the organization. Historically, the auto companies have excelled at creating perquisites that separate executives. Typical auto executives get cars that are specially built, so that they do not have to experience the "thrill" of owning standard production models. They park in a special heated garage when they come to work, and their cars are serviced and gassed for them. They eat in a special executive dining room and work in a special executive office area. The net effect is that they are insulated from their product, from their dealer network, and from the employees who work in the organization. Is it any wonder, given these conditions, that executives make decisions that seem naive and misguided to the employees in the organization? In essence, the executives and the employees are experiencing totally different worlds.

An example of just how bad executive decision making can get is provided in a widely reported story from a General Motors plant in Livonia, Michigan. The plant's management sent out a memo telling salaried employees who owned cars not manufactured by GM to park them in the hourly employees' parking lot. This one act managed to upset both hourly and salaried employees. Clearly, this action did not serve to produce a unified, committed workforce.

Ross Perot, a former member of the GM board and founder of EDS, has suggested radical elimination of perquisites for all GM corporate executives. As he has pointed out, the perquisites tend to separate executives from their consumers and their employees. He has talked about abolishing executive office floors and doing a number of other things to cause employees to regularly come in contact with their managers. According to him, this would result in significant cost savings as well as improved relations between organizational levels.

There are a number of organizations that do an excellent job of facilitating communication between all levels of the organization. Federal Express, for example, expects all of its managers to do production jobs on a regular basis. Office layouts and the organization's general way of operating minimize the role of perquisites, so that indeed managers do not lead a charmed or privileged life within the organization.

I think that it is particularly important in service organizations that senior managers experience the actual service delivery of their own organization. They can do this in one of two ways: as a customer or as an employee delivering the service. Federal Express has its managers deliver their service on a regular basis so that they can understand what is involved, while Volvo had all the senior managers at its new assembly plant work for a time as assembly operators so that they could learn what assembly work is like.

American Steel and Wire is another example of an egalitarian organization. Everybody there gets perks equally, whether vacation, profit sharing, or health insurance. According to the CEO, the organization does this to produce a culture of teamwork and shared success. In a *Fortune* magazine interview he noted, "There are a lot of executives at other companies who will not give up perks. It's like telling your kids not to smoke with a cigarette in your mouth. If you tell your workers, 'We love you, you're good and we want to listen to you' but you're doing it from a fancy car and the country club, they're not going to believe you" (Dumaine, 1989, p. 54).

Kodak and Herman Miller, the highly regarded furniture manufacturer mentioned earlier, are two companies that have an egalitarian approach to protecting employees against loss of jobs due to a takeover. Most companies have installed so-called golden parachute plans that provide lavish income protection for a few senior executives. Kodak and Herman Miller on the other hand, have installed a "tin" parachute plan that covers all employees. Clearly, these two approaches send very different messages to employees.

Egalitarian treatment with respect to perquisites inevitably raises the question of whether an organization should also be egalitarian with respect to pay for performance—that is, whether all pay-for-performance systems should equally affect everyone in the organization. There is no single right approach to this issue.

An organization that is highly participative runs a significant risk if it has compensation programs that are restricted to the senior levels. There is credibility, however, to the argument that having the same *percentage* of compensation at risk for all levels in the organization is not wise. For example, the top—even in a high-involvement organization—*does* have more influence on corporate profitability, and it typically has a much higher total compensation level. Thus it probably makes sense to have a greater percentage of senior executives' compensation at risk based on organizational performance, perhaps through profit sharing. At the lower levels in the organization other means—for example, gainsharing—can be used to put appropriate amounts of compensation at risk.

This suggests an approach for the high-involvement organization that puts compensation at risk at all levels in the organization, with the kind of compensation at risk varying somewhat from level to level. Organization-wide plans, perhaps including stock option plans and profit-sharing plans, would have a big impact at the top of the organization but relatively little at the bottom. On the other hand, gainsharing plans and divisional profit-sharing plans would have a significant impact at the bottom of the organization but no impact at the top. Taken in total, this means that people at the lower levels of an organization might be affected more by compensation-at-risk plans than people at the top. However, in most cases it probably makes more sense to have a lower percentage of total compensation at risk at the lower levels than at the top. The pay levels for these lower jobs are typically close to the minimum amount of money needed to maintain an acceptable life-style.

Perhaps the best way to summarize this discussion on the effects of level on compensation mix is to repeat that how an organization varies compensation mix needs to be driven by the structure of the organization and by its management style. As has been noted, different approaches to structure and style call for radically different approaches to total compensation mix. The traditional top-down bureaucratic organization quite appropriately has radically different types of compensation at different levels in the organization. On the other hand, a participative, egalitarian organization that bases its management strategy on having everyone feel responsible for the success of the business cannot tolerate a hierarchical system. Rather, it needs to move strongly away from the type of system that differentiates people in the organization by level of management.

Line of Business. In a diversified organization, such as the classic conglomerate, it often makes sense to vary the compensation mix of individuals by their line of business. The issue here is basically the same as it is with level of total compensation. The simple fact is that different lines of business, like different organizations, cultivate different cultures and face different external environments. If a compensation system does not recognize this by adjusting the compensation mix, the organization runs a decided risk of being out of touch with its competitive environment. Indeed, this often occurs when large organizations with high benefit costs acquire businesses that have low benefit costs. If management decides to install a single, corporate-wide benefit program, the extra cost of benefits may well create significant problems for the acquired organization.

Targeting compensation mix to each line of business can produce some interesting dilemmas for the organization that wants to be participative and egalitarian in its practices. For example, it can lead to a situation in which the employees in each business of an otherwise egalitarian organization end up with somewhat different compensation mixes because particular businesses call for it. One alternative is to adopt a flexible compensation approach, which we will discuss later. Another is to center the participation activities and the egalitarianism within particular business units. This inevitably has the effect of separating the business units from each other and from the executives responsible for multiple business units, but this may not be a serious problem if the business units operate relatively autonomously and if people within each unit are treated in an egalitarian way. If appropriate, corporate-wide profit-sharing and stock purchase plans can be used to produce a total organizational culture that transcends the different business units.

Function. Most organizations do vary the total compensation mix
that people receive by the type of work they do. Individuals in sales
jobs, for example, are usually paid bonuses, engineers earn technical recognition awards and patent awards, and production employees earn production incentives and are paid for overtime. And
in many traditional organizations there are strong arguments in
favor of these variations in compensation mix. Clearly, there are
different things that can be measured in each function, and employees in the different functions have somewhat different needs.

In an organization that relies on functional excellence—that
is, on the effectiveness of its separate functions—differences make a
great deal of sense. On the other hand, in an organization that needs
a high degree of integration and in which individuals are expected
to move from one function to another, significant differences by
function may be counterproductive. For example, pay-for-performance plans that distinguish between functions may cause the functions to maximize their own performance rather than the
performance of the organization, and they may cause people to have
career tracks that are largely single-function-oriented.

Moves from one function to another often end up being punished in such a system, because individuals who move get lower
performance rewards while learning a new function. This encourages individuals to progress up the hierarchy of a particular function without getting a broad perspective on the business. A very
functional orientation can be a particularly critical problem when
decision making is required that demands integrating the behavior
and the expertise of the different functions. It can also be a serious
problem if an organization lacks individuals with multifunctional
experience to fill positions in senior management.

In short, a red flag should be raised with respect to compensation programs that are unique to one function of an organization.
Compensation variation by function makes sense only with some
organizational structures and business strategies; it definitely does
not make sense with others. Indeed, in organizations where a high
sense of identity with overall organizational performance is desired,
the best approach may well be to have minimal or no differences
across functions. In such areas as R & D it may make sense to offer
special technical rewards and technical ladders. Similarly, in some

of the sales areas it may make sense to have bonus programs that tie into the more measurable results that are possible in this area. Going much beyond these differences, however, may be more dysfunctional than functional.

Seniority. Historically, many organizations have structured their compensation programs to be influenced by seniority. Benefits such as retirement plans and vacation time typically improve as a function of seniority. The longer an individual is with an organization, the more his or her benefit coverage improves. As a result, seniority effectively makes benefits a larger portion of the total compensation package.

Seniority-based rewards send a clear message to the workforce that seniority is valued and that the organization wants individuals to have a relatively permanent and long-lasting relationship there. Directly rewarding tenure motivates senior individuals to stay with the organization because no other firm is likely to reward them as well. It also helps the organization create a culture in which people think of themselves as having a *career* with the organization, not just a job. Thus seniority-based rewards make sense in an organization that has a business need for a culture that emphasizes long-term employment and stability.

Seniority-based benefits do not fit entrepreneurial organizations, however, or organizations that want to have some employee turnover in order to bring new ideas and technology into the organization. One technology company I studied had no benefit plans because it did not want employees to stay with the organization; it wanted turnover so that it could hire new graduates who would know the latest technologies.

Allowing Individual Choice

Historically, organizations have given individuals little choice with respect to their total compensation mix. When individuals were assigned to jobs they were told their base pay, how much compensation was at risk, their eligibility for stock option plans and profit-sharing plans, the array of benefits they would receive, and the kind of working conditions and perquisites they would enjoy. The practice of offering flexible benefit plans, a radical and interesting alternative to the traditional fixed compensation mix, was developed in the 1960s.

Research indicates that employees differ widely in the preferences that they have for the typical fringe benefits (Nealey, 1963). These differences are quite sensible and indeed predictable, given the differences in people's life-styles and personal situations. For example, older employees value retirement plans more than younger ones do, and they are willing to put more money into retirement. Young employees with families, on the other hand, are particularly concerned with medical insurance and life insurance, while single individuals tend to be particularly concerned with time off and vacations.

Research also reveals that the typical benefit package is valued by employees at a level that is less than its actual cost to the organization (Nealey, 1963; Lawler and Levin, 1968). Even though individuals value a benefit package at perhaps 30 percent less than its cost, the organization still has to pay full cost for it. What this phenomenon leads to is a situation in which the organization is, in essence, wasting money; it is buying things for people that they do not value. In that situation benefits are not contributing to attraction, retention, and motivation the way they should given their cost.

Fixed benefit plans send some interesting messages to individuals. They may, for example, seem to say, "We know what's best for you, and we're going to give it to you whether you want it or not." In effect, they put the organization in a paternalistic role and prevent individuals from making what could be important decisions about their personal finances. They may also send the message that the organization is relatively unconcerned about its costs, because it is willing to buy things for individuals even though the individuals do not want them. Finally, they may tell those individuals with a nontraditional life-style that they are not particularly valued by the organization. It is, of course, those with a nontraditional life-style who are particularly disadvantaged by most fixed benefit plans. Such plans are targeted to individuals who have families and are in the middle of their working careers. Although this used to be the dominant group in many organizations, it is a dwindling fraction as more and more dual-career families have appeared, divorce has increased, and women have entered the workforce (Johnston, 1987).

The solution to the benefit problem—in some ways an obvious solution, but one that has been relatively slow to win acceptance—is to give individuals the option of picking the benefits that they want. Such flexible or "cafeteria" benefits have now been installed in a number of U.S. corporations—over 30 percent of the *Fortune* 1,000 (Lawler, Ledford, and Mohrman, 1989).

The typical flexible benefit program allows individuals to pick from among an array of benefits based on a budget of dollars that reflects the organization's willingness to spend money on that employee. In many cases this creates a win-win situation. Individuals win because they can choose those benefits that are particularly attractive to them. And the organization wins because it does not have to increase its costs; it simply takes its traditional costs and gives those to the employee to spend. In addition, individuals choosing their own benefits may be more attracted to the organization and are potentially more positive about the organization as a place to work.

The advantages of flexible benefit plans, however, go significantly beyond attraction and retention. Ultimately, such plans can help drive an organizational culture that says, "We value individuals and their right to make their own life-style decisions, and we trust individuals to behave in mature ways as they manage their own lives." As was mentioned earlier, the traditional fixed benefit program tends to send the opposite message; it suggests paternalism and control on the part of the organization.

There seems to be little question that many organizations that have installed flexible benefit programs have ultimately realized some cost savings (Boden, 1989; Bloom and Trahan, 1986). That is, by controlling the amount of money that they allow individuals to spend on benefits, they have been able to cap their total compensation costs more effectively than organizations that provide a fixed benefit package. Organizations offering fixed benefits have to either go along with increases in benefit costs or reduce benefits. The flexible benefits-based organizations, on the other hand, can simply raise the cost of the benefits from which employees choose; then individuals cover the increase out of their benefit allotment.

There are some definite disadvantages to flexible benefit plans, however. There are start-up costs, ongoing maintenance costs, and adverse selection costs (that is, costs that result when individuals who are high users of a given benefit select it). In addition, if an organization has only a few employees who choose certain benefits, it may lose out on large-group cost savings; thus those benefits will be costly for those who choose them. These disadvantages are not to be dismissed, but in my mind they are small compared to the win-win possibility that exists with flexible benefit plans. They are perhaps most valuable in organizations that practice a participative management style. In organizations that treat employees as knowledgeable human beings, it makes sense to allow them to choose from among a wide variety of benefits. Expecting employees to make important decisions is consistent with the way they are expected to behave in their day-to-day work life.

My disappointment with most of the flexible benefit plans that I have seen stems from the limited choices that they provide. Most companies have followed the approach taken by the first plan, which was established by TRW in 1974 (Fragner, 1975). It allows individuals a very limited choice in benefits. In essence, every employee has to take a package of benefits that includes life insurance, health insurance, retirement, and vacation. They can then go on to enhance their coverage by adding additional levels of these benefits or by buying benefits that are not part of the core package. They cannot, however, take all cash, nor can they buy many of the perquisites that are available to others in the organization. (We will turn to the perquisites issue a little later. For now let me focus a bit more on the idea of true flexibility in buying benefits.)

The argument for mandating a minimum level of key benefits is based on a combination of paternalism and legal liability. Companies talk about how bad they would feel if someone did not have life insurance and left impoverished survivors. They talk about the problem of someone's becoming ill and having no health insurance. They talk about the potential lawsuit brought by an employee who made a bad or poorly informed decision. These are all important concerns, but they are also concerns that can put organizations in a parental role that is inconsistent with a philosophy that believes employees are adults and can make mature decisions.

Despite the limited choices that are available in most flexible benefit programs, what little research there is suggests that they are in fact highly effective. Studies of employees on such plans tend to suggest that 90 percent or more prefer them to traditional plans and would like even greater flexibility (Bloom and Trahan, 1986). As would be expected, flexible plans tend to have a positive cultural impact and to increase the organization's ability to attract and retain employees. In short, they seem to be one of those unique practices that succeed both for the employee and for the organization.

Earlier I noted that employees at different levels in the organization may have somewhat different needs for benefit coverage. Senior executives, for example, may have a greater need for tax counseling and financial advice than individuals at lower income levels. With flexible benefits there is no reason why all the typical executive benefits (such as premium health-care coverage) could not be available to *everyone* in the organization. If they are differentially selected by senior managers, so be it. At least the distinctions are being made by individual choice rather than by organizational prescription.

Some perks could also be offered as part of a flexible benefit plan. For example, if an individual wanted a reserved or heated parking place because he or she had a special car, this could be made available for a price in the flexible program. Similarly, if an individual particularly wanted the organization to pay club dues or first-class airfare, this too could be deducted as part of the flexible benefit program. This model could also be applied to office furnishings and other kinds of perquisites that are traditionally allocated by organization level. Although to many this might seem to be carrying flexible benefits too far, I think it fits in an organization that wishes to create an egalitarian culture.

One of the disadvantages of the flexible plan, high administration costs, can be largely overcome by use of computers (Boden, 1989). Employees can be given annual opportunities to sit at a terminal or personal computer and cost-effectively record their choices. Ultimately, an expert system could be developed that would gather data from each individual and then suggest benefit packages. This approach undoubtedly would raise some liability questions, but if these can be answered it would seem to be the best approach to decision making about benefits.

Overall, it seems clear that flexibility and individual choice are the right way to go with many benefit and perquisite programs. It seems to particularly fit organizations that are knowledge-work-oriented and that need to employ professional and technical individuals, because such employees are eager to make these decisions for themselves. Flexible benefit programs also seem to be particularly appropriate for employee involvement-oriented organizations. The movement to flexibility is well under way, and it is likely to continue—assuming that the movement toward employee involvement continues and that tax laws do not change in a way that negatively affects flexible practices.

The Right Choice

It is clear from the discussion above that there is no *right* total compensation mix for all organizations. The mix needs to be driven by the type of business the organization is in and the type of management style that it wishes to practice. At one extreme, an organization that is participative, is in a single business, and wishes to have everyone involved in organizational success and failure needs a highly egalitarian and homogeneous approach to compensation. If that same organization is highly entrepreneurial, it probably also needs considerable amounts of at-risk compensation for everyone in the organization, and it would appropriately have few differences in compensation that relate to such things as function, level in the organization, and seniority. Indeed, it would focus quite heavily on providing individual choice and on egalitarianism. In contrast to this type of organization is the organization that is hierarchical, large, and involved in many lines of business. In this kind of organization, mixes may appropriately vary by level, by function, by type of organization, and by line of business, and they may provide only limited choices for individuals.

Chapter Twelve

Managing Decision-Making and Communication Processes

So far we have looked at two of the three components of a pay system that need to be in alignment: core principles and structures. Now we are ready to consider the third component: the processes that are used to design and operate a pay system. We will focus on decision making and communication—issues that have tremendous power to influence pay system effectiveness. Their major impact is on how the plan is perceived. And because, as was stressed earlier, the impact of a pay system is strongly influenced by how it is perceived to operate, perception is particularly critical.

Perceptions do not influence costs, of course, but they very much influence the ability of a play plan to reinforce a particular culture, to motivate performance, and to attract and retain individuals. Effectively managed pay systems call attention to the key issues that the organization needs to address and reinforce key beliefs and motivational patterns in the organization. No pay system can work effectively simply because it has the "right" objective characteristics, however.

Time after time I have heard managers say that their organization pays for performance, and that is what counts. The truth of the matter is it may *not* be what counts. The behavior of people is a function of what they perceive, not what others perceive or how things actually are. If employees do not perceive that the organization pays for performance, it matters little that managers and the administrators of the program believe that they have an effective pay-for-performance system.

I am convinced that perceptions of pay systems typically deteriorate as distance from the top increases. This happens because those at progressively lower levels in the organization are further and further away from the people who designed the system, who administer it, and who have most of the data about how it operates. It may be impossible to close the gap between the top and the bottom completely. However, with better management of the decision-making process concerning pay, and with better communication practices, it is possible to close it significantly. There certainly is evidence that a great deal can be done. Let us first consider the decision-making process, and then we will consider communication.

Participative Decision Making in Pay System Design

The evidence on participation strongly suggests that there are some definite advantages to having individuals involved in the design of systems that will affect them (Lawler, 1986b; Coch and French, 1948). Perhaps the most important advantage has to do with their acceptance of a system and their commitment to seeing that it operates effectively. Time after time the literature has shown that commitment to a decision is increased with participation, and that commitment is crucial to effective implementation. This finding has some important implications for the area of pay system design. Virtually every pay system and every reward structure in an organization depends on the commitment of a number of individuals. Probably the clearest evidence of this dependence is in the case of merit-based pay programs and bonus programs. These are typically administered by supervisors; thus the commitment of supervisors at all levels in the organization is required.

The advantages of participation do not stop with individual acceptance of and commitment to a decision, however. A participative decision-making process also builds understanding of the decision. Individuals who participate in the design of any program are much more knowledgeable about it when it is installed, and they can often operate it more effectively for that reason. This advantage is very important to pay systems, because they are often complicated and require a great deal of understanding throughout the organization if they are to operate effectively.

Finally, the evidence on participative decision making suggests that the decisions themselves may change for the better when a broad range of individuals participate. The simple fact is that individuals from various parts of an organization often have information that is not held by others. Participative decision making typically means that more issues are considered and better data are brought to the process. Similarly, when the design of a pay system is participative, issues come to the forefront that would not have been considered otherwise.

The key determinant of whether participation will pay off in better decisions is information. Participation works only when individuals have adequate data relevant to the issue. In the case of pay systems, individuals throughout the organization clearly do have data that are relevant. If nothing else, they have their own perceptions, beliefs, values, and preferences. Because these subjective factors are critical to the design process, it is easy to make the case that employees should be involved in pay system design.

So far I have argued that participation can lead to a better-designed system, a better understanding of the system, and a greater commitment to seeing that the system operates effectively. These are results that organizations want in pay systems, and the data suggest that they are attainable if a participative design process is used (Lawler and Hackman, 1969). Thus it seems that participation is an obvious right choice when it comes to designing pay systems.

Historically, few organizations have seen pay system design and implementation as a process in which participation is appropriate, however. Design has typically been handled by staff groups, with approval by senior line managers; understanding has been handled by top-down communication programs; acceptance has been created by imposing the plan on the organization. There is evidence that organizations are changing their practices in this area, however (Lawler, 1981; Mohrman, Resnick-West, and Lawler, 1989).

Increasingly, individuals who will be affected by pay plans are being included in the design process. This is most frequently happening in organizations that are interested in changing to a more participative management style and that see pay system design as a logical place to practice participation (Lawler, Ledford, and Mohrman, 1989; O'Dell, 1987). In such organizations the payoff from successful participation can be great: not only can it lead to a better reward system; it can also reinforce the credibility of the entire participative management idea and build a higher level of trust in the organization. The risks, however, are significant.

The key risks in participation revolve around how much individuals will be motivated by narrow self-interest considerations. If their behavior is dominated by concern for how much they are paid and whether they are going to be treated well by the new system, participation is likely to fail. On the other hand, if they can be counted on to place high importance on the impact of the system on the organization and its effectiveness, there is a good chance that a participative design effort can succeed.

Many of my questions about the ability and willingness of individuals to design pay systems that are good for organizations were answered by a study I did years ago with Richard Hackman (Lawler and Hackman, 1969; Scheflen, Lawler, and Hackman, 1971). We were asked by a janitorial company to do something that would reduce their high rate of absenteeism. The company paid minimum wages and employed a part-time workforce. Like its competitors, it had very high turnover. Not exactly the ideal situation for participative pay system design! Nevertheless, in the spirit of scientific inquiry we proceeded to help several janitorial crews design attendance bonus systems. Somewhat to our surprise, they designed rather good systems that provided in some cases for smaller bonuses than the company was willing to offer. The systems reduced absenteeism throughout the company, but the effect was greatest in the crews that designed them.

One last point needs to be made about participation and the design process. Typically, participative design is slower than top-down design. Time is needed initially to get the individuals who will be involved up to speed in what is known about pay system design, and the actual decision process that follows often takes longer. In the typical top-down design effort (which is generally supported by expert consulting help), little educational effort is needed, and decisions can often be made quickly by senior executives. This leads to the obvious conclusion that if time is at a premium, participation may not be the right approach. One caveat: although this conclusion is obvious, it may be not correct. Top-down design may be the fastest way to *develop* a pay system, but it may not be the fastest way to get a pay system operating *effectively*. With top-down design, the communicating, selling, and understanding process has just begun when the design is completed. With participative design, on the other hand, it is well under way when the design is completed.

Actually, participative design can go rather quickly if there is a commitment to speed. I helped design a gainsharing plan in an organization that had a history of participative decision making and a bias for action. This airline designed a rather good plan in less than a month by committing a group to work on it almost full-time. The results were positive, too: load factors increased on the planes, as did food and beverage sales.

Given the complexities of participative pay system design, organizations should probably use it only if they have an overall strategy of managing participatively and having individuals committed to and involved in the overall operation of the business. Pay system design can be a place where participation starts, but it should not be a place where participation ends. Indeed, if participation is successfully used in the area of pay system design, a strong message can be sent to the organization that participation is possible even when tough issues and tough decisions are involved, and it can give participative decision making a powerful push forward (Lawler, 1981). On the other hand, if participative decision making is used in other areas first, it is almost inevitable that employees will want to influence the pay system. This system is such an important part of an organization that it is impossible and undesirable to separate it from a general move toward participative decision making.

One final comment needs to be made about the participative design of pay systems. As the reader has probably concluded by now, it goes hand in hand with the idea of decentralizing corporate decision making about pay. Unless there is considerable decentralization of the pay system, it is virtually impossible to allow much local decision making about plan design. Unfortunately, a desire for local autonomy and decentralization can come in direct conflict with the idea of a single corporate culture and vision.

Sometimes the conflict between participation and a single culture can be handled in general corporate guidelines that include core values and pay principles that apply to all parts of the organization. Within this unified structure, local units can still be allowed to design their own performance appraisal systems, gainsharing plans, and so on. A good example of this is the work that Dana has done with its gainsharing plans. The organization has a broad commitment to gainsharing plans but has allowed local units to do much of their own design work. Similarly, in much of the performance appraisal work that I have done, only the broad principles of how a system should work are *corporate* principles (Mohrman, Resnick-West, and Lawler, 1989). Local units are allowed to work on the details of timing, coverage, meetings, and so on. In general, this two-level approach has worked well where it is desirable to combine some central consistency and structure with local involvement and decision making.

Structuring Participative Design Processes. Time after time, in working with organizations to design performance appraisal plans, flexible benefit plans, gainsharing plans, skill-based pay plans, and other pay programs, I have used diagonal slice task forces—groups made up of individuals from all levels of the organization. Membership cuts across the different functions, departments, and levels of the organization. Diagonal slice task forces do not have to have final decision-making authority in order to be an effective form of participation. For example, they can be asked simply to recommend a plan to senior management. The key success factor is whether the individuals who are on the task force feel that their recommendations will be given serious consideration and will be rejected only if there is a clear and glaring flaw in them.

There are a number of things that need to be done to assure that the diagonal slice task force model works effectively. First, individuals on the task force need to be chosen carefully. They need to be opinion leaders from the organization, and they need to be seen as objective. If the individuals on the task force are opinion leaders, they will be able to convince the rest of the organization that whatever plan is designed is potentially an effective plan for the organization, while their credibility with the rest of the organization is key to helping other employees feel that their interests have been well and fairly represented.

It is usually desirable to start the task force with team-building activities. These are particularly important when task forces deal with pay, because of the strong self-interest factor that may come into play. Team-building activities should recognize the self-interest factor, discuss it, and develop norms about the willingness of individuals to challenge each other about it.

Finally, task forces dealing with pay issues operate best when they are given an extensive educational program in compensation system design. This can take a considerable amount of time, because people on a task force do not often have a background in this area. On the contrary, they have been in situations where compensation information is kept secret.

One final point needs to be made about the establishment of a task force. The organization needs to make it very clear what decisions can be made. If certain decisions are not acceptable, then the task force needs to be told this up front. In talking about this issue when I deal with organizations, I use the box concept: I try to get the managers who establish the task force to be very clear about the characteristics of the "box" that outlines the decision-making latitude that the task force has. If the organization is designing a gainsharing plan, I press senior managers to specify what would not be acceptable to them in a gainsharing plan. For example, if it would not be all right for the plan to cover only a few people in the location, this needs to be said. Similarly, if it would not be okay for the plan to measure only labor costs, this needs to be said.

Once the size and shape of the box have been determined, it is important to look at it and see if meaningful decision-making areas are left for the task force. If they are not, there is no sense in going ahead with a task force. Indeed, if a task force is commissioned but given little discretion, employees will perceive it as a pseudo-participative activity and it will probably do more harm than good.

If senior management is unable to define what are acceptable and unacceptable task force decisions, I am hesitant to go ahead with a participative design activity. The risk is that the task force will come up with what seems like an ideal plan to them, only to have senior managers reject it because it is not what they "had in mind." This is the worst possible outcome for any participative decision-making process. It increases the level of mistrust and cynicism in the organization and typically turns the task force (and subsequent task forces) into a group that tries to figure out what senior management wants. If this is all the task force tries to do, there is clearly no reason for its existence. Senior managers can do the work themselves, avoid the time and hassle of dealing with a task force, and develop a plan that better fits what they want.

Applying Participative Design Processes. Virtually any piece of an organization's pay system can be designed in a participative way. As I mentioned earlier, I have frequently used task forces in the design of all types of pay-for-performance systems, performance appraisal systems, skill-based pay systems, and attendance incentive systems. In each case the result has been similar. It has taken time (from three to six months, typically) to design the system, but once it has been designed, implementation has gone smoothly, acceptance has been high, and the plan has usually been effective.

Gainsharing plans are particularly good candidates for the task force design approach (Lawler, 1988). Their effective operation requires that people throughout the organization understand the plan and accept it as fair and valid. In addition, many of the design decisions need to be influenced by the characteristics of the local situation. Issues such as how to handle absenteeism and who to cover with the plan need to take into consideration specifics of the local work situation and the preferences of the local workforce. A task force is the ideal vehicle to get these inputs into the plan. What's more, once the plan has been designed, a task force is an effective vehicle for helping communicate the plan and convincing others that trying to make the plan pay off is worthwhile.

Gainsharing plans typically require high levels of maintenance, ongoing communication, and support—another reason why participative design works especially well with gainsharing plans. Participatively designed plans are better able to handle maintenance issues than top-down designed systems are, because the participative design process helps develop the skills that are needed to maintain the plan. In fact, the same group that designs the plan can stay in place and operate as maintainers of the plan. When changes in the plan are needed, it is not necessary to go outside and hire an "expert" to alter the plan; there is already in place a credible, informed group of individuals who can make changes in the plan and be seen as trustworthy.

All too often, in top-down organizations I have seen "trusted outside experts" come in, design a gainsharing plan, and sell it to the workforce. If things go right, this often leads to a fast, successful start-up of the plan and significant gains for everyone. Problems often develop several years later, however, when the plan needs to be changed. If it was designed by an outsider, it is hard for the organization to do its own redesign. It generally has to pay the cost of having the outsider come in again to work his or her magic.

Several years ago I saw a classic example of the problems that can arise when an expert design is used. The company consulted me when it had a change in product mix that resulted in unwarrantedly high gainsharing payments. Executives knew that they needed to change the plan, but because the plan had been designed by an outside expert and approved by management, no one there knew how to handle redesign. I could tell them how to redesign the plan, but the real issue was *acceptance* of the new design. If the plan had not been paying out, change would have been easy; but this plan was paying out a 30 percent bonus. Many individuals had become quite comfortable with the existing plan, even though they knew that things were not quite right. An ongoing, credible task force could have stepped in to point out that the plan was not performing as it should and to make the changes; unfortunately, there was no task force. Management had to step in and say that the plan was being redesigned because it was paying out unfairly—a tough situation for managers to be in, and one that could not help but decrease some of the trust that existed between management and the workforce.

The major *dis*advantage to using task forces in gainsharing design is that conflicts can develop within the task force over such sensitive issues as how gains should be split between the company and the workforce and whether individuals who perform well should receive larger bonuses than others. These issues usually are manageable, however, and as a result diagonal slice task forces are my preferred way to go in designing gainsharing plans.

As was mentioned earlier, performance appraisal is another area in which a participative design process makes a great deal of sense. There is no right answer to how performance should be appraised in an organization. Local factors need to be taken into consideration, and the commitment of individuals is critical to the effective operation of any appraisal plan. Thus, in working with organizations to design performance appraisal systems, I always use diagonal slice task forces made up of individuals who will be administrators of the plan and individuals who will be appraised by it. Needless to say, the two groups bring some opposing views of what the appraisal system should look like, but consensus is possible. Typically, task forces develop appraisal plans that the rest of the organization is willing to accept simply because the plans were developed by peers.

One final area in which participative design is highly desirable is skill-based pay. Participation is optional in the development of job evaluation plans, because many well-developed programs are available that can simply be installed. The situation is quite different with respect to skill-based pay, however. A lot of local development and refining of such plans needs to be done. In my experience it is almost impossible for this process to be done effectively by people who are not actually performing the jobs. Thus participation is essential.

As was mentioned earlier, the key to an effective skill-based pay system is the definition of skills and a clear specification of the tests that will be used to determine whether each skill has been mastered. Both these components are usually best done by a combination of the individuals performing the work and a technical expert for that particular part of the work process. Thus I typically use an organization-wide committee to develop the broad structure of the skill-based plan and then allow each work area to develop the details of the plan as it applies to their jobs. This produces a two-tiered participative process that allows almost all individuals to participate directly in the design of the skill-based pay system. With this kind of process, the plan is typically quite well understood and accepted by everyone. In addition, because of the broad range of people involved, the plan is usually well designed and appropriate for its particular situation.

Participation in Pay Administration

The ultimate participative approach to pay administration is to have each individual determine his or her own pay. Individuals could decide what their base pay should be, make choices about which benefits fit their situation, and decide on the amount of bonus they should receive. This approach is probably a bit radical for most organizations and is not likely to be practiced by many in the near future. However, there are a number of forms of participation in pay administration that are possible and reasonable for many organizations. Not surprisingly, they are particularly appropriate for organizations that are otherwise committed to employee involvement.

Let us first look at the general areas in which individuals can be involved in making decisions about their pay. Perhaps the place where it makes most sense to have individuals make decisions is in the mix of cash and benefits they receive. As was noted earlier, flexible benefit programs actively involve individuals in decision making concerning how their benefit dollars will be allocated.

In theory, there is every reason for individuals to make mix decisions without substantial constraints. However, flexible benefit programs typically substantially limit the amount of flexibility an individual has. The decision-making box that individuals are put in is usually a very small one, allowing them to pick from among only a limited number of benefits. Basically, either an organization decides to trust its employees and treat them like mature, independent human beings (and therefore enforces few constraints in benefit flexibility), or it decides to exercise some degree of paternalism. What an organization decides about the flexibility of benefits needs to be guided by its overall approach to management. Even the most traditional top-down organization can usually live with *some* flexibility on the part of individuals. But only in the case of highly participative organizations committed to hiring mature individuals, treating them as adults, and educating them in financial planning does it make sense to go to extreme flexibility in benefit choice.

In many respects the decision to let individuals choose the kind of benefits they want is a no-risk decision: regardless of the decisions individuals make, the organization's total cost structure is not affected. This is not true of individual decisions in other pay areas—for example, decisions about merit increases, how a job is evaluated, and when someone gets a skill-based pay increase. If these decisions are given to individuals and they substantially raise their own pay, the organizational cost structure *is* affected. Thus decisions in these areas are particularly sensitive from an organizational point of view and are rarely, if ever, made totally by the individual whose pay is affected.

On the other hand, it is possible and often desirable to get input in these areas from the individuals whose pay will be affected. The research I have done with Monty Mohrman and others on performance appraisal clearly shows that performance appraisals go best when the individual being appraised has a chance to give input to the decision process (Lawler, Mohrman, and Resnick, 1984). Similar findings have come out of the work on skill-based pay (Lawler and Ledford, 1985). An important component of the effective operation of a skill-based pay system is the opportunity for individuals to call for a review of their skills when they feel they are ready to be certified and to have input into the decision about whether they have acquired a particular skill. The absence of an opportunity for individuals to participate in this decision process can erode the plan's credibility.

The data on goal setting for sales incentive plans and performance reviews also strongly suggest that individuals ought to have an active role in the setting of goals. This helps ensure that they see the goals as fair and reasonable, and it helps elicit their commitment to achieving the goals (Locke and Latham, 1984; Vroom, 1964).

The key to having individuals effectively participate in decisions affecting the administration of their pay lies in providing checks and balances in the decision process. Just as an individual needs the right to challenge a supervisor who makes an arbitrary and capricious decision about a pay increase, a supervisor needs the ability and willingness to challenge an individual's input concerning what he or she should be paid. Decision making cannot be abdicated by management; management has to monitor the decision process and, where appropriate, intervene.

Sometimes the basic economics of the business situation can

provide a powerful check on the demands of individuals for higher wages. For this to happen, individuals must understand the negative impact of higher wages on the business. When I first visited Donnelly Mirrors in the early 1970s, I was impressed by the approach the firm used to decide annual pay increases, because it helped individuals understand the economics of the business. At the time Donnelly had a number of fixed-price contracts, and it had a gainsharing plan. Thus wage increases in effect had to be funded out of performance improvements or they would simply reduce the bonus payments. Each year Donnelly used an active participation process to set pay-increase levels and to get individuals to commit to cost reductions that would fund the pay increases. It worked; raises tended to "fit" what could be saved through cost reductions.

There are also examples of employees who have refused raises because they would have made the organization noncompetitive. A building insulators' union in New Jersey even went on strike for a lower wage because the insulators were afraid of losing out to nonunion labor!

Perhaps the most interesting case of workers setting their own pay occurred at the Friedman-Jacobs Company. Friedman, a small firm, decided to allow employees to set their own wages, make their own hours, and take their vacations whenever they felt like it. Apparently, this rather radical approach has worked well for Friedman, as was reported in an article in the *Washington Post* ("Arthur Friedman's Outrage," Feb. 23, 1975, pp. C-1 and C-8):

> "It was about a month before anyone asked for a raise," recalls Stan Robinson, 55, the payroll clerk. "And when they did, they asked Art first. But he refused to listen and told them to just tell me what they wanted. I kept going back to him to make sure it was all right, but he wouldn't even talk about it. I finally figured out he was serious."
>
> "It was something that I wanted to do," explains Friedman. "I always said that if you give people what they want, you get what you want. You have to be willing to lose, to stick your neck out. I finally decided that the time had come to practice what I preached."
>
> Soon the path to Stan Robinson's desk was heavily trav-

eled. Friedman's wife, Merle, was one of the first; she figured
that her contribution was worth $1 an hour more. Some asked
for $50 more a week, some $60. Delivery truck driver, Charles
Ryan, was more ambitious; he demanded a $100 raise.

In most companies, Ryan would have been laughed out
of the office. His work had not been particularly distin-
guished. His truck usually left in the morning and returned
at five o'clock in the afternoon religiously, just in time for him
to punch out. He dragged around the shop, complained constantly, and was almost always late for work. Things changed.

"He had been resentful about his prior pay," explains
Friedman. "The raise made him a fabulous employee. He
started showing up early in the morning and would be back
by three o'clock, asking what else had to be done."

Instead of the all-out raid on the company coffers that
some businessmen might expect, the fifteen employees of the
Friedman-Jacobs Company displayed astonishing restraint
and maturity. The wages they demanded were just slightly
higher than the scale of the Retail Clerks union to which they
all belonged (at Friedman's insistence). Some did not even take
a raise. One serviceman who was receiving considerably less
than his co-workers was asked why he did not insist on equal
pay. "I don't want to work that hard," was the obvious
answer.

Why did this approach work for Friedman? Probably because
the employees realized that if they took too much pay, the organization would not be able to function. The employees were aware
that the firm operated on the margin between selling prices, which
were known to all, and the cost of goods, which was also known.
Because most Friedman employees met customers, they realized that
higher prices meant less business. They were also aware that sales
costs (salaries) could go only so high before the company would go
out of business. And salaries were public, allowing group pressure
to be used against anyone whose pay was too high and who was
therefore harming the business and jeopardizing the pay of all.

It seems that, when management does a good job of creating
a cooperative setting and employees are given the responsibility for

decisions about something as important as pay, employees behave responsibly. This is in contrast to adversarial relationships (for example, most union-management negotiations), in which large demands are the norm. The crucial difference seems to be that in negotiations the workers are *bargaining* for salaries, not *setting* salaries.

Increasingly, peers are playing a role in the administration of pay. This is perhaps most dramatically illustrated by the peer role in many skill-based pay plans. In a number of plants that have these plans, peers review the skills of an individual and decide whether that individual does or does not deserve a pay increase (Lawler, 1981). In a smaller number of cases, peers are used to decide whether an individual deserves a merit pay increase.

The peer evaluation process has been handled in a number of different ways in the organizations that I have studied. In the most dramatic examples, each individual's performance was discussed at a meeting of the appropriate work group, and all individuals present were expected to comment on whether they thought the individual deserved the raise or not. In some cases, the individual was present for this discussion; in others, he or she was not.

Clearly, the toughest process to handle well is one where the individual is present at the peer evaluation and has a chance to listen to the comments. This process runs the risk of becoming so highly politicized that the true opinions of individuals are not expressed. Although a "secret" process can be less politicized, it runs the very great risk of having little credibility in the eyes of the individual whose pay is being assessed, in large part because less chance for being heard exists.

In some organizations peer groups simply fill out questionnaires or performance appraisal documents and submit these to the supervisor, who summarizes the results and incorporates them into his or her own overall performance review. This is clearly the least participative way to get peer input into a performance review. However, in a more traditional organization it may be the most appropriate. It is clearly the least threatening for most individuals and for that reason may be more acceptable than other methods. Its major problem is that it offers little direct accountability for what peers say; that is, there is little chance for the individual to hear directly what is said and to challenge the views of others.

To be effective, appraisers must be expert in the performance they are judging and have a chance to see the individual perform. These two conditions may be better met by peers than bosses, because peers have more opportunity to see the individual's behavior (and they often see it during "unguarded" times).

Particularly if an individual is part of a team, other team members often have the best data on how cooperative and team-oriented he or she is. Thus a strong case can be made that in many situations peers have the kind of data that should be incorporated into a performance appraisal judgment.

The success of peer evaluation depends on the willingness of individuals to contribute valid data to the appraisal process. There are a number of reasons why peers may not be willing to give valid data (Kane and Lawler, 1978). If they feel in competition with an individual, for example, they may be tempted to provide unfairly negative data. On the other hand, if they do not trust what management will do with the data, they may present unreasonably bland data or simply refuse to participate in the decision process.

In my experience it is easiest to get peer input when professional employees, such as lawyers, professors, or accountants, are involved. They have professional standards to which they are committed, and they are often competent to judge the performance of their peers. Problems may result even in these situations, of course—particularly if the professionals do not trust management to use the data fairly or if they feel they are competing for the same rewards or recognition. When work teams assess whether or not an individual has mastered a skill a number of conditions are favorable to peer input. First, the decision process is in the public domain, so there is little concern about the data being misused by management. In addition, there is little competition among individuals, because typically everyone can acquire every skill. The major issue, therefore, is whether the individual actually has mastered the skill. In such situations political and personal considerations can generally be put aside so that work teams can reach good decisions about skill acquisition.

I have seen discussions about skill acquisition done extremely effectively by peer groups that had the guidance of a skillful team leader. Yes, I have seen tears, anger, disappointment, and strong emotions; but I have also seen honest communication, deep caring for individuals, and extremely constructive feedback—indeed, better feedback and more constructive caring than are usually present when a supervisor evaluates an employee. The simple fact of the matter is that groups—particularly peer groups—can do things that a supervisor cannot do because of the group members' relationship to the individual and because of the number of people involved. Different individuals can take different roles and provide different pieces of the emotional support and feedback.

Peer-group decision processes can clearly be used in areas other than performance judgments and skill-acquisition judgments. They offer a good way to evaluate jobs and to help ensure the credibility of a job evaluation system. Similarly, they can be used to determine membership in certain pay plans and eligibility for certain benefits and perquisites. Finally, as was illustrated in the example of the engine manufacturer mentioned earlier, employees can participate in salary-survey data gathering and in pay budget recommendations.

No discussion of participative pay administration would be complete without some mention of subordinates' evaluation of their bosses' skills and performance. In many cases subordinates have the best information about how their bosses operate, so ways need to be found to include the information they have in overall evaluations. The least threatening way (for both sides) is probably to have employees fill out attitude questionnaires that ask for their opinions of the boss. This approach has been used for years by Sears, IBM, and a host of other companies. One step beyond this is the approach in which subordinates are interviewed as part of the appraisal process. Because this makes it clear that subordinates' views count, it is probably the best process for organizations that are interested in practicing participative management.

Overall, there is a lot to be gained from the participative administration of pay systems. The credibility of systems can be greatly enhanced when individuals are involved in administering their own pay and peer groups are involved in administering the pay of their members. There is no doubt that individuals have the relevant data. The challenge is to create an organizational culture in which individuals see employee involvement as a reasonable way to handle rewards and in which they understand the economic realities of the business. When this type of culture exists, pay plans can be administered more fairly and in a way that is more acceptable to all levels of the organization.

Communication of Pay Information

It is impossible to separate communication of pay information from decision making about pay. Both are essentially power issues within an organization. Decision making *directly* involves power; in participative decision making individuals are being given power that has traditionally been held by management. Moving to a more public approach to pay also involves a transfer of power, though less obviously. The simple fact of the matter is that when individuals get more information about pay, they have more power than they do under a highly secretive approach. They have, for example, the power to challenge management's interpretation of how the pay system operates, and in some cases that power may galvanize them to try to gain additional power through unionization. In the absence of valid data—that is, without good communication—individuals may feel that their pay is not being well administered but lack the ability to "prove" the point and unite their peers in collective action.

I first became aware of just how important some organizations think pay information is when I was doing my doctoral dissertation (Porter and Lawler, 1968). Among other issues, I was studying the effects of pay secrecy. I collected attitude data from a chemical plant in California and then sought information on how much the survey respondents were paid. I had trouble getting permission from the organization to see these data; and even once I got permission, it was not easy to actually put my hands on the data. Management payroll information was kept separate from payroll information about production employees; in fact, it was locked in the company safe. Once a month the checks were written by the secretary of the plant manager and signed by the plant manager; no one else had access to information about management salaries. In fact it was kept in the manager's personal safe. Finally I did get the data, but I had to sign a release form promising that they would be seen by no one else.

Not all organizations are this secretive about pay, of course. Indeed, there is reason to believe that most organizations are slowly moving toward openness. Information about merit budgets and pay ranges is increasingly being made public by organizations. Nevertheless, even today many organizations have strict policies and norms about the secrecy of pay—particularly management pay. It is seen as inappropriate in most companies for employees to talk about what they earn, and data are rarely given out (even internally) on salaries. Some organizations even fire individuals who release salary data. This is one way to make it very clear that the organization means it when it says it believes in pay secrecy!

The intriguing question, from an organizational effectiveness point of view, is whether or not secrecy is a good idea. In many respects the question is relevant only in traditional top-down organizations. I have never seen it become a major issue in participatively managed organizations. Once an organization commits itself to having employees participate in the design of pay systems, it follows naturally that management will openly distribute financial information. It is hard to imagine how individuals could meaningfully participate in the design of a pay system without being given data about how employees are currently paid.

The one sticky issue in participative systems is how extensive the openness should be. Some participative organizations believe that *individual* pay data are best kept secret. In most cases, however, individuals recognize that for participation to be meaningful and for the reward system to be credible, individual pay rates need to be in the public domain. I have worked in two organizations that make all pay rates public. At times this policy has caused pay decisions to be challenged and required additional explanations, but it has been well worth it to the organizations because of the additional credibility and trust that the openness builds.

Openness is a more complicated issue in traditional top-down organizations. Secrecy clearly reinforces the supervisor's power and is consistent with the top-down approach to pay and decision making in the organization. However, before we decide that secrecy is automatically the best policy for more traditionally managed organizations, there are a couple of issues that need to be explored.

Secrecy is not neutral with respect to people's perceptions of the pay practices in an organization. On the contrary, the evidence that has been gathered over the years suggests that secrecy leads to consistent distortions of people's perceptions of how pay is administered (Lawler, 1972). To be specific, it leads to overestimates of the pay of others, so that (in comparison) individuals feel more poorly paid than in fact they are. Some may become so dissatisfied with their pay that they look elsewhere for employment. This problem can be partially solved by releasing information on pay ranges and midpoints—that is, by giving individuals a general idea of how others are paid—without releasing individual pay rates. Thus organizations can overcome some of the disadvantages of complete secrecy without releasing individual salary data. A number of organizations in the last ten years have done just this. They have released salary ranges and told everyone where different jobs fall in the range system.

One organization, Bell Labs, has gone a bit further than this. It actually shows the distribution of salaries within each pay range. In essence, it shows individual salaries but does not attach names to those salaries. This makes it very clear to individuals where they stand relative to others in the organization. Going this far toward public salaries is a step that I think many organizations should take. It may eliminate the ability of supervisors to be all-powerful with respect to pay system matters, but this is not necessarily bad—particularly if supervisors are abusing their power by misrepresenting the pay system to make themselves look good.

Supervisors sometimes mislead subordinates by telling them that a particular pay raise is the best they can do, though they would *like* to treat the person better. Supervisors may also try to portray an employee as better paid than he or she really is. With somewhat more open data, it is impossible for supervisors to engage in this kind of behavior. Thus I typically recommend that, unless the organization has a terribly indefensible pay system, it should go to at least a level of openness that gives out pay-range information. I usually go on to add that even the indefensible system perhaps ought to reveal information just to create the pressure for change.

A compensation manager once told me that he would be happy to open up his company's pay information for scrutiny once he had four or five years to get his system in order. I countered by saying that unless he made it open, in four or five years the system would probably *still* be indefensible. I think that secrecy corrupts pay systems. The more secret the pay is, the more management is tempted to make indefensible pay decisions.

Now let us return to the issue of making individual pay information public even in a traditional top-down organization. There is evidence that employees in these organizations do not want their pay to be made public (Lawler, 1972). Many individuals also feel that making pay public in such an organization runs counter to the management style. I agree that it does in one respect: it moves some power downward in the organization—power that typically would rest completely at the top. On the other hand, it makes a great deal of sense from a motivational point of view to do this.

As was noted in our discussion of motivation and pay for performance, effective pay-for-performance systems must build the perception that pay and performance are related. In the absence of public pay information, all that the individual can rely on is vague claims that a pay-for-performance system exists. Public pay information that shows that high-performing individuals are getting larger increases is a dramatic way to increase the credibility of any pay-for-performance system. Releasing pay-range information does not accomplish this purpose. It gives individuals information about how they stand relative to others, but it does not finally and ultimately demonstrate that the people paid the most are in fact the best performers. Only releasing individual pay data can accomplish this. Thus, in traditionally managed organizations that rely heavily on pay-for-performance systems as a source of motivation, I often argue for at least making pay increases public.

I should add that most organizations are not persuaded by the argument that public pay can lead to better and clearer pay-for-performance systems. The apparent conflict between their overall top-down management style and the releasing of individual salary information overwhelms the motivational arguments in favor of putting pay data in the public domain.

Another argument against making pay-increase information public at the individual level focuses on the impact of public pay on the behavior of decision makers. It is assumed that supervisors will be less willing to give widely varied pay increases to good and poor performers if they know that their actions will be public. If this is true—and I suspect it often is—the organization has a supervision problem that needs to be addressed before *any* pay-for-performance system can be made to work. Even though secrecy may lead supervisors to give more varied pay raises, what difference does this make? If only the supervisors see that pay and performance are related, how will the employees be motivated by the pay system? If they do not see the pay-for-performance relationship, the "good" decisions of the supervisors have been wasted.

Overall, decisions about releasing pay data are probably best thought of as second-order decisions. That is, they are probably best thought of as decisions that should be driven by the overall management style of the organization. As I have indicated, secrecy rarely seems to be an issue in participative organizations; it is automatically assumed that at least general pay information will be in the public domain. Conversely, in traditional top-down organizations it is automatically assumed that pay information will *not* be in the public domain.

It is certainly possible to argue with the point that traditionally managed organizations should keep pay secret, but those arguments are usually futile. There is a certain irony in the decision of top-down organizations to keep pay secret. In many ways traditionally managed organizations need pay for performance as a motivator more than do participative organizations. Yet they are the organizations that have the greatest difficulty using pay-for-performance systems, because they are unwilling to release data that could establish the credibility of such systems.

 **Part Five**

Applying Pay Strategies

Chapter Thirteen

A Pay Strategy for Acme Corporation: A Traditional Manufacturing Company

Acme Corporation is a traditional manufacturing concern. Its several different divisions make unrelated products for three cyclical domestic markets. Although Acme executives have heard about such practices as self-managing work teams, quality circles, flat organizational structures, total quality, and open information systems, they are quite comfortable with a rather traditional, but enlightened, top-down management style. Indeed, the organization is operating quite successfully this way. What executives primarily want from their pay system is reasonable labor costs, the ability to motivate individuals to perform their jobs well, and the ability to attract and retain good performers. They are currently a nonunion company and would like to remain so.

In many respects Acme Corporation is typical of many organizations in the United States. Despite all the writing about flat organizations and involvement and participative leadership, most organizations are still managed in a traditional manner and require a traditional pay system (Lawler, Ledford, and Mohrman, 1989). The issue to be addressed in this chapter is what that traditional pay system should look like. The emphasis here is on the *total* pay system. So far we have talked about individual pieces of the pay strategy; we have not put the pieces together to build an overall strategy. In this chapter and the next we will put the pieces together to create an overall pay program for two quite different fictitious organizations.

Core Principles for Acme

The starting place for any compensation system should be a set of core principles that drive particular pay practices and directly reflect the needs of the business. Acme is in a manufacturing business, where labor costs are a critical determinant of the organization's effectiveness. Similarly, individual performance effectiveness is a critical driver of business success. Because issues of motivation and labor costs are paramount, Acme's core principles need to emphasize pay for performance and pricing jobs to the external market. Finally, given the trend toward litigation in the area of pay, Acme's core principles should also emphasize that individuals have the right to appeal decisions about their pay.

The following are examples of some specific core pay principles that fit Acme.

- Pay increases will be based upon job performance.
- The performance of all employees will be assessed on a regular basis, and employees will be told how they are performing.
- Organizational pay levels will reflect the competitive marketplace.
- The success of the business will influence the pay levels of the organization.
- Individuals will be paid fairly based on the work that they do and on the level of pay the same work receives in other organizations.
- Individuals have the right to know how their pay was determined and to have decisions regarding their pay reviewed by the personnel department and by senior management.
- Benefit plans will be provided to cover the important needs of the workforce.
- A competitive benefit program will be available to all individuals in the organization.

Now that we have identified some core principles for the organization, the challenge is to bring them to life in actual pay systems and pay practices. We will first look at the structural dimensions of the pay system and then look at the process issues.

Structural Issues

Pay for Performance. The core principles of Acme emphasize pay for performance, and with good reason. In a traditionally managed organization, pay needs to be one of the most important motivators. In the absence of the high levels of intrinsic motivation that can be brought about by involvement and job enrichment, a good deal of emphasis needs to be put on extrinsic motivation. As was noted in our earlier discussion of motivation, this usually means a concentration on individual pay for performance and performance appraisal. In the case of Acme there also is a need for an organization-wide pay-for-performance system, because Acme is in cyclical businesses. It needs to adjust its costs to its ability to pay on a regular basis. This strongly suggests at least a two-pronged approach to pay for performance.

First, the organization needs to have a profit-sharing plan that adjusts the pay costs of the organization to its ability to pay. Given that Acme is a multidivisional organization and does not believe in participative management, a profit-sharing plan is not likely to be a source of motivation; it is too difficult for most employees to establish a clear line of sight. Profit-sharing can still be a way to adjust labor costs to match organizational performance, however. And in the case of senior management a profit-sharing plan can clearly be a potential motivator; at that level it should be designed to be motivational.

How should the profit-sharing plan be structured? It should pay out annually, although quarterly reports of its condition should be made available to all employees. More frequent payouts are desirable when motivation is a major factor, but because in this case the plan will be motivational only at the top, annual payouts at all levels are appropriate. The plan should be a first-dollar profit-sharing plan—that is, all employees should begin to get a share of profits as soon as Acme makes any money—but they should get a small percentage of the profits (from 1 to 5 percent). This is in contrast to plans that pay out profit sharing only after a rather high level of profitability has been reached. In cyclical business settings a high profit standard often means that in many years no payouts are made, and in those years there is no motivation for anyone, including executives. A high profit standard also tends to produce fluctuations in pay that are greater than those of the business, thus giving individuals a false impression of how the business actually operates.

At the top of the organization, where individuals do have the ability to influence performance, a considerable amount of total compensation (from 30 to 40 percent) should depend upon corporate profitability. Division managers should also be put on a bonus plan that is based on their division's profit performance. A focus on divisional performance is appropriate for them and can motivate them to focus on what they can influence: their division's performance.

At the lower levels of the organization a relatively modest amount of pay should depend on corporate or divisional profits. For example, the range might be from 0 percent of base pay in a bad year up to 10 or 15 percent in an outstanding year. This amount of variance should provide some cost reduction for the organization when its business performance falters, allowing it to offer a little more job security than can be offered in an organization that cannot reduce its labor costs without layoffs.

In addition to profit sharing, the executive pay package at Acme should include a stock option plan. It makes sense to limit stock options to the senior executives in this organization because of Acme's traditional management style. People further down in the organization are simply not in a position to influence stock values, so a stock option plan would have no incentive value for them. And because Acme is not interested in building an employee involvement culture, such a plan is also not needed as a symbol of shared responsibilities.

One large risk with any profit-sharing plan is the negative impact it can have on retention in a difficult period. This can be countered by giving various forms of deferred compensation to high performers who are needed for future senior management positions in the organization. For example, Acme might want to give a few rising stars in the organization some deferred stock grants as a retention device. The intention here is simply to lock in key human resources so that the organization does not risk losing them in years when the profit-sharing plan does not pay off. I suggest giving stock rather than stock options as deferred compensation, because shares are unlikely to lose all their value when the company performs poorly. Stock options, on the other hand, can lose all their value and thus cease to be an effective retention device.

Acme's management style does not demand an ESOP, but the organization may still decide to adopt one for purely financial reasons. If Acme needs the financing and can take advantage of what ESOPs offer, such a plan should be established. Acme might also want to adopt an ESOP to protect itself against a hostile takeover effort. Because the firm is in multiple cyclical businesses, it is possible that its breakup value could be higher than its stock price reflects, making it a prime takeover candidate.

Let us now turn to the individual pay-for-performance system at Acme, which needs to motivate strongly. Acme does not use teams, and it strongly believes in individual job descriptions and individual accountability. This means that an individual performance appraisal system needs to be a key feature of the Acme organization. Earlier we discussed what is needed to make an individual performance appraisal system operate effectively. Acme needs to follow these guidelines religiously. Particularly important, because Acme is a top-down-managed organization, is leadership from the top. Top managers must support the system by using it themselves and demanding that others use it.

Even though Acme is a traditionally managed organization, the performance appraisal system does not have to be completely top-down. It is important that individuals have some influence in setting the goals and performance measures that will be used to appraise their work. Similarly, it is important to give them an input opportunity at the end of the performance period so that they feel that their supervisor has all the relevant information needed to make an accurate performance judgment.

Because Acme needs to rely heavily on individual pay for performance, a significant amount of money needs to be at risk for all individuals in the organization. At the top levels of the organization this should involve annual payments that can vary from 0 to 35 percent of base pay, depending upon the performance of the individual during that year. At the bottom levels of the organization the range should be at least 0 to 10 percent—and perhaps more like 0 to 15 or 20 percent. Clearly, a traditional salary-increase system cannot accomplish this. What is needed is a bonus system (or other variable compensation system) that allows the performance appraisal judgments to determine how much of a bonus each individual will receive.

The best way to structure an individual pay-for-performance system so that a considerable amount of pay will be at risk for each individual is to have a base pay rate that is below market for the jobs of all individuals. In the most extreme pay-for-performance systems, the same salary or base wage is paid to all individuals in a job, regardless of seniority or performance. This base amount changes only as the market changes for that particular job. Typically, of course, this still means an annual adjustment in everyone's pay— but a market adjustment that in no way reflects performance. Keeping this adjustment separate from performance-based pay actions prevents the confusion that is so common in "merit-based" pay systems. In the latter, merit and market movement get combined, and as a result the relationship between pay and performance is not clear.

The separate performance-based variable payment is used to position individuals in the market according to their performance. With this approach it is possible to match both market position and size of bonus to current performance. An outstanding performance appraisal rating should put an individual well above the market through the payment of a large annual bonus or other variable pay amount. On the other hand, a poor performance appraisal should result in no bonus payment; as a result, the poor performer's total pay package will be below the market. Thus the best performers are always the best paid overall and always get the largest bonuses. In merit-based salary-increase systems, on the other hand, individuals are often paid below their market value and are therefore confused about the pay-for-performance relationship.

The combination of a profit-sharing plan and an individual bonus plan creates the possibility for relatively high levels of variable compensation. An individual who performs well in a year when the company performs well can end up with a substantial amount of pay above and beyond base salary. Similarly, an individual who performs poorly in a year that is bad for the company can end up receiving virtually no additional pay.

It makes a substantial difference just how profit-sharing and individual bonus plans are combined. One option is to let the profit-sharing plan create the bonus pool and then to divide it up based on individual performance. This has some important advantages over a merit-based salary-increase system because, among other things, it reduces some of the competitiveness that is built into a merit salary system. The pot is not fixed, as it is in merit plans. Cooperation and better organizational performance can lead to more for all. However, this approach can be risky in a cyclical business. In a bad year it may produce no bonus awards, forcing everyone below market. This in turn creates the risk of an organization losing its best individuals. Thus the profit-sharing plan either needs to be funded in such a way that there is always *some* money to distribute, or it needs to be separate from the individual bonus plan. If the latter approach is used, the bonus pool can be budgeted for just as merit salary increases are; profit sharing then becomes an extra that rewards cooperation and leads to high total pay in good years.

Because Acme relies heavily on individual performance and motivation, it probably also makes sense for the firm to give special incentive rewards for individual performance. These incentive awards should be used to recognize outstanding one-time individual accomplishments, such as technical breakthroughs, significant cost savings, and extraordinary responses to crises and business problems. One option is to pay these out in cash, but another is to use stock or stock options in ways that will lock individuals into the organization for the long run. My preference is to use some form of deferred compensation for these particular awards and to make everyone in the organization eligible for them.

A combination of bonuses, profit sharing, and individual incentive awards should create a performance-oriented culture for Acme. Because outstanding individual performance is rewarded, the organization should attract and retain individuals who are strong in achievement needs and strong in needs for individual recognition. This pay combination should also have the advantage of making the total pay costs of the organization partially variable as a result of organizational performance. In short, it fits both Acme's need to motivate individuals and its need to vary labor costs as a function of the ability to pay. The key link in this system is the individual pay-for-performance bonus. If Acme is able to execute performance appraisal well, the system should be effective in motivating individual performance. Thus the organization should emphasize activities that will make the performance appraisal system effective.

Job-Based Pay. Acme is not an organization that fits the skill-based pay model. It clearly should rely on job-based pay, and—because labor costs are a critical issue—it needs to do an excellent job of administering its job-based system. Acme could go to an extensive job evaluation system, but my preference is to simply take every job in the organization to the market directly. Indeed, because labor costs are so important to Acme, the firm needs to strongly emphasize external equity rather than internal equity. This means that its divisions should ignore each other and focus on the external market. Any corporate job evaluation plan would be counterproductive to the overall strategy of Acme Corporation, which is to keep itself focused on its competitors and keep its costs in line with theirs.

Because Acme is a multidivisional company, there is no single set of competitors. Different divisions have different competitive needs and therefore should focus strongly on local competitive issues and not on intracompany comparisons and pay rates. Multiple job evaluation plans, each locally owned and managed, could encourage this focus on local competition; however, the best solution is to simply take individual jobs to the market and test them against the pay rates of competitors.

In some companies key individual employees are part of the corporate (rather than divisional) pay system to facilitate moving them from one division to another. In fact, some companies put *most* salaried employees on the corporate system for just this reason. However, in most cases this is not advisable. Usually only a few individuals are ever moved, and they can be handled on an exception basis. Thus, in the case of Acme, virtually all employees in the various divisions should be on their division's pay plan. The situation with senior management is somewhat different, however. Upper-level managers need to be on a corporate pay system that is based on comparisons to similar companies.

So far we have not considered the wages of local-market employees in our discussion of Acme—and perhaps Acme should not consider them either. A strong case can be made for having each division target its pay to those companies with which it competes rather than targeting it to community wage levels. This may be a difficult policy to implement, however, depending upon the wage rates in the communities where Acme operates. If the industry rate is above the local community rate, of course setting wages at the industry rate is not difficult! Indeed, Acme could have a strong competitive edge in attracting individuals and would probably experience little turnover.

The situation is considerably more difficult to manage when local pay rates are *above* industry wage rates, although even then industry rates can be paid and defended. The key here is to do an educational job that effectively shows the negative consequences of paying the community rates and places a great deal of emphasis on the competitive environment in which the business operates. If executives are to be credible in presenting this approach, they must apply it to their own pay as well, exercising considerable restraint in both pay and perquisites.

Market Position. Acme faces an interesting challenge with respect to market position. Because costs are so important, it is not necessarily advisable for the firm to simply say that it is going to pay above the market in order to attract and retain the best individuals. This is a possible strategy, of course, but one that very much runs the risk of overpaying a number of individuals and therefore raising pay costs to a noncompetitive level. A more reasonable strategy is to be sure that the best performers are paid significantly above market; and indeed, if the individual bonus plan works, this should happen. With this plan operating and funded every year, even in down years the best performers should be positioned well above the market. Retention of the best performers should also be helped by the individual special awards, which target outstanding individual performance with deferred compensation.

Positioned correctly, the profit-sharing plan can have the effect of changing the market position of most individuals' total compensation according to the performance of the organization. Thus the overall pay rates of the organization should be above market in a year when Acme does well. This fits one of Acme's core principles: "The success of the business will influence the pay levels of the organization." In years when Acme is not highly profitable, the market position may fall to average or below average. This will happen automatically, because the profit-sharing plan will bring compensation costs down to reflect the ability of the organization to pay. This may cause some turnover; but if, as is often true in cyclical businesses, all organizations in the same business have poor performance at the same time, turnover may not occur. After all, related organizations will not be in a position to hire employees away from Acme.

Decentralization of the Pay Structure. Acme's organizational structure calls for some decentralization in the way pay is administered. Because it is a multiple business company, with each division being a profit center, certain pay decisions need to be delegated to the divisions. As was noted earlier, each division faces different competitors; thus divisions need to target their wage costs to different cost structures and different competitors. This suggests that the corporate compensation group should have responsibility for executive pay, the pay of some high-potential individuals, and the corporate profit-sharing plan. The pay system for all others should be decentralized to the divisions. In addition, the units should run their own bonus plans and performance appraisal plans. General corporate guidelines can be used to give indications about how the systems should operate, however.

I did not recommend gainsharing plans for Acme in our discussion of pay for performance because of the organization's lack of interest in participative management. As was noted in Chapter Seven, gainsharing plans tend to work well only when participative management is practiced. Acme may want to consider using gainsharing on a decentralized basis, however, in those divisions that badly need an additional form of variable compensation in order to compete effectively in particular local labor markets. A gainsharing plan in one of Acme's manufacturing plants, for example—a traditionally managed unit, but one that is small enough and simple enough that gainsharing could produce some incremental motivation—might pay off. It could have some incentive value with respect to individual performance, and it could stimulate suggestions and ideas that would improve overall organizational effectiveness.

Benefits. How decentralized should the benefit plan be at Acme? The organization would be best served by a limited flexible benefit program, designed and managed at the corporate level but administered in each of Acme's divisions. Flexible benefits are ideal for companies like Acme—companies that need to focus on labor costs and get good value for the dollars they spend on compensation. In addition, because Acme's divisions face different competitive markets, they have different benefit coverage needs. Flexible benefit plans are a way to handle this situation. They can allow the corporation to purchase benefits (enhancing savings by large-group purchases), and they can give individuals a wide range of benefit choices. Different divisions can still budget for different benefit costs; businesses that are in high-benefit-paying industries can simply match their competitors by allocating more dollars for the purchase of benefits, while divisions in low-benefit-paying industries can allocate less. Thus the company can adjust its benefit costs on a division-by-division basis and still get the advantages of central administration and central purchasing.

How much flexibility should be built into the Acme plan? Because Acme is not a highly participative company and is not interested in educating its employees in the economics of financial management, only limited flexibility is appropriate. For example, all employees should be required to take a certain amount of health insurance, life insurance, pension, vacation, and disability benefits. They should also be given the option of buying additional benefit coverage in return for reduced cash compensation. This type of plan assures that the company and the individual are protected against catastrophic situations, yet it allows individuals to use some of their benefit dollars as they see fit.

Degree of Hierarchy. There is nothing about Acme that suggests that it should be egalitarian in the way it manages its reward system. With respect to total compensation, it is appropriate for Acme to simply match the degree of hierarchy present in its competitors. Thus senior executives with Acme should be paid at least fifty times more than production workers. This is the norm in most large manufacturing organizations in the United States. In addition, executives should also be eligible for special stock plans and perhaps even for some special perquisites. Their particular benefit needs can be covered under the flexible benefit program.

In traditional organizations perquisites are usually based on hierarchical position. Parking spaces, office size, office furniture, flights on the company plane, and so on are all strongly driven by hierarchy. Given that Acme wants to manage in a relatively traditional top-down way, there is no reason to have an egalitarian workplace. Still, Acme should limit the number of visible expensive perquisites associated with management and supervisory positions. For example, luxurious offices and special dining rooms should probably be downplayed. I suggest this because of the profit-sharing feature of the Acme reward system, and the fact that Acme needs to be a highly cost-competitive organization. Even in a traditional top-down organization, it is hard to get employees to take seriously the idea that costs are a critical factor when management consistently and regularly indulges itself with costly visible perquisites and benefits. From a symbol-management point of view, it is important that Acme managers emphasize the importance of reducing costs whenever and wherever possible. This means a small corporate staff and few luxuries at the corporate offices.

Acme might want to give serious consideration to having an all-salaried workforce. For an all-salaried plan to work, however, there needs to be some trust in the organization, and a nonadversarial relationship between management and the workforce, although such a plan does not require a highly participative work environment. All the evidence suggests that this is a low-cost but attractive approach to pay that appeals to a large number of workers. Actually, the difference between a workforce that has hourly and salaried employees and one that has only salaried is more in terminology and how hours of work are recorded than in cost. An all-salaried workforce does not punch timeclocks. They are trusted to report the hours they have worked so that, in compliance with federal law, all nonmanagement employees (called nonexempt by the law) can be paid for overtime.

Cost is an issue with a shift to an all-salaried workforce only if hourly employees have traditionally been given lower cost benefits than salaried employees. Because everyone at Acme can be covered by the same flexible benefit program however, there should—with the possible exception of sick pay—be no cost problem. All-salaried pay plans usually pay all employees a fixed salary whether they come to work or not. This means that employees who under many hourly pay systems would not be paid when they are absent are paid. If this benefit is abused it can be costly. Research indicates that in most cases it is not abused in organizations that monitor attendance and have a positive work culture (Lawler, 1981).

Overall, we have designed a pay system for Acme that is less hierarchical than the ones in most traditional companies. Although slightly against the general tendency of Acme to manage in a top-down manner, this degree of egalitarianism is probably desirable. It reinforces the importance of everyone's working together and fits with the fact that Acme requires a culture that values cost control.

Process Issues

Acme's management style clearly calls for pay programs that are designed and administered in a hierarchical fashion. As far as design is concerned, the only question is whether pay plans are best designed at the corporate level or at the divisional level; there is no reason to push pay system design any lower in the organization. Given that Acme's various business units face different markets, it makes sense for them to design their own pay plans—guided, of course, by corporate rules and procedures and supported by a very small central compensation staff.

In terms of the ongoing administration of the plan, some of the programs that have been recommended in preceding pages require that individuals exercise some decision making, do some financial planning, and have some input. The flexible benefit program, for example, gives individuals a choice. The profit-sharing and individual bonus plans should lead to variable pay, and individuals need to be able to cope with the personal financial impact of this. The performance appraisal system depends upon individuals having ongoing input and an opportunity to challenge seemingly unfair or unreasonable decisions. Thus some education of individuals about performance appraisal and financial planning is needed at the plant level. An appeal process also needs to be set up to deal with individuals who feel unfairly treated.

A policy of strict secrecy with respect to individual pay rates would seem to be the correct one for Acme. Given the strong emphasis on pay for performance, however, it does not necessarily follow that *all* pay information should be kept secret. Indeed, Acme should release pay-range information and fully acquaint individuals with how their pay relates to the pay of Acme's competitors. In addition, Acme needs to release enough organizational performance data so that everyone understands how the profit-sharing plan works and how their payout is actually determined.

Finally, a great deal of information should be communicated about how the performance appraisal system works and how it drives individual pay rates. The emphasis should be on showing a clear relationship between performance and the bonuses that individuals receive. Without a high level of communication, it is hard for individuals to understand the impact of their performance on pay. Thus a noncommunicative organization can lose a great deal of the positive impact that is available with this type of highly variable individual bonus plan.

The Acme Strategy in Review

Now that we have covered the major features of the Acme pay strategy, we need to look back and see if they fit together to create a coherent whole. Overall, I think the answer is yes. They have been designed to fit a business that is in a very competitive market and in which costs—particularly labor costs—are critical determinants of economic effectiveness. Acme has determined that the best way to compete in this environment is to operate with a traditional, tightly controlled management style. The pay system reinforces this by having considerable amounts of compensation at risk and by minimizing perquisites and visible symbols of spending. It also places a considerable emphasis on controlling costs relative to its business competitors'. Pricing jobs to business competitors helps to keep the individuals at Acme focused on the competitive marketplace rather than on internal comparisons.

Finally, the process issues are handled in a way that is consistent with a top-down management style. Individuals are in the position of having minimal input to the pay systems but are given enough information so that they know how the systems are being administered and what they can reasonably and fairly expect. In addition, they are given the opportunity to challenge decisions that they think are unreasonable.

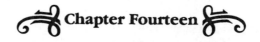

Chapter Fourteen

A Pay Strategy for HiTech International: A Global Technology Company

HiTech International is a midsized company that makes and services a variety of electronic instruments. These instruments are used in factories, labs, and other locations to gather and analyze sophisticated technical data. Although HiTech is a leader in its field and has grown very rapidly, it has a number of tough international and domestic competitors. It has approximately 20,000 diverse but generally young workers.

After an extensive strategic analysis of its business, HiTech has decided that it can gain competitive advantage by being a high-quality manufacturer and servicer of its instruments. Service is a key selling point, because the kind of instruments the organization sells need continuing support (including regular maintenance and occasional software programming). The field is very dynamic, with new products coming out rapidly, so HiTech has also decided that it needs to be quick to market with new products and highly flexible in its manufacturing operations. Because the cost of developing new products is high and the life expectancy relatively short, HiTech needs to be a worldwide seller of its products. Finally, technology leadership is critical to selling HiTech's products; thus the organization is committed to incorporating the latest technological advances.

HiTech's labor costs are a significant portion of its total cost of doing business. Few employees are directly involved in manufacturing; most are in R & D, engineering, service, and administration. HiTech has decided that the best way to control its labor costs is to have a relatively flat organization with a highly flexible and committed workforce. Most of the employees, even in the manufacturing area, do knowledge work or operate relatively sophisticated equipment. This means that HiTech needs employees who constantly learn in order to keep up with the technology, flexibly adapt their behavior to new technology, work cooperatively to integrate R & D and manufacturing, and operate in a high-involvement way that reduces the need for supervision.

Finally, because HiTech is a technology company, it has decided to make a substantial investment in information technology. Thus all its employees are given access to computer terminals and an electronic bulletin board and mail system. Electronic mail, seen as the basic communication device in the organization, is used extensively for exchanging information among employees (including those who are in the field). It is designed to reduce the need for supervision and overhead support.

What type of pay structure is likely to produce the commitment-oriented, learning-oriented, and flexible employee behavior that HiTech has decided it needs? The system that was designed for Acme in the previous chapter is clearly not likely to accomplish this. It fits a company that wants highly motivated employees who operate within a rather traditional organizational structure that is focused on labor-cost reduction and wants relatively predictable bureaucratic behavior. HiTech needs to take a substantially different approach to compensation—one that fits its very different business strategy and management style. With this in mind, let us look at what fits HiTech.

Core Principles for HiTech

HiTech needs a highly skilled workforce, which suggests a core principle that emphasizes paying individuals according to their skills, knowledge, and market value. Pay for performance is needed at HiTech, although a strong emphasis on individual pay for performance may be counterproductive. Research evidence shows that in high-technology work, team and group pay-for-performance programs make the most sense, because the work demands cooperation and teamwork (Schuster, 1984; Von Glinow and Mohrman, 1989). Thus HiTech International should have a core principle that emphasizes pay for team and organizational performance. This principle can be tied directly to the issue of market position. To attract the best and the brightest and establish technology leadership, HiTech needs to pay above-market wages. But should it *guar-*

antee above-market wages? Probably not. It needs a system that, to a degree, relates market position to the success and effectiveness of the organization.

Because HiTech is a knowledge-based organization, it must have decision making that is based on who has the expertise rather than on hierarchically driven formal authority. Many of its most valuable human assets are its engineering and technical people. Thus it needs to be strongly committed to a core principle that calls for egalitarian rewards and perquisites, so that *all* its human assets feel valued and appreciated.

HiTech wants to have a committed and highly involved workforce that is self-managing. Its workforce is highly educated and wants to understand and influence the organizational policies that affect it. Thus HiTech needs a core principle that strongly supports its commitment to participation in the development and administration of its pay plans. It also needs a core principle affirming open information about how the pay system operates and pay is determined. All pay policies and practices need to be in the public domain. Without a principle of open communication, general participation in decision making is impossible.

Finally, because of the nature of HiTech's workforce, a core principle that emphasizes individual choice in pay and reward system treatment fits the organization well. Educated, knowledgeable employees are in an excellent position to choose their benefit programs and to influence their career tracks. Thus it is appropriate to have a core principle that stresses individual participation in determining rewards and career tracks.

Structural Issues

Base Pay. Paying the person rather than the job fits HiTech International's approach to business. In the case of its manufacturing operations, this means a straightforward pay-for-skills approach. With frequent product changes and the need to be quick to market, skill-based pay is a natural here. Experience has shown that skill-based pay leads to a flexible workforce that is fast to adapt to new technologies and new products. It also reduces the resistance that employees often feel to work restructuring, because with skill-based pay people do not "own" jobs or parts of the production process and thus are not as threatened by change. In addition, because skill-based pay encourages growth and learning, it reinforces the needed organizational commitment to lifetime learning and the constant development of new knowledge and skills.

Knowledge-based pay in the form of technical ladders fits well in HiTech's R & D areas. These ladders should reward depth of knowledge in key technology areas in order to assure that HiTech attracts and retains the technology experts who will give it leadership. These plans also need to emphasize some horizontal learning so that individuals are trained to follow products from conception to market. Such training is a critical factor in getting products to the market quickly and in ensuring that products do not just get "thrown over the wall" from development to manufacturing.

Knowledge-based pay also fits well in HiTech's service organization. It can be used there to reward individuals for becoming more versatile in their ability to sell and service the instruments that HiTech makes. This is particularly important, because customers want people with solutions, not people who just fix hardware. Knowledge-based pay can be used to encourage individuals in the service function to learn various features of the systems HiTech sells so that they become better problem solvers and responders to customer concerns.

As is true in any organization, it is least clear how HiTech can apply the idea of paying the person to its managerial and support personnel. One possible use of knowledge-based pay is to encourage people to move horizontally in the organization and become more familiar with all features of the organization's operations. This breadth of knowledge should be quite valuable because of the business demands that HiTech faces. Again, organizations want *solutions* from HiTech, not just hardware, and they want those solutions quickly. Individuals who are broadly trained in different areas of the company are in the best position to manage the overall operation of the company and to provide customers with integrative solutions that involve the right hardware, software, and personalization of HiTech's products.

In those situations where the horizontal learning model does not fit HiTech's way of doing business, the correct approach is probably simply to pay individuals their market value based on those skills that they are actually using. The compensation department should evaluate market value frequently—perhaps twice each year—by scanning the environment to determine what it would take to replace key individuals in the organization. This should lead to a base pay that represents the market value of each individual's skills and abilities. From an administrative point of view, this can be handled by creating a wide pay range for each responsibility level (no more than a few, and preferably only one, for each management level) and then allowing individuals to progress within this range based on skill development and learning. Admittedly, obtaining market data can be difficult when pay is based on individuals rather than jobs, because salary-survey data are not collected this way. Nevertheless, by doing regular salary surveys and by constantly looking at hiring pay rates, HiTech should be able to get a good sense of what the market is for people with the kind of skills it needs.

Pay for Performance. Pay for performance needs to be a critical part of the reward system at HiTech International. HiTech is a commitment-based organization; thus the pay-for-performance system needs to reinforce individuals' understanding of and commitment to the organization's overall success. In short, it needs to create an environment throughout the organization in which individuals share in HiTech's success and feel personally identified with and concerned about its performance.

In order to focus the attention of individuals on organizational performance, a series of performance-based pay systems are needed. A corporate-wide profit-sharing plan is clearly called for. This plan, which should pay out any time the organization is profitable, should be the major vehicle that brings the pay of all employees up to (and perhaps slightly above) the market for their skills. At the top level of the organization, it should be a substantial piece of the total compensation package—perhaps as much as 30 or 40 percent. At the middle management level it should be a much smaller percentage—perhaps 20 percent—while at the nonmanagement level it should be a still smaller percentage.

In addition to a profit-sharing plan, HiTech needs equity

vehicles that affect everyone in the organization. It would make sense to require that all employees own at least 100 shares of stock in the company, for example. This requirement for employment can be reinforced and supported by a stock purchase plan once the employees join the organization. Finally, options should be used liberally to reinforce equity participation and (to a lesser degree) individual and team performance. Rather than giving across-the-board options to senior managers only, HiTech should give options throughout the organization to individuals and teams that have particularly outstanding years or accomplish singularly important breakthroughs. The options should be structured both as a reward for good performance and a retention device; the latter can be accomplished by making them exercisable over a ten-year period.

Because it is strongly committed to pay for performance, HiTech needs to have gainsharing plans in all of its operating locations. Each manufacturing plant, for example, can have its own stand-alone gainsharing plan that covers all employees in that location.

Gainsharing need not stop with just the manufacturing locations, however. It can and should be installed in the sales and service offices as well. Installing gainsharing in service units requires some custom design work, because most existing plans are targeted at manufacturing plants. The key to making gainsharing successful in sales and service units, as has been shown by Xerox and some other companies that have used it in their service units, is the measurement of both cost of service and customer satisfaction. Customer satisfaction needs to be tracked on an ongoing basis, and it needs to be built into the plan as a critical determinant of whether a gainsharing bonus is paid or not. If customer satisfaction is ignored, there is an enormous danger that costs will be reduced but that inferior service will erode customer loyalty.

Finally, HiTech needs a reward system that recognizes unusual one-time individual and group performance at the time the performance occurs. Because of the significant monetary rewards that have already been called for, these rewards need not necessarily have much monetary value. Perhaps the best approach is to make them largely recognition rewards (for example, a dinner for two or tickets to a game or play). The challenge with any plan like this is to administer it in a way that is congruent with the organization's commitment to fair and meaningful rewards for performance. The value of the recognition award very much depends on its scarcity and on whether it is given to the "right" individuals under the right conditions. Particularly during the plan's initial operating period, the status of the recipients in the eyes of other employees influences the value of the reward as much as the reward gives status to individuals. That status is not unlimited, however. If such awards are so overused that they become standard operating procedure, they cease to be a form of recognition.

Recognition reward programs are usually most useful in sales and service areas, because there is a tradition there of recognition for outstanding performance. In these areas the rewards can have some significant financial value—perhaps a vacation trip—but if they do, individuals should be given the choice of the cash or the "prize." This ties directly back to the organization's principle of giving people a say in how they are treated and what their rewards are.

Because its employees are valuable, HiTech should avoid layoffs and reductions at all costs. Replacing individuals is a major problem when high-technology workers are involved. Thus the organization needs to have a way of reducing its total labor costs that does not involve laying individuals off. (A combination of profit-sharing and gainsharing plans can help.) Avoiding layoffs is not enough, however, if low pay leads to high turnover. This is why it is important to combine variable pay with approaches such as stock options and stock ownership plans, which give individuals a financial reason to stay with the organization.

Noticeably missing from our discussion of pay-for-performance systems has been any mention of merit pay or individual bonuses. This is not an oversight. These approaches do not fit the style at HiTech. The strong emphasis on teams and teamwork means that individual rewards should be downplayed. Stock option and recognition reward plans allow the organization to reward individuals for performance; thus merit increases and individual bonuses are not needed. Performance appraisals, however, are still needed, because they can guide employees' skill development and support promotion decisions (Mohrman, Resnick-West, and

Lawler, 1989). The performance appraisals should be done in a very participative manner. For example, the appraisal of managers should involve the use of peer and subordinate evaluation data.

Overall, the pay-for-performance systems at HiTech should be designed to create a world in which senior managers have as much as 50 percent of their total compensation dependent upon performance and have a significant ownership interest in the company. Even at the lower levels, a substantial amount of the total compensation should be dependent upon performance, and ownership interest should be encouraged. It is interesting to note that individuals at the lower levels of the organization would participate in more performance-based pay systems than individuals at the top. The typical nonmanager could own stock, have stock options, participate in the profit-sharing plan, and participate in a gainsharing plan. The purpose of this mix of pay-for-performance systems is to emphasize the performance of the organization at different levels and to help reinforce and build a commitment-oriented organization.

Degree of Hierarchy. Hierarchical reward structures simply do not fit HiTech International's business strategy or its emphasis on a management style featuring involvement and technical leadership. Thus the reward system should be designed to minimize differences that are based on organizational level. All employees should be salaried and receive the same flexible benefit plan. No special perquisites should be available to managers or executives. The policy prohibiting special treatment based on organizational level should cover a broad range of things, from whether individuals have secretaries to where they park, eat, and sit on an airplane. In short, a ruthless approach to egalitarian rewards is appropriate.

A small point, but one that can be of symbolic importance, has to do with the provision of secretaries. Individuals often get secretaries simply because of their level in the hierarchy. As a result, higher-level employees often have secretaries with virtually nothing to do, while lower-level employees share overworked secretaries with a number of other individuals. The problem is compounded when secretaries are paid based on the level of the person they report to rather than on their own skills and duties. This is seen as unfair by the secretaries and unduly emphasizes the importance of organizational hierarchy. This practice has no place at HiTech. Secretaries should be allocated according to need and paid based upon their skills.

Benefits. A flexible benefit plan fits HiTech perfectly, because its workforce is knowledgeable and well educated. Such a plan can also help ensure that the organization meets the needs of individuals while remaining egalitarian. By providing a wide range of benefit choices, HiTech can meet the needs of individuals at different levels and with different family situations without creating a hierarchically driven plan.

The typical management perquisites can be included in HiTech's flexible program. For example, individuals who want a car could get one through the flexible benefit program, or they could get a thicker carpet, special parking, new office furniture, or even a secretary. It is worth thinking about including a few of the existing traditional executive benefits in a flexible benefit program as well. For example, extensive financial counseling could be made available through the program, as could certain additional kinds of life and health insurance.

HiTech International is one organization in which a *completely* flexible benefit program appears to be appropriate. Individuals could take cash and opt out of all benefits, for example. As was noted earlier, most organizations resist this because they are afraid employees will make mistakes. There is a tendency for them to be paternalistic when it comes to employee welfare. This conservative stance is probably appropriate in a traditional top-down organization, but it is not necessarily a good fit with the kind of culture that HiTech wishes to develop and the kind of relationship it wishes to have with its employees. Its whole management style is based on the assumption that individuals are self-managing, mature adults. This fits with a benefit program that maximizes the options that individuals have and educates employees to make informed choices.

Market Position. The management style and structure of HiTech International calls for total compensation levels that are less hierarchically driven than is true in traditional organizations. In essence, because HiTech is a commitment-driven organization that believes in broad involvement and decision making, it makes sense to pay nonmanagement employees slightly more than they would be paid in a top-down organization. After all, they are expected to do more, take more responsibility, and be more involved in the business. Higher base pay typically does come about as a result of the kind of skill-based pay system that we have already suggested that HiTech adopt.

On the other hand, at the more senior levels of management it is appropriate to pay individuals less than they would be paid in the traditionally managed organization—at least in terms of base pay—because the differences in power and role are not as great in an organization practicing high-involvement management as they are in more traditional organizations. Thus a smaller range from top to bottom makes sense. One qualification is in order here, however: managers in an organization such as HiTech should be able to make more than their counterparts in other organizations if the organizational performance of HiTech is truly outstanding. Given outstanding performance, individuals at *all* levels should make more than individuals in other organizations. Thus, although the total compensation levels for HiTech could potentially exceed those of other firms, the ratio from top to bottom would still be less than is typically found in a traditionally managed organization such as Acme.

Centralization of the Pay Structure. HiTech is an integrated organization; its products and services need to work together for the organization to meet customer needs. It does not have product lines that go to entirely different markets and face different competitors. Thus it should not decentralize its pay structures. It does not make sense, for example, to have radically different pay systems for different functions or for identical functions in different parts of the country or world. The core principles should be *corporate* core principles, and the same pay practices should exist throughout the firm. Not surprisingly, a corporate staff of significant size will be needed to develop, maintain, and administer the multifaceted pay system.

The pay system needs to be an integrator, because the technology calls for an integrated approach to meeting customer needs. Thus, although gainsharing plans and skill-based pay plans can be developed locally, most pay issues need to be managed at the corporate level. For example, the flexible benefit program should be a corporate plan, and the profit-sharing plan and stock option plans should be corporate-driven. Pricing individuals and skills to the market should be a corporate function, with pricing left to local units only when exclusively local-market skills are involved.

Process Issues

Participation. In order to be consistent with the management style of HiTech, the design and administration of the pay system must be handled in a participative manner. Participation also fits the type of workforce that HiTech has. Highly educated knowledge workers are not only capable of having but want to have a role in determining how their reward systems are structured and operated. In many cases they are the most knowledgeable about whether someone has or has not learned a new skill and whether a co-worker does or does not deserve a special performance reward. Thus it makes sense to involve employees in both the design and administration of the pay system.

What kind of pay decisions should be made in a participative way? The skill-based pay plans should be developed participatively to fit the kinds of skills that they need to reinforce and develop. As is true in many high-involvement organizations, individuals should also be involved in deciding whether their peers have acquired a new skill and deserve the pay increase that is associated with it. Similarly, gainsharing plans should be developed in a participative manner. In the case of those pay plans that are corporate-wide, diagonal slice task forces should be used to develop and maintain the plans.

Communication. As was mentioned in our discussion of HiTech's core principles, information about the critical elements of the reward system needs to be in the public domain. Openness about pay is needed to create a culture of trust and involvement. Without factual information about pay practices and rates, pay issues will be subject to speculation and misinterpretation. This can lead to reduced trust.

Openness is also needed to allow individuals to participate in decision making about pay and so that individuals can make informed judgments about whether other individuals deserve rewards. It is also necessary so that individuals can participate meaningfully in the design and ongoing administration of the profit-sharing plans, gainsharing plans, flexible benefit program, and so forth.

Communication is particularly needed in efforts to make corporate-wide programs meaningful to individuals. And communication is not just a matter of the books being open and accessible; *active* communication, education, and frequent meetings are needed to reinforce the understanding and importance of organizational performance. Individuals need to be encouraged to ask questions about the different costs that the organization encounters, its strategies and how they relate to the profitability of the company, the price of the stock, and the operation of local gainsharing plans. Passive, open-book communication runs the risk of substantially neutralizing the potentially positive impact of profit-sharing and gainsharing plans.

The New Pay

There is no company that looks exactly like HiTech. There are companies that have many of the characteristics of HiTech, however, and some of these have many of the same pay practices that I have prescribed above. For example, Compaq Computer, Apple, Digital, Tandem Computer, and Sun Microsystems all bear a resemblance to HiTech and have some of the same pay practices. But the total system that I have designed for HiTech does not exist, and thus I cannot say that it is a proven approach. I am convinced, however, that the approach is one that fits the strategy and technology of organizations like HiTech International.

The HiTech system contains an internally consistent set of pay practices that reinforce a particular management style—high involvement—and a particular business strategy. The pay system should be accepted as a whole rather than be partially implemented.

The danger of partial implementation is that it can lead to a situation in which pay practices cancel each other out. This can happen if one practice is more consistent with a traditional management style while another fits better with a high-involvement style, for example. Partial implementation can also lead to gaps in the pay system that fail to support certain behaviors that are needed for organizational effectiveness.

Taken together, the practices recommended for HiTech represent a "new pay." All the fundamental characteristics of the pay structure are different from those in a traditional organization. But more than that, they are different in a way that is internally consistent and supportive of a high-involvement management style and a different type of organizational behavior. Because they are internally consistent, they can have a particularly strong impact on organizational performance. As I said, this is not a proven approach, however. Pieces of the system are in place and have proven to be effective, but this is not enough. Acceptance of the total system and application of the total system are necessary to finally establish that the pieces fit together and have their desired effect on performance. My prediction is that systems like the one suggested for HiTech International will be implemented by organizations and will prove to be extremely effective.

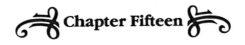

Chapter Fifteen

Strategic Pay and Public Policy: The Need for Change

The design of pay systems in all countries is impacted by a number of laws. Laws can be used to mandate or prohibit certain pay practices as well as to encourage or discourage them. Making certain benefits tax free, for example, is one way to encourage companies to offer those benefits. Requiring that companies pay for overtime is a way to ensure that they have structured overtime pay programs. In this chapter I will consider some of the key public policy issues with respect to organizations' adopting pay systems that are strategically advantageous.

In considering the role of government in determining pay practices, I start with a viewpoint that favors minimal government intervention. My core principle is that pay practices should be adopted because they will help the organization operate effectively, not because they are tax advantaged or government mandated. I also believe that in most cases organizations are in the best position to decide which pay system is best for them. There are a number of reasons why I take these positions, not the least of which is my belief that to be internationally competitive, organizations need the ability to pay in whatever way offers competitive advantage. In addition, there are numerous examples of well-intentioned governmental efforts to regulate pay policies that have had dysfunctional impacts.

There are, however, some major exceptions to my belief that government should neither mandate or prohibit specific pay practices nor encourage or discourage them through tax advantages. When individual rights are concerned—for example, when there is a possibility of discrimination based on race, sex, religion, or age—there is justification for government action. In the case of overt discrimination or other unfair treatment of individuals and groups, the government should mandate protective practices and, when those fail to ensure equality, bring lawsuits.

273

Pay for Performance

There is no current law in the United States that requires or substantially encourages any organization to pay for performance. I
believe that this is as it should be. Not everyone agrees, however,
Over the years there have been calls for tax incentives in this country
to increase the prevalence of such pay-for-performance systems as
profit-sharing plans and stock ownership plans. A number of other
countries, including France and England, have already either encouraged or mandated profit sharing legislatively. One argument
for this type of legislation is that societies are better off when companies have profit-sharing plans—better off because, as Weitzman
(1984) argues in his book *The Share Economy*, such plans reduce
the tendency of organizations to lay off individuals in bad times.

Although I generally favor profit-sharing and gainsharing
plans, I am not convinced that every organization should be forced
(or even encouraged) to have them. They should be adopted because
an organization feels that they will improve organizational performance. In short, the government should create a "level playing
field" for competing approaches to paying for performance rather
than trying to motivate or mandate the adoption of some (for example, profit sharing) while ignoring others.

Employee Ownership

Most large U.S. companies have well-funded retirement plans, in
part because retirement plans are tax favored in several ways. For
example, if money in a company retirement plan is invested in
stock, gains in the stock are not taxed until an individual retires (or
otherwise withdraws the stock)—a tax process that encourages employee ownership as well as the creation of retirement plans. Because tax is ultimately paid on retirement funds, and because
offering incentives for individual retirement planning has a number
of macroeconomic advantages, including increasing the savings
rate, it is hard to argue against this particular piece of tax policy.

Much more controversial than the tax advantages favoring
retirement plans and stock ownership in retirement plans are the
provisions concerning employee stock ownership plans (Blasi,

1988). Because they have had several strong advocates in Congress, as well as a number of articulate spokespersons in the business world, ESOPs are tax favored. They allow companies to borrow money at a significantly lower real interest rate than would be available to them in the free market. This feature has had the effect of significantly increasing the number of ESOPs created. As far as individuals are concerned, there is no real tax advantage to being a member of an ESOP (except that again taxes are deferred until the stock is received). The policy question is whether organizations should receive tax advantages simply because they set up an ESOP.

As with profit sharing, I am not convinced that ESOPs should be given special tax treatment. As Blasi (1988) and others have pointed out, if organizations are going to get tax advantages for setting up ESOPs, at least there should be a related requirement that companies install participative management practices that encourage employee involvement and give employees the right to vote the stock they own. Employee voting is not possible with most ESOPs, because the stock is held by the ESOP rather than directly by the employees. Thus, rather than encouraging participation, ESOPs can end up being antiparticipative and can disenfranchise other stockholders by putting more power in the hands of management.

If ESOPs put more power in the hands of employees—and some do—they would be advancing shared national values concerning democracy in the society and in the workplace. Without this feature, however, they are simply a means by which companies can reduce their taxes, gain a competitive advantage in the marketplace by obtaining cheaper capital, and fend off unwanted takeover efforts. Companies such as Polaroid have discovered that substantial ESOPs can make it much more difficult for the company to be taken over and for management to be unseated. Thus, rather than making management more accountable to the employees and to the shareholders for how well it runs the firm, ESOPs can help ensure that the present management—regardless of its competence, performance, and management style—is maintained.

I am not suggesting, however, that ESOPs be banned—simply that they not be tax advantaged to companies. It is hard to see why companies should get favorable tax treatment for creating

ESOPs that fail to contribute to employee well-being, participative management, or any other social goal.

Skill-Based Pay

Currently, there are no tax regulations that strongly encourage organizations to use either traditional job evaluation-based pay or person-based pay. There is, however, one important and volatile issue that could ultimately lead to legislation mandating a specific approach to base pay. Study after study has shown that the pay of women lags far behind that of men. Estimates suggest that in 1988 women made somewhere between 65 and 70 percent of what men earned (Patten, 1988). This gap between men and women has been closing for a number of years, but it is still enormous; and no one can predict when, if ever, it will close completely. Because of this gap, and the slow movement toward equality, numerous groups have argued for legislation that would operate to close the gap. The sex discrimination laws already in effect have targeted this inequality and they have probably helped close the gap, but too large a gap still remains.

There are a number of reasons why women still have lower pay levels. One is that they have not had access to many of the higher-paying positions, such as those in top management. Another is that relatively low pay rates are associated with the types of work that have traditionally been done by females. Studies using job evaluation have shown that work traditionally done by women tends to be paid less relative to its job evaluation score than is work traditionally done by men (Patten, 1988). A classic example is the job of secretary, which has always been relatively low paid but which involves considerable responsibility and a high level of skill. In comparison, assembly-line work is often paid more but can be learned in a relatively short period of time. I could list many similar examples of work that is traditionally done by women and is underpaid, but I do not think I need to. There is little doubt that the phenomenon is real; the issue is how to correct it.

Proponents of "comparable worth" have argued that the best way to correct the problem is to mandate job evaluation systems in all government and private-sector organizations. They argue that if a similar job evaluation system is used across all parts of an organization, pay can be set to truly reflect job worth, not historical patterns of sex discrimination. This argument has fallen on receptive ears in some states—and indeed in some countries. Some city governments have mandated that job evaluation be used in this manner, as have some states, but they have restricted their mandate to government employees rather than mandating job evaluation for all organizations that operate within the city or state.

The Canadian province of Ontario has gone further than any state government in the United States. In 1987 it passed a pay-equity act mandating structured job evaluation programs in all public- and private-sector organizations that operate in Ontario. The law also requires that organizations take positive action to erase historical differences that seem to be based on sex discrimination and report to the government on their job evaluation programs and on how different groups are paid. The law specifically identifies certain factors that need to be looked at in job evaluation and in essence mandates a point-factor type of system.

So far arguments in favor of comparable-worth legislation have not met with the same success in the United States that they have in Canada. In most cases the arguments against comparable work have won the day. These arguments are essentially twofold. One line of argument maintains that the gap is diminishing and will be further closed by the continued opening of more high-paying jobs to women. It goes on to argue that freeing up these better jobs should be the major focus of government intervention into the private sector.

The second line of argument warns of the potential horrors of the government's legislating job evaluation practices, auditing them, and then holding organizations accountable for inequities. Not only is this intervention likely to produce enormous bureaucratic regulations and inefficiencies, the argument runs; it could also increasingly take organizations out of touch with a market. Instead of pay being driven by the marketplace and the supply of and demand for talent, it would be driven by internal evaluation systems. This shift runs the risk of producing tremendous inefficiencies in the allocation of labor and organizations' ability to hire individuals. Finally it could significantly raise the wage bill of many organizations.

No one has good numbers to indicate how much of a wage increase comparable worth would produce. My guess is that in the case of some jobs that are traditionally done by women, organizations might have to increase wages by 20 or even 30 percent. At a time when international competition is a key concern, this is a cost that most organizations would be hesitant to take on. If *all* organizations were to incur this cost, it would be a very different situation, of course. The increase might well cause some inflation but would not put a particular firm at a competitive disadvantage. In markets that are exclusively national, U.S. companies could indeed absorb this kind of extra cost without any one of them necessarily being at a competitive disadvantage. In areas such as electronics and autos, however—areas in which the competition is international— substantial extra costs could be a serious problem for U.S. companies. They would have to absorb a cost that their foreign competitors would not.

I have a concern with comparable worth that goes beyond the bureaucracy it might create and the cost disadvantages it might inflict on U.S. corporations. This concern has to do with its potential impact on the use of skill- or person-based pay. Some of the comparable-worth proposals that have been suggested would make skill- or knowledge-based pay difficult or impossible to implement. Needless to say, I feel that handicapping skill-based pay would be a substantial mistake. As I said earlier, I am opposed to favoring one compensation approach over another. The playing field should be level in the choice between person-based pay and job-based pay. There is no compelling reason to argue that the government should intervene and make one the required or preferred approach to administering pay. Thus any system that mandates job evaluation is undesirable.

Overall, I am convinced by the arguments against comparable-worth legislation and would not like to see it become the law of the land. If a law is passed designed to increase the pay in the types of work traditionally done by women, I think it is important that it allow for skill-based pay. Skill-based pay is not itself in opposition to comparable worth; it does not necessarily operate in ways that reduce pay for the skills traditionally possessed by women. Thus, if comparable worth becomes a legislative mandate, the resulting law could and should allow for both skill-based plans and job-based plans designed to produce comparable worth.

Flexible Benefits

Benefit plans are subject to extensive regulation and special tax treatment. Benefits such as retirement, health insurance, and life insurance are tax advantaged as a way of encouraging organizations to offer them. When flexible benefits were proposed in the 1970s, there were some tax complications that made them difficult to install. Specifically, it was unclear whether the Internal Revenue Service would treat them as tax neutral or would instead convert certain nontaxable benefits to taxable benefits in an organization that had a flexible benefit program. This has since been clarified: at the present time there are no significant tax advantages or disadvantages to having a flexible benefit program. However, there is a continuing debate over how flexible benefit programs should be taxed.

Much as I favor the idea of flexible benefits, I do not think there is a compelling reason for the government to encourage organizations to adopt them. I would like to see a situation in which specific benefits are selected because they are seen as a good purchase by individuals who have the freedom to pick them or refuse them, but this situation should not come about by mandate. Rather, flexible benefits ought to be installed because they demonstrate their effectiveness and their positive impact on organizational performance.

But what about the tax-advantaged treatment of certain benefits? This is a tough issue, but I come down on the side of treating all benefits equally from a tax point of view. Specifically, I favor treating all benefits like cash. This is a rather radical view, and one that could raise the tax bill of those individuals who now receive extensive tax-free fringe benefits. It could also raise additional revenue for the government, although this is not my intention. Indeed, the change to exclusively taxable benefits could be neutralized by simply lowering overall tax rates.

Problems could arise, however, if all benefits were taxable. Perhaps the major one is that the increased cost of benefits due to taxation could decrease the number of individuals throughout society who have access to adequate health care, life insurance, and basic retirement protection. Yet giving individuals tax advantages in order to encourage organizations to offer benefit plans is a weak and inefficient way to see that society has adequate health-care protection. These tax advantages merely reduce the taxes of some and in many cases ensure health care to those individuals who are least in need of tax reductions. They ignore the large number of individuals who work in organizations that do not offer benefits and those individuals who do not work regularly. Health care for them is probably best provided through either government-sponsored health-care insurance programs or by government-sponsored and -provided health-care programs. The situation for retirement benefits is different than it is for other tax-advantaged benefits. Retirement benefits are taxed when received, and thus, as I mentioned earlier, it probably makes sense to continue their tax-advantaged status.

Egalitarian Reward Practices

In various ways and at various times, the government has intervened in company pay practices to encourage organizations to be more egalitarian in their treatment of employees. Many of these interventions have focused on the issue of benefits and have tried to ensure that individuals throughout the organization have equal access to tax-free benefits. The policy concern here is that high-paid employees can take advantage of the tax laws and get tax-free benefits while lower-paid employees get either no tax-free benefits or fewer tax-free benefits.

If my earlier recommendation that all benefits become taxable were accepted, the concern about equal access to benefits would become less important. If all benefits are taxable, offering them to just one group does not favor that group over others with respect to tax laws. In other words, upper-level employees are not getting something tax free that others in the organization cannot. Certainly, they gain something, but they have to pay taxes on that gain just as they currently have to pay taxes on other compensation. My recommendation, then, is that if benefits are made taxable, it is not necessary to mandate that benefits be available to individuals at all levels in an organization on an equal basis.

I am somewhat sympathetic to the view that benefits offered to one individual in an organization should be made available to all on an equal opportunity basis. Probably the most sensible legislative approach—if legislation is needed at all—is to require that any benefit that is part of a flexible benefit program be made available to all members of the organization and that the cost be the same for all members of the organization. In other words, all individuals would be able to buy benefits, regardless of their hierarchical position in the organization. Much as this appeals to me, I think that it carries government intervention too far, thus I would prefer to see no legislation.

Any discussion of egalitarianism in pay has to look at the issue of executive compensation levels. Should legislative action should be taken to control them? At the present time there is no legislation or tax policy in the United States that operates to discourage companies from having enormous cash compensation differences between top executives and lower-paid employees. Legislation that would place tax penalties on excessively high levels of executive compensation has been proposed, however. For example, it has been suggested that executive compensation rates that exceed a fixed dollar amount or a certain ratio between the top and the bottom of the organization (say, fifteen to one) be treated as a non-tax deductible expense for the corporations paying them.

In essence, most proposals on excessive executive compensation would say to an organization that it can pay executives $1 million or more a year if it wants, but that the government will not help pay part of the bill by making those excessive compensation costs tax deductible for the corporation. (In fact, legislation such as this has already been passed with respect to executive gold parachutes.) On the surface this type of legislation has a certain appeal, but it certainly disrupts the free market with respect to executive pay rates. Thus it fails the level-playing-field test with respect to compensation rates and practices.

There is an obvious alternative to the idea of trying to use tax laws to discourage organizations from paying their senior executives excessively high salaries: tax the individuals who receive these salaries. The concern that these individuals are profiting too much from being senior executives and that society is helping to fund their pay by making it tax deductible for corporations can at least partially be met by increasing their tax rates. This could be easily done by adding higher tax brackets for earned income that exceeds $500,000 a year, $1 million a year, and so on. Obviously, these tax brackets would impact relatively few individuals, but they would be at least a partially effective way of dealing with what is perceived as a social inequity.

Another approach to controlling executive pay is to try to make the pay-setting process for senior executives more responsible. The problem in setting executive salaries today is that there are no effective constraints. It is hard for any individual or group in the organization to say no to executive requests for additional stock options, profit-sharing plans, and so on. Legally, decision making in this area rests with the board of directors and shareholders, but all too often the board is not independent enough or powerful enough to effectively manage the pay of senior executives.

The answer would seem to be to require that the compensation committees of all corporate boards be made up of independent outside directors. Indeed, for large corporations, the regulation should perhaps go so far as to specify that compensation committee members not be officers or directors of other large, publicly traded corporations. Above all, though, they should not be executives who have overlapping board memberships with the individuals whose salary packages they are setting.

One interesting idea is to have representatives from the union (or, in the case of a nonunion company, selected representatives of the workforce) review executive salaries. The argument favoring this approach rests on the view that executives are in their positions to serve the multiple stakeholders of an organization, so their rewards and performance ought to be reviewed by those multiple stakeholders. In the case of large organizations, the key stakeholders include the employees as well as the stockholders. At the present time, however, in most cases the stockholders are poorly represented by the board of directors and the employees are not represented at all.

In conclusion I think something *does* need to be done about executive salaries in the United States. They are out of control, and in many respects unjustifiable. The challenge is to produce checks and balances that subject them to the same kind of review process that occurs elsewhere in the organization. If this kind of review process were in place, it is unlikely that executive salaries would progress so much more rapidly and be so much higher than the salaries of individuals elsewhere in the corporation. Tax penalties for excessive salaries are one way to go, but I favor them only as a last resort. As a first step I favor the idea of creating more meaningful board-of-directors reviews so that pay levels at the top are subject to the same types of review that exist for other employees. This is a simple step toward fair and equal treatment of all employees and does not constitute an unreasonable entry of government into company pay practices.

Overtime Pay

One piece of legislation currently in effect creates a hierarchical differentiation in U.S. organizations. The Fair Labor Standards Act of 1938 requires that employees in an organization be divided into exempt and nonexempt classifications. Nonexempt employees are eligible for overtime pay and are covered by a set of protective regulations that separate them from the managerial and professional employees in the organization. The legislation, originally written to guard against exploitation by organizations, was badly needed when it was passed. Unfortunately, it is still badly needed in some organizations that are managed in an autocratic and exploitative way.

The rules requiring exempt-nonexempt classification simply do not make sense in high-involvement organizations, however. They create a dysfunctionally hierarchical distinction in organizations that are working hard to eliminate them. The classification can be partially offset by making all employees salaried (as opposed to hourly) members of the workforce. The resulting "egalitarian" workforce still has to be divided into exempt and nonexempt employees, however. The question, therefore, is whether the law should be changed to allow organizations to drop this distinction entirely. I think that the law should be revised.

Exemption from the act should not be quickly or easily extended to organizations. Determining precisely which organizations should have the option of an all-exempt workforce is not a simple task. Perhaps the best way to make that determination would be to set a number of conditions that an organization would have to meet.

These conditions should include such things as having similar pay and benefit treatment for all employees in the organization—in other words, having an all-salaried workforce. They should also include having participative decision-making processes that are accessible to all employees and that affect decisions about wages, hours of work, and work design. In addition, exemption should probably be limited to work situations in which all individuals have substantial skills that have to do with how the business operates and access to information about the financial and operating results of their units. Finally, it probably makes sense to limit exemption to organizations in which individuals are on gainsharing plans and profit-sharing plans and own stock, so that all employees will gain from any overtime hours worked.

My proposed list of conditions that would qualify an organization for an all-exempt workforce is subject to debate—and indeed, it should be debated. But at least it provides a starting point by suggesting situations in which the old exempt-nonexempt distinction should be eliminated. The new management practices and the new technologies that demand high levels of employee involvement and high levels of knowledge also require that our labor laws and our pay laws progress. One law that clearly needs to evolve is the Fair Labor Standards Act.

Pay Disclosure

It can be difficult for an individual to gather evidence of pay discrimination. Particularly given the secrecy about pay practices and pay rates found in most organizations, it is hard for people to know whether they are being treated fairly in the area of pay. Information about pay is needed if individuals are to monitor the fairness of an organization's pay system and hold the organization accountable for its pay practices. Thus it makes sense to require that organizations at least provide documents explaining their pay practices. These should include information about pay ranges, job classification systems, pay-increase budgets, and whatever other financial and pay system information individuals need in order to assess how they are being treated relative to their co-workers. I stop short of saying that organizations should be required to reveal the pay rates of all individuals, however. Admittedly, this information can be helpful to someone considering whether there is a pattern of discrimination and whether individuals are treated fairly, but because it invades the individuals' right to confidentiality with respect to pay, it should not be mandated.

One final point about pay information. In all publicly held U.S. corporations, the pay of the top five officers must be reported to the shareholders once a year. This seems to have done little to discourage high pay at the executive level, but at least it helps to make executive pay visible to shareholders and employees. In order to allow shareholders to understand better what is going on at the executive level, perhaps the number of executives whose pay is in the public domain should be increased rather substantially. After all, in many large corporations the five top-paid individuals give a relatively poor picture of what is going on in the area of executive compensation. A much more meaningful number of employees would be one hundred. With information about this number of executives, shareholders and employees could have a reasonably good picture of how senior executives are being paid.

Participative Decision Making

There is little legislation in the United States that either favors or discourages the participative design of pay systems. The big exception here, of course, is legislation that allows employees to form unions and collectively bargain on matters of pay and hours. The problem is that most employees in the United States are not in unions and therefore are not affected by this legislation. The U.S. situation is a notable contrast to that in western Europe, where considerable legislation (in Germany, Sweden, and Norway, for example) requires that representative employee groups have a voice in setting wage rates, hours of work, and a number of other employment conditions.

There is one piece of U.S. legislation that, in some cases, can punish organizations for having employees participate in pay decisions. A provision of the National Labor Relations Act of 1935, which was designed to prevent the creation of company-dominated unions, makes it an unfair labor practice for organizations to have groups of employees meet to discuss wages and working conditions (Tuller, 1973; Sangerman, 1973). The original intent of this legislation was to prevent companies from using pseudo-participation as a way to make union organizing more difficult. This was and is a real concern, of course, but the potential negative effects of the law are greater than its potential benefits. In some cases this legislation makes organizations hesitant to discuss changes in pay practices with employees, even though discussion is necessary as gainsharing plans and other new pay programs are established. The answer to this problem is a relatively simple one: the law should be changed so that organizations are neither punished nor rewarded for involving employees in decision making about their pay and working conditions.

I do not favor mandating participation as is done in Europe, even though that approach has some attraction. Proponents make the case that employees have a right to discuss and provide input into decisions that concern their pay and working conditions. They go on to argue that in a democratic society, participation is a basic right—one that should be guaranteed to employees by the government, not subject to organizational whim. At one level this is an attractive and compelling argument, but in reality it is difficult to mandate participative decision making. In fact, even in those European countries where participation in the form of work councils and other representative groups has been mandated, charges and countercharges often fly about whether participative decision making actually occurs. All too often organizations go through the ritual of asking for comments only because this is mandated by the government. Without weighing the submitted comments, they then announce whatever decision they had already made. Therefore, my level-playing-field position extends to participation in pay decisions: they should be neither mandated nor punished. I remain hopeful that organizations will increasingly become convinced that participative decision making is simply good management practice.

References

Adams, J. S. "Toward an Understanding of Inequity." *Journal of Abnormal and Social Psychology*, 1963, *67*, 422–436.

Adams, J. S. "Injustice in Social Exchange." In L. Berkowitz, (ed.), *Advances in Experimental Social Psychology*. Vol. 2. Orlando, Fla.: Academic Press, 1965.

"Arthur Friedman's Outrage: Employees Decide Their Own Pay." *The Washington Post*, Feb. 23, 1975, pp. C-1 and C-8.

Blasi, J. R. *Employee Ownership*. Cambridge, Mass.: Ballinger, 1988.

Blinder, A. S. *Paying for Productivity*. Washington, D.C.: Brookings, 1990.

Bloom, D. E., and Trahan, J. T. *Flexible Benefits and Employee Choice*. Elmsford, N.Y.: Pergamon Press, 1986.

Boden, W. D. "Flexible Benefits: One Company's View." *Compensation and Benefits Review*, 1989, *21*, 11–16.

Bullock, R. J., and Bullock. P. F. "Gainsharing and Rubik's Cube: Solving System Problems." *National Productivity Review*, 1982, *2* (1), 396–407.

Bullock, R. J., and Lawler, E. E. "Gainsharing: A Few Questions and Fewer Answers." *Human Resource Management*, 1984, *5*, 197–212.

Coch, L., and French, J.R.P. "Overcoming Resistance to Change." *Human Relations*, 1948, *1* (4), 512–533.

Conte, M., and Tannenbaum, A. *Employee Ownership*. Ann Arbor: Institute for Social Research, University of Michigan, 1980.

Davis, S. M., and Lawrence, P. R. *Matrix*. Reading, Mass.: Addison-Wesley, 1977.

Deming, W. E. *The Merit System: The Annual Appraisal, Destroyer of People*. Paper presented at "A Day with Dr. W. Edwards Deming," University of Minnesota, 1987.

Dumaine, B. "What the Leaders of Tomorrow See." *Fortune,* July 3, 1989, *120,* 54.

Ellig, B. K. *Executive Compensation: A Total Pay Perspective.* New York: McGraw-Hill, 1982.

Ewing, D. E. *Freedom Inside the Organization.* New York: Dutton, 1977.

Ewing, D. E. *Do It My Way or You're Fired.* New York: Wiley, 1983.

Fay, C. H. "External Pay Relationships." In L. R. Gomez-Mejia (ed.), *Compensation and Benefits.* Vol. 3. Washington, D.C.: BNA, 1989.

Finkelstein, S., and Hambrick, D. C. "Chief Executive Compensation: A Synthesis and Reconciliation." *Strategic Management Journal,* 1988, *9,* 543–558.

Fragner, B. N. "Employees' 'Cafeteria' Offers Insurance Options." *Harvard Business Review,* 1975, *53* (6), 2–4.

Frost, Carl F., Wakeley, John H., and Ruh, Robert A. *The Scanlon Plan for Organizational Development: Identity, Participation, and Equity.* East Lansing: Michigan State University Press, 1974.

Galbraith, J. *Designing Complex Organizations.* Reading, Mass.: Addison-Wesley, 1973.

Ghiselli, E. E., and Brown, C. W. *Personnel and Industrial Psychology.* New York: McGraw-Hill, 1955.

Gifford, D. L., and Seltz, C. A. *Fundamentals of Flexible Compensation.* New York: Wiley, 1988.

Giles, B. A., and Barrett, G. V. "Utility of Merit Increases." *Journal of Applied Psychology,* 1971, *55,* 103–109.

Gomez-Mejia, L. R., and Welbourne, T. M. "Compensation Strategy: An Overview and Future Steps." *Human Resource Planning,* 1988, *11,* 173–189.

Goodman, P. S. "An Examination of Referents Used in the Evaluation of Pay." *Organizational Behavior and Human Performance,* 1974, *12,* 170–195.

Graham-Moore, B., and Ross, T. *Productivity Gainsharing.* Englewood Cliffs, N.J.: Prentice-Hall, 1983.

Grayson, C. J., and O'Dell, C. *A Two-Minute Warning.* New York: Free Press, 1988.

Grove, A. "Keeping Favoritism and Prejudice Out of Evaluation." *Wall Street Journal,* Feb. 27, 1984.

Gupta, N., Schweizer, T. P., and Jenkins, G. D., Jr. "Pay-for-Knowledge Compensation Plans: Hypotheses and Survey Results." *Monthly Labor Review,* 1987, *110* (10), 40–43.

Guzzo, R. A., Jette, R. A., and Katzell, R. A. "The Effect of Psychology-Based Intervention Programs on Worker Productivity: A Meta-Analysis." *Personnel Psychology,* 1985, *38,* 275–291.

Hackman, J. R., and Oldham, G. R. *Work Redesign.* Reading, Mass.: Addison-Wesley, 1980.

Hall, D. T., and Lawler, E. E. "Unused Potential in R. and D. Labs." *Research Management,* 1969, *12,* 339–354.

Henderson, R. I. *Compensation Management: Rewarding Performance.* (4th ed.) Reston, Va.: Reston, 1985.

Hills, S. F. "Internal Pay Relationships." In L. R. Gomez-Mejia (ed.), *Compensation and Benefits.* Vol. 3. Washington, D.C.: BNA, 1989.

Jacques, E. *Equitable Payment.* New York: Wiley, 1961.

Johnston, R., and Lawrence, P. R. "Beyond Vertical Integration: The Rise of the Value-Adding Partnership." *Harvard Business Review,* 1988, *66* (4), 94–101.

Johnston, W. B. *Work Force 2000.* Indianapolis, Ind.: Hudson Institute, 1987.

Kane, J., and Lawler, E. E. "Methods of Peer Assessment." *Psychological Bulletin,* 1978, *85* (3), 555–586.

Kerr, J. "Diversification Strategies and Managerial Rewards: An Empirical Study." *Academy of Management Journal,* 1985, *28* (1), 155–179.

Kerr, J., and Slocumm, J. W. "Managing Corporate Culture Through Reward Systems." *Academy of Management Journal,* 1987, *1* (2), 99–108.

Kerr, S. "On the Folly of Rewarding *A,* While Hoping for *B.*" *Academy of Management Journal,* 1975, *18,* 769–783.

Lawler, E. E. "Managers' Attitudes Toward How Their Pay Is and Should Be Determined." *Journal of Applied Psychology,* 1966, *50,* 273–279.

Lawler, E. E. "Equity Theory as a Predictor of Productivity and Work Quality." *Psychological Bulletin,* 1968, *70,* 596–610.

Lawler, E. E. *Pay and Organizational Effectiveness: A Psychological View.* New York: McGraw-Hill, 1971.

Lawler, E. E. "Secrecy and the Need to Know." In M. Dunnette, R. House, and H. Tosi (eds.), *Readings in Managerial Motivation and Compensation*. East Lansing: Michigan State University Press, 1972.

Lawler, E. E. *Motivation in Work Organizations*. Pacific Grove, Calif.: Brooks/Cole, 1973.

Lawler, E. E. "The New Plant Revolution." *Organizational Dynamics*, 1978, *6* (3), 2–12.

Lawler, E. E. *Pay and Organization Development*. Reading, Mass.: Addison-Wesley, 1981.

Lawler, E. E. "What's Wrong with Point-Factor Job Evaluation." *Compensation and Benefits Review*, 1986a, *18* (2), 20–28.

Lawler, E. E. *High-Involvement Management: Participative Strategies for Improving Organizational Performance*. San Francisco: Jossey-Bass, 1986b.

Lawler, E. E. "Gainsharing Theory and Research: Findings and Future Directions." In W. A. Pasmore and R. Woodman (eds.), *Research in Organizational Change and Development*. Vol. 2. Greenwich, Conn.: JAI Press, 1988.

Lawler, E. E., and Drexler, J. A. "Entrepreneurship in the Large Corporation: Is It Possible?" *Management Review*, 1981, *70* (4), 8–11.

Lawler, E. E., and Hackman, J. R. "The Impact of Employee Participation in the Development of Pay Incentive Plans: A Field Experiment." *Journal of Applied Psychology* 1969, *53*, 467–471.

Lawler, E. E., and Ledford, G. E. "Skill-Based Pay." *Personnel*, 1985, *62* (9), 30–37.

Lawler, E. E., Ledford, G. E., and Mohrman, S. A. *Employee Involvement in America*. Houston, Tex.: American Productivity and Quality Center, 1989.

Lawler, E. E., and Levin, E. "Union Officers' Perceptions of Members' Pay Preferences." *Industrial and Labor Relations Review*, 1968, *21*, 509–517.

Lawler, E. E., and Mohrman, S. A. "Quality Circles After the Fad." *Harvard Business Review*, 1985, *85* (1), 64–71.

Lawler, E. E., and Mohrman, S. A. "Quality Circles: After the Honeymoon." *Organizational Dynamics*, 1987, *15* (4), 42–55.

Lawler, E. E., Mohrman, A. M., and Resnick, S. M. "Performance

Appraisal Revisited." *Organizational Dynamics,* 1984, *13* (1), 20–35.

Lincoln, J. F. *Incentive Management.* Cleveland, Ohio: Lincoln Electric Company, 1951.

Locke, E. A., and Latham, G. P.. *Goal Setting: A Motivational Technique That Works.* Englewood Cliffs, N.J.: Prentice-Hall, 1984.

McCaffrey, R. M. "Employee Benefits and Services." In L. R. Gomez-Mejia (ed.), *Compensation and Benefits.* Vol. 3. Washington, D.C.: BNA, 1989.

Metzger, B. L. *Profit Sharing in Perspective.* Evanston, Ill.: Profit Sharing Research Foundation, 1964.

Meyer, H. H., Kay, E., and French, J.R.P., Jr. "Split Roles in Performance Appraisal." *Harvard Business Review,* 1965, *43* (1), 123–129.

Miles, R. E., and Snow, C. "Organizations: New Concepts for New Forms." *California Management Review,* 1986, *28,* 62–73.

Mirvis, P. H., and Lawler, E. E. "Measuring the Financial Impact of Employee Attitudes." *Journal of Applied Psychology,* 1977, *62* (1), 1–8.

Mirvis, P. H., and Lawler, E. E. "Accounting for the Quality of Work Life." *Journal of Occupational Behavior,* 1984, *5,* 197–212.

Mobley, W. H. *Employee Turnover: Causes, Consequences, and Control.* Reading, Mass.: Addison-Wesley, 1982.

Mobley, W. H., Hand, H. H., Meglino, B. M., and Griffeth, R. W. "Review and Conceptual Analysis of the Employee Turnover Process." *Psychological Bulletin,* 1979, *86,* 493–522.

Mohrman, A. M. *Deming Versus Performance Appraisal: Is There a Resolution?* Los Angeles: Center for Effective Organizations, University of Southern California, 1989.

Mohrman, A. M., and Lawler, E. E. "Motivation and Performance-Appraisal Behavior." In F. Landy and S. Zedeck (eds.), *Performance Measurement and Theory.* Hillsdale, N.J.: Erlbaum, 1983.

Mohrman, A. M., Resnick-West, S. M., and Lawler, E. E. *Designing Performance Appraisal Systems: Aligning Appraisals and Organizational Realities.* San Francisco: Jossey-Bass, 1989.

Mowday, R. T., Porter, L. W., and Steers, R. M. *Employee-Organization Linkages.* New York: Academic Press, 1982.

Nalbantian, H. *Incentives, Cooperation, and Risk Sharing.* Totowa, N.J.: Rowman and Littlefield, 1987.

Nealey, S. "Pay and Benefit Preferences." *Industrial Relations,* 1963, *3,* 17–28.

O'Dell, C. *People, Performance, and Pay.* Houston, Tex.: American Productivity Center, 1987.

O'Reilly, C. A., Main, B. G., and Crystal, G. S. "CEO Compensation as Tournament and Social Comparison: A Tale of Two Theories." *Administrative Science Quarterly,* 1988, *33,* 257–274.

O'Toole, J. *Vanguard Management.* New York: Doubleday, 1985.

Patten, T. H. *Fair Pay? The Managerial Challenge of Comparable Job Worth and Job Evaluation.* San Francisco: Jossey-Bass, 1988.

Peters, T. *Thriving on Chaos.* New York: Knopf, 1987.

Peters, T. J., and Waterman, R. M. *In Search of Excellence,* New York: Harper & Row, 1982.

Porter, L. W., and Lawler, E. E. *Managerial Attitudes and Performance.* Homewood, Ill.: Irwin-Dorsey, 1968.

Porter, L. W., Lawler, E. E., and Hackman, J. R. *Behavior in Organizations.* New York: McGraw-Hill, 1975.

Prince, J. B., and Lawler, E. E. "Does Salary Discussion Hurt the Developmental Performance Appraisal?" *Organizational Behavior and Human Decision Processes,* 1986, *37,* 357–375.

Risher, H. W. Job Evaluation: Validity and Reliability. *Compensation and Benefits Review,* 1989, *21,* 22–36.

Rock, M. I. *Handbook of Wage and Salary Administration.* (2nd ed.) New York: McGraw-Hill, 1984.

Rosen, C., Klein, K., and Young, K. *Employee Ownership in America.* Lexington, Mass.: Heath, 1986.

Rosow, J. M., and Zager, R. *Employment Security in a Free Economy.* Elmsford, N.Y.: Pergamon Press, 1984.

Sangerman, H. "Employee Committees: Can They Survive Under the Taft-Hartley Act?" *Labor Law Journal,* Oct. 1973, pp. 684–691.

Scheflen, K. C., Lawler, E. E., and Hackman, J. R. "Long-Term Impact of Employee Participation in the Development of Pay Incentive Plans: A Field Experiment Revisited." *Journal of Applied Psychology,* 1971, *55,* 182–186.

Schuster, J. *Management Compensation in High-Technology Companies.* Lexington, Mass.: Lexington, 1984.

Schuster, M. "Forty Years of Scanlon Plan Research." In C. Crouch and F. A. Heller (eds.), *International Yearbook of Organizational Democracy.* Vol. 1: *Organizational Democracy and Political Processes.* Chichester, England: Wiley, 1983.

Tosi, H., and Tosi, L. "What Managers Need to Know About Knowledge-Based Pay." *Organizational Dynamics,* 1986, *14* (3), 52–64.

Tuller, M. "New Standards for Domination and Support Under Section 8(a)(2)." *Yale Law Journal,* 1973, *82,* 510–532.

U.S. General Accounting Office. *Productivity Sharing Programs: Can They Contribute to Productivity Improvement?* Washington, D.C.: U.S. General Accounting Office, 1981.

Varadarajan, P., and Futrell, C. "Factors Affecting Perceptions of Smallest Meaningful Pay Increases." *Industrial Relations,* 1984, *23,* 278–285.

Von Glinow, M. A., and Mohrman, S. A. *Managing Complexity in High-Technology Organizations.* New York: Oxford University Press, 1989.

Vroom, V. H. *Work and Motivation.* New York: Wiley, 1964.

Walton, R. E. "Establishing and Maintaining High-Commitment Work Systems." In J. R. Kimberly, R. H. Miles, and Associates, *The Organizational Life Cycle: Issues in the Creation, Transformation, and Decline of Organizations.* San Francisco: Jossey-Bass, 1980.

Weitzman, M. L. *The Share Economy.* Cambridge, Mass.: Harvard University Press, 1984.

Whyte, W. F. (ed.). *Money and Motivation: An Analysis of Incentives in Industry.* New York: Harper & Row, 1955.

Work in America. Report of a Special Task Force to the Secretary of Health, Education, and Welfare. Cambridge, Mass.: MIT Press, 1973.

Yankelovich, D., and Immerwahr, J. *Putting the Work Ethic to Work.* New York: Public Agenda Foundation, 1983.

Index

A

Absenteeism, 162, 224, 234, 257
"Acme Corporation" (case study), 245-259, 261, 269; core principles for, 245-246; market position, 253-254; structural issues, 246-257
Adams, J. S., 24, 48, 186
Administration, pay. *See* Human resources administration
Aerospace Industry, 184-185, 189
AFG Industries, 109
Age-based pay, 45, 154, 159
Airline industry, 127, 172-173, 196, 200
America West Airlines, 127
American Airlines, 200
American Express, 85, 127, 128
American Steel and Wire, 211
Amoco, 85, 99, 111
Apple Computer, 44, 49, 129, 207, 271
Applicability, pay system: future, 66-69, 178, 271-272; gainsharing, 116-123, 130-131, 254-255; merit pay and, 81-85; organizational impact and, 4, 29-36, 48-49, 125-126, 145-146, 207; performance appraisal-based rewards, 92-94, 98-100; skill-based pay systems, 170-176, 230, 236-237, 268-269. *See also* Culture, organizational
Appraisal, performance. *See* Performance appraisal
ARCO, 159, 190
Assessment. *See* Performance appraisal
AT&T, 28, 30, 34, 125, 148, 151

At-risk compensation. *See* Compensation, at-risk
Attitudes, workforce, 174; changing expectations and, 10, 64-65, 78; and fears, 49, 60; pay design team, 226-228; toward gainsharing plans, 115-117; toward pay levels, 24-26, 41, 65-66, 71-72, 143-144, 149-150, 191-192; toward pay secrecy, 238-242; toward performance appraisal, 89-92. *See also* Credibility
Attracting employees. *See* Retention and attraction, employee
Auditing: job description, 146, 147; wage rate, 137-138
Auto industry pay practices, 9, 171, 209-210. *See also Names of individual companies*
Avis, 127
Awards, special, 18, 84-85

B

Baby-food industry, 59
Banking industry, 15, 67, 124, 144, 172
Barrett, G. V., 17, 203
Base pay. *See* Compensation levels
"Beating" the pay system, 59-61, 145-146
Bell Labs, 240
Ben and Jerry's Homemade, Incorporated, 197
Benchmarks. *See* Comparisons, pay
Benefits, employee, 65, 279-280; flexible, 5, 49-50, 216-220, 255, 268, 279-280; pay costs and, 35, 49, 78, 181-183, 216

Blasi, J. R., 126, 128, 275
Blinder, A. S., 13-14, 58, 125, 127
Bloom, D. E., 217, 219
Boden, W. D., 217, 219
Bonus plans, 82-83, 108-110, 194; influence of, 21, 119-121, 206, 249-251. *See also* Gainsharing
Box, decision-making, 227, 231
Brown, C. W., 27
Bullock, P. F., 113
Bullock, R. J., 113, 116
Bureaucratic management. *See* Organization, business
Butler Manufacturing, 113, 115

C

"Cafeteria benefits." *See* Benefits, employee, flexible
Canada, 277
Career: mobility and pay systems, 147-148, 176, 214, 215; planning and performance appraisals, 91-92, 97, 106-107
Carter, J., 34, 70
Cash voucher rewards, 81
Centralized administration. *See* Pay practices, centralization of
CEO pay. *See* Senior management
Change: acceleration of, 9; organizational, 33-34, 121, 144-145, 161, 169-170, 177, 260, 263; societal, 9, 63-66; technological, 169. *See* also Individual development
Chaparrel Steel, 109
Chemical industry, 190
Civil Service Reform Act, 70
Coch, L., 222
Commission plans, 67
Communication: among job appraisers, 105-106; gaps, 221-222; pay disclosure, 284-285; of pay information, 190-191, 238-242, 258-259; of pay principles, 38-43, 70, 99, 117, 143, 221-222, 225-226, 269-271, 284-285; secret pay systems and, 17-18, 20, 46, 50, 191, 238-242; statement samples, 41-43, 99, 143

Community pay rates. *See* Geographic factors; Market-based pay
Compaq Computer, 271
Comparable worth issues, 276-279
Comparisons, pay: benchmark, 142-143, 186-192. *See also* Labor market comparisons
Compensation, at-risk, 203-207, 212
Compensation levels: attitudes toward, 24-26, 41, 65-66, 71-72, 143-144, 149-150, 191-192; basis for, 44-45; control of inequitable, 280-283; different pay, 195-198, 206-213, 264; impact of total, 181-183; merit pay, 71-76, 82; organizational performance and, 192-195, 205-206; setting total, 183-200
Compensation mix: designing a, 246-252; factors influencing the, 205-215, 220; impact of the, 202-205; individual choice of, 215-220; organizational level and, 207-213
Compensation staff. *See* Human resources administration
Competitiveness, economic, U.S. pay and global, 4, 7-8, 66-67, 187-189, 260-261
Computer industry compensation, 182-184, 260-261. *See also names of individual companies*
Computerized pay systems. *See* Human resources administration
Conglomerates. *See* Diversified businesses
Conoco, 105
Conte, M., 127
Contract, performance, 101
Control Data, 198
Cost objectives, organizational, 34-36, 232-233, 256-257; cost effectiveness and flexibility, 204-205, 251-252, 260-261; employee replacement, 199; flexible benefits and, 217-218; gainsharing plans and, 119-121; incentive pay and, 62; job-based pay and, 143, 145-147, 245-246; 278; pay-increase

budget, 47-48; skill-based pay and, 165

Credibility: of performance measures, 14, 119-121; of reward systems, 19-20, 38-40, 52-53, 70, 83, 118-119, 123; of selection for reward, 18. *See also* Communication

Crystal, G. S., 181

Culture, organizational, 5, 94, 127, 182; belief in the, 38-40, 145-146, 164; negative influences on, 61, 63, 144, 146, 196; pay system match to, 31-34, 164, 196, 220, 251-252; risk taking in the, 22, 33, 140-141, 193-194; subcultures and, 61-62, 125, 200, 208. *See also* Values, organizational

Customer satisfaction, 40, 67, 111-112, 186; measurement of, 15

Cyclical businesses, 207, 247

D

Dana, 111, 226

Davis, S. M., 77

Decision making, organizational: employee participation in, 10, 50-51, 68-69, 122-123, 163-164, 208, 218-219; participative pay administration and, 83, 231-238, 262; participative pay design and, 222-230, 262, 285-287; unilateral, 68

Deming, W. E., 77

Demographics, workforce, 10, 64-65, 216-217

Description, job. *See* Job evaluation systems

Diagonal slice task force, 226-228

Digital Equipment Corporation (DEC), 32, 40-41, 127-128, 156, 159, 183-184, 200, 209, 271

Discrimination: job, 273, 276-279; pay, 88, 284-285

Diversified businesses: varied pay strategies for, 46, 124, 131, 144, 199-200, 213-214, 252-253. *See also* "Acme Corporation" (case study)

Donnelly Mirrors, 44, 111, 120, 233

Dow Chemical, 41, 43-44, 83, 129

Drexler, J. A., 22

Dual-career families, 217

Due process, 51-52, 78, 83

Dumaine, B., 211

DuPont, 83, 124

E

Eaton, 159

EDS, 210

Education and learning: about the business, 125, 154-158, 175-176, 211; about compensation, 227, 271; costs of, 166; cross-training, 162, 174, 211; levels of, 9-10; on-the-job, 154-158. *See also* Communication; Skill-based pay

Egalitarian businesses, 197, 210-214, 219, 260-262, 267, 280-284. *See also* Pay equity, internal

Electronic industry. *See* High-technology industry

Ellig, B. K., 181

Employee ownership plans, 129, 249, 274-276; ESOPs, 126-128, 249, 275-276; gainsharing and, 129-131

Energy industry, 189-190

Entrepreneurship, 204, 205, 215; rewards for risk taking and, 21-22, 33, 49, 177, 193-194, 207

Equity, pay. *See* Pay equity

ESOPs. *See* Employee ownership plans, ESOPs

European pay practices, 188, 274, 285-286

Ewing, D. E., 78

Excellence, organizational, 5, 33, 143-144, 182; service quality and, 122, 260, 263, 266

Executives. *See* Senior management

Exempt-nonexempt classification, 283-284

Exxon, 47, 138, 190

F

Fair Labor Standards Act of 1938, 283–284
Fast-food industry, 27–28
Fay, C. H., 186
Fears, employee. *See* Attitudes, workforce
Federal Express, 32, 40, 211
Finkelstein, S., 181
Firestone, 111
"Fit." *See* Applicability, pay system
Fixed-cost pay practices, 35–36
Flat organization. *See* "HiTech International" (case study)
Ford, H., 209
Foreign companies: pay practices of, 8–9; U.S. workforce compensation by, 8–9
Formula-driven pay. *See* Pay-for-performance, formula-driven
Fortune, 108, 211
Fortune 1,000 companies, 57, 70, 111, 123, 158, 217
Fragner, B. N., 218
French, J.R.P., Jr., 91, 97, 222
Friedman-Jacobs Company, 233–234
Fringe benefits. *See* Benefits, employee; Perquisites (employee)
Frost, C. F., 110
Futrell, C., 17
Future pay trends, 66–69, 81–85, 178; the new pay, 271–272

G

Gaines, 112–113, 115
Gainsharing systems, 5, 110–123; critical elements of, 118–123; organizational openness and, 20; participative management and, 113–115, 226, 228, 229, 265; profit sharing and, 129–131, 206; research on, 115–118; situational factors, 116–117, 130–131, 254–255
Galbraith, J., 175
"Gaming" by workers, 59–61

General Electric (GE), 102, 106, 111, 138, 143, 149, 159, 171, 199–200
General Foods, 113, 159
General Motors (GM), 30, 88–89, 125, 159, 171, 210
Geographic factors, pay and, 46, 113, 190–191, 252–255
Ghiselli, E. E., 27
Gifford, D. L., 50
Giles, B. A., 17, 203
Golden parachute, 211
Gomez-Mejia, L. R., 35, 181
Goodman, P. S., 186
Government intervention issues, 7, 66, 111, 273–287
Government service, 34, 277
Graham-Moore, B., 116
Grayson, C. J., 4, 7, 141
Grievances: due process and pay, 51–52, 78, 83; union, 60
Griffeth, R. W., 24, 182
Group bonus plans. *See* Bonus plans; Gainsharing
Grove, A., 94
Gupta, N., 158
Guzzo, R. A., 58

H

Hackman, J. R., 57, 64, 91, 93, 156, 223, 224
Hall, D. T., 89–90
Hambrick, D. C., 181
Hand, H. H., 24, 182
Hay system job evaluation, 135, 137
Henderson, R. I., 135
Herman Miller, 5, 44, 108, 109, 111, 197, 211
Hewlett-Packard, 26–27, 39, 44, 47, 125, 182, 184, 190, 198
Hierarchical pay levels, 6–7, 23, 30, 41, 125, 141–142, 147–148, 152, 206, 207; gap in worker-executive, 6–7, 23, 125, 188, 196, 208, 255–256, 280–283; overtime classification and, 283–284
High-involvement plants. *See* Manufacturing industry
High-technology industry, 9, 22–23,

64, 112, 142, 148, 157, 198–199, 209–210, 215, 262–263
Hills, S. F., 135
"HiTech International" (case study), 260–261, 271–272; core principles for, 261–262; process issues, 270–271; structural issues, 262–270
Holiday Inns, 111
Honda, 171, 209
Honeywell, 41–42, 112, 159
Hotel industry, 15
Human resources administration: centralized, 137–139, 151, 254–255, 269–270; computerized, 80, 176, 219–220, 261; decentralized, 254–255; participative administration and, 231–238; participative design and, 228–230; pay system effects on, 146–147, 152, 219–220

I

IBM, 26–27, 32, 33, 39, 44, 47, 85, 138, 182, 183–184, 190, 200, 237, 239
Immerwahr, J., 43, 57, 66, 80
Impact, reward system: on the individual, 13–29. See also Applicability, pay system
Improshare Plan, 110, 114, 118
Incentive pay, 57–58, 251; future uses of, 66–69; problems with, 58–63. See also Pay-for-performance
Individual development: compensation choice and, 215–220, 224, 231–235, 262, 268; discouragement of, 62, 140–142, 147–150; of knowledge, 22–23, 215, 260–263; motivation of, 13–15, 18–23, 74–75, 93, 153, 171, 194–195, 202–203, 247, 249, 253; multifunctional experience, 161–164, 171–173, 211, 214, 263; quantifiability of, 103–106, 154–155; self-management and, 155–156, 164–165. See also Mobility; Skill-based pay
Industrywide pay practices, 8, 24, 47–48, 142–143, 187, 189–190

Inflation: job evaluation, 146; pay and economic, 72–73, 76, 79, 194
Information processing work. See Knowledge-based work
Intel, 94
Interesting work, importance of, 16–17
Internal Revenue Service, 279–280
International competition. See Competitiveness, economic

J

Jacques, E., 100
Janitorial work, 224
Japanese pay practices, 8–9, 126, 135, 187, 188, 198, 209; in U.S. plants, 171
Jenkins, D., 161
Jenkins, G. D., Jr., 158
Jette, R. A., 58
Job evaluation systems, 92–93, 135–136, 145, 276–279
Job evaluation-based pay: advantages of, 136–139; disadvantages of, 139–150, 277–278
Job switching. See Mobility
Job-based pay, mix, 44, 135–136, 198–199, 214–215; point-factor approach, 135–136, 141, 145, 147–148, 150, 151
Johnson & Johnson, 40, 159, 161
Johnston, R., 77
Johnston, W. B., 9, 65, 217
Just-in-time manufacturing, 161–162

K

Kane, J., 80, 167, 236
Katzell, R. A., 58
Kay, E., 91, 97
Kerr, J., 35
Kerr, S., 13–14
Klein, K., 127
Knowledge-based work, 9, 22–23, 64, 112, 142, 148, 157, 198–199, 209–210, 262–263; technical "ladders" and, 158–159, 176, 178, 215, 263

Knowledge-development motivation, 22–23, 215, 260–263
Kodak, 83, 129, 211

L

Labor costs: pay systems and 34–36, 126, 186–192, 204–205. *See also* Cost objectives, organizational
Labor legislation and pay practices, 283–284, 286
Labor market comparisons, 34–36, 186–192, 204–205. *See also* Market-based pay
Ladders. *See* Knowledge-based work
Latham, G. P., 97, 98, 232
Lawler, E. E.: (1966), 43; (1968), 24; (1971), 13, 16, 17, 45, 57, 58; (1972), 240, 241; (1973), 18, 24, 34; (1978), 112, 154, 159; (1981), 4, 83, 223, 225, 235, 257; (1986a), 65, 139; (1986b), 8, 10–11, 77, 80, 142, 148, 159, 163, 222; (1988), 110, 228; Bullock, R. J., and, 113, 116; and Drexler, J. A., 22; and Hackman, J. R., 223, 224; Hall, D. T., and, 89–90; Kane, J., and, 80, 167, 236; and Ledford, G. E., 23, 232; Ledford, G. E., and Mohrman, S. A., 5, 50, 57, 70, 111, 123, 153, 158, 217, 223, 245; and Levin, E., 216; Mirvis, P. H., and, 27; Mohrman, A. M., and Resnick, S. M., 102, 232; and Mohrman, S. A., 86, 163; Mohrman, A. M., Resnick-West, S. M., and, 71, 88, 93, 95, 106, 223, 226, 266–267; Porter, L. W., and, 238; Porter, L. W., Hackman, J. R., and, 91; Prince, J. B., and, 92, 96; Scheflen, K. C., Hackman, J. R., and, 224
Lawrence, P. R., 77
Leading companies: bonus-paying, 108–110; high-paying market position of, 47–48, 182, 184–185, 190; skills-based pay in, 176
Ledford, G. E., 5, 50, 57, 70, 111, 123, 153, 158, 165, 191, 217, 245; Lawler, E. E., and, 23, 232

Legal aspects of pay practices, 7, 65–66, 218–219, 246, 273, 286; due process, 51–52, 78, 83; employee lawsuits, 88; overtime pay, 283–284
Levels, pay. *See* Compensation levels
Levels, performance: organizational, 195–198, 207–213; profit sharing and, 130–131; rating of, 104–106
Levin, E., 216
Life-styles, employee. *See* Senior management; Workforce, the
Lincoln, J. F., 108
Lincoln Electric, 5, 44, 106, 108, 109
Lincoln National Life, 112
Line of business. *See* Diversified businesses
"Line of sight" from performance to rewards, 14, 67–68, 114, 116, 119–121, 127, 206; weak, 20, 75–76, 124, 128, 250
Locke, E. A., 97, 98, 232
Low-wage countries, 7
Low-wage strategies, 185–186, 194–195, 197, 233, 267

M

McCaffrey, R. M., 181
Main, B. G., 181
Management: new approaches to, 10–11; participative, 113–115, 156, 164–165, 170, 175, 177, 196; self-, 155–156, 164–165
Managers: compensation of mid-level, 6; market pay rates for, 46–47; mobility of, 147–148, 156, 210, 211; skill-based pay for, 156–157, 160, 170–171, 173–176; subordinate evaluation and, 78, 87–90, 93–94, 237, 242. *See also* Senior management
Manufacturing industry, 111–112, 154–156, 159–160. *See also* "Acme Corporation" (case study)
Marital status and benefits, 216–217
Market-based pay, 45–48, 71, 151–152, 157, 186–195, 246, 250–252,

261-262, 264; industrywide, 8, 24, 47-48, 142-143, 187, 189-190. *See also* Labor market comparisons
Mead, 111, 129, 159
Measurement of performance: approaches to, 14-15; complexities in, 63-64, 90-91, 119-122, 203. *See also* Performance appraisal
Mechanic skills (vehicle), 173
Meglino, B. M., 24, 182
Merit-based rewards, 34, 70-71; forces favoring, 79-81; forces threatening, 76-78; future uses of, 81-85; problems with, 71-76, 250-251, 266
Metzger, B. L., 123, 124
Meyer, H. H., 91, 97
Miles, R. E., 77, 175
Military service reward systems, 106
Minimum-wage laws, 7
Minnesota Mining and Manufacturing (3M), 22, 111, 177
Mirvis, P. H., 27
Mobil, 190
Mobility: horizontal, 148, 156, 161, 163, 263; incentives, 147-149, 174-175, 204, 208; multifunctional, 161-164, 171-173, 211, 214, 263; skills directed to, 156, 165; vertical, 163, 214. *See also* Diversified businesses
Mobley, W. H., 24, 182
Mohrman, A. M.: (1989), 77; Resnick-West, S. M., and Lawler, E. E. (1989), 71, 88, 93, 95, 106, 223, 226, 266
Mohrman, S. A.: Lawler, E. E., and, 86, 163; Lawler, E. E., Ledford, G. E., and, 5, 50, 57, 70, 111, 123, 153, 158, 217, 223, 245; Von Glinow, M. A., and, 84, 92, 142, 261
Money reward systems: individual performance and, 13-14; relative importance of, 16-17
Motivation, individual: performance reward system, 13-15, 18-21, 114, 140-141; skill-based pay, 22-24,

153, 232, 262-263. *See also* Individual development
Motorola, 108-109, 111, 124, 159, 176
Mowday, R. T., 24
Multibusiness organizations. *See* Diversified businesses

N

Nalbantian, H., 13-14, 57
National labor market, U.S. *See* Competitiveness, economic
National Labor Relations Act of 1935, 286
Nealey, S., 216
Nissan, 171
Nobel Prize, 18, 20, 84-85
Nordstrom, 40, 67, 195
Northern Telecom, 159
Nucor Steel, 109

O

Objectivity, of job evaluation plans, 138-139
O'Dell, C., 4, 5, 7, 50, 111, 141, 158, 223
Off standard work, 60-61
Office space rewards. *See* Perquisites (employee)
Office work skills, 173
Oldham, G. R., 57, 64, 93, 156
Olsen, K., 32, 209
Ontario, Canada, 277
Openness. *See* Communication; Reward systems
O'Reilly, C. A., 181
Organization, business: bureaucratic, 6-7, 11, 30, 139-142, 196, 204, 239-242; centralized, 137-139, 151, 254-255, 269-270; decentralized, 80, 111, 124, 199-200; effects of pay systems on, 4, 29-36, 48-49, 125-126, 145-146, 207; egalitarian, 197, 210-214, 219, 260-262, 267, 280-284; matrix or networking, 77, 175; multiskilled employees and, 163-164; participative, 122-123, 196-198, 208, 210-

213, 218-219, 285-287; participative pay administration and, 83, 231-238, 262; participative pay design and, 222-230, 262, 285-287. *See also* Decision making, organizational
O'Toole, J., 10-11
Outside consultants, using, 112-113, 116, 119, 123, 224, 229
Overtime pay, 283-284

P

"Parachute" plans, 211
Parking spaces. *See* Perquisites (employee)
Paternalism, organizational, 49, 209, 216-218, 231
Patten, T. H., 276
Pay administration. *See* Human resources administration
Pay equity: comparable worth and, 276-279; external, 48-49, 137-139, 186-195, 252; internal, 48-49, 137-139, 142-144, 151, 183, 186, 188, 191, 195-198, 211
Pay-for-performance, 192-195, 205-206, 214; achievability of, 20-21, 52-53, 76-81, 241-242, 264; as a core principle, 44-45, 246, 261-262; formula-driven, 19-20; gainsharing and, 130-131; multiple level, 206, 212; productivity and, 66; U.S. belief in, 79-81, 274. *See also* Incentive pay; Performance motivation
Pay gap: and labor markets, 186-188, 196-197, 268-269; men-women, 276-279; worker-executive, 6-7, 23, 125, 188, 196, 208, 255-256, 280-283
Pay practices: centralization of, 137-139, 151, 254-255, 269-270; comparing, 3, 5, 24-26, 50, 142-143, 186-198, 240; egalitarian, 280-283; government-influenced, 273-274, 285-287; industrywide, 8, 24, 47-48, 142-143, 187, 189-190; of labor markets, 34-36, 186-192,

204-205; public policy and, 273-287; publicized, 238-242; traditional approaches to, 3, 6-9
Pay principles, organizational: communication of, 38-40, 70, 221-222, 269-271, 284-285; development of, 40-43; key issues in, 41-52, 226, 245-246; sample statements of, 41-43, 99, 143, 225-226
Pay raises, 19, 47-48, 233-234. *See also* Gainsharing systems; Pay-for-performance
Pay-range systems, 73
Pay strategy: choice of a, 11-12, 40, 151-152, 183-201, 278; organizational excellence and, 143-144, 192-195. *See also* Culture, organizational
Pay system design: changing the, 33-34, 200; for a global technology company, 260-261, 269-272; participative decision making in, 222-230, 270, 286; steps in, 11-12, 37-38; task force, 113, 119, 226-228; for a traditional company, 245-246, 257-259
Paying the person. *See* Skill-based pay
Peer evaluation: rewards based on, 18, 20, 80-81, 84-85, 115, 124, 130, 230, 235; of skills acquisition, 155, 167-168, 270
PepsiCo, 127, 128
Perception of pay. *See* Attitudes, workforce
Performance appraisal, 72, 77, 83-84, 157-158, 229-230, 232, 249-250, 266-267; career planning and, 106-107; difficulty of, 89-92, 167; effective, 92-94; forms for, 103-106, 235-236; goals of, 86-87; problems with, 87-89. *See also* Peer evaluation
Performance appraisal-based rewards: deciding to use, 98-100; designing effective, 92-94, 100-103, 128-131, 246-252; pay actions related to, 19, 51-52; problems with, 87-89, 235-236; situational factors

and, 92-94, 98-100; substitutes for pay-linked, 97-98

Performance effectiveness (organizational): compensation mix and, 18-20, 109, 205-207, 246-254, 261-262; historical basis of, 110, 120-121; pay budgets and, 47-48; total compensation for, 44, 192-195, 203, 247-248. *See also* Gainsharing

Performance effectiveness (work): competitiveness and, 7, 194-195; external visibility of, 29; history, 120-121; norms and levels, 59-61; setting goals for, 20-21, 44, 249. *See also* Measurement of performance; Teamwork

Performance motivation: reward systems and, 13-15, 18-21. *See also* Individual development

Perot, R., 210

Perquisites (employee), 202-205, 219, 268; costs of, 181; hierarchical, 30, 208-211, 256, 267; job-based, 150. *See also* Benefits, employee

Personnel administration. *See* Human resources administration

Peters, T. J., 10-11, 140, 142

Piece-rate pay. *See* Incentive pay

Point factors, job evaluation, 135-136, 141, 145, 147-148, 150, 151

Polaroid, 51, 275

Pool, bonus, 111

Porter, L. W., 24, 91

President's Task Force on Industrial Competitiveness, 111

Prince, J. B., 92, 96

Principles of reward administration. *See* Pay principles, organizational

Problem solving by employees, 115, 122, 163-164

Procter & Gamble, 5, 40, 61, 159-160

Production work skills, 153-156, 159, 161, 177-178

Productivity and incentive pay, 57-58

Profit-sharing plans, 110, 123-126, 206, 274-275; advantages of, 125-126, 206, 207; designing, 247-251, 266; gainsharing and, 127, 129-131; organizational openness and, 20; weak motivation by, 19-20, 124

Promotions, job, 74, 149-150, 174

Public Agenda Foundation, 57-58, 66

Public pay systems. *See* Communication

Public policy issues and legislation, 273-287

Punishment, performance motivation by, 21-22

Q

Quality Improvement, 77-78, 163-164

Quantifiability: of individual development, 104-106; job evaluation plans and, 138-139

R

R & D work (research and development), 84-85, 157, 159

Raises. *See* Pay raises

Recruitment. *See* Retention and attraction, employee

Red-circle-rate approach, 171

Refunds, customer, 112

Rehiring, 74

Reorganization, organizational, pay system changes and, 31

Repetitive task jobs, 63-64, 67-68, 185-186

Research on pay practices, 5, 216, 219, 261; gainsharing studies, 115-118; skill-based pay and, 160

Resnick, S. M., 102, 232

Resnick-West, S. M., 71, 88, 93, 95, 106, 223, 226, 266

Retail Clerks Union, 234

Retention and attraction, employee, 27-29, 72, 189, 194-195, 197, 203; flexible benefits and, 215-220,

224, 266; turnover *vs.*, 26–29, 49, 190–191, 193–194, 215, 266

Retirement benefits, 49–50, 207, 216, 274–276

Review, performance. *See* Performance appraisal

Reward systems: core principles of, 41–52; open *vs.* secret, 17–18, 20, 46, 50, 78, 191, 238–242, 258, 262, 270–271, 284–285; performance-related, 18–20; valued, 16–18

Rights, employee, due process and, 51–52

Risher, H. W., 150

Risk taking. *See* Compensation, at-risk; Entrepreneurship

Rock, M. I., 135

Rockwell, 111

Rosen, C., 127

Rosow, J. M., 206

Ross, T., 116

Rucker Plan, 110, 114

Ruh, R. A., 110

S

Salary surveys, 50, 264

Sales jobs, 173; compensation, 21, 62, 67, 193–195, 232, 265, 266

Sangerman, H., 286

Satisfaction, individual pay, 24–25

Scanlon, J., 113–114

Scanlon Plan, 110, 113, 115, 116, 120, 122

Scarcity, reward, 18, 266

Scheflen, K. C., 224

Schuster, J., 84, 92, 261

Schuster, M., 116

Schweizer, T. P., 158

Sears, 237

Secrecy. *See* Communication; Reward systems

Secretarial work, 267–268, 276

Security, job, 206

Selection, employee, 27–29; for rewards, 18. *See also* Peer evaluation; Performance appraisal

Seltz, C. A., 50

Senior management: compensation comparisons, 186–188, 194, 196–198, 238, 241–242; excessive compensation of, 280–283, 285; pay task force and, 227–228; perquisites and pay gap of, 6–7, 23, 125, 188, 196, 204, 210, 255–256, 280–283; rewards to, 6, 125, 148, 170–171, 181, 206, 207–208, 219, 247–248, 267–269; separateness of, 210–211, 252. *See also* Managers; Perquisites (employee)

Seniority-based rewards, 28–29, 34, 154, 215

Service quality, business, 118, 122, 260, 263, 266

Shareholders, corporation, 282–283, 285

Shell Canada, 156

Shenandoah Life, 173

Single workers, 216–217

Skill-based pay, 5, 35, 45, 50; advantages of, 160–166, 197; applicability of, 170–176, 230, 236–237, 268–269; disadvantages of, 166–170; effectiveness of, 160; in high-involvement plants, 159–166; the incidence of, 158–160; individual motivation with, 22–24, 153, 163–164, 232, 262–263; the nature of, 154–158; new approaches to, 176–178, 278–279; the workforce and, 9–10, 64–65, 177–178. *See also* Individual development

Slocumm, J. W., 35

Smith, F., 32

Snow, C., 77, 175

Societal changes, 9–10, 65–66

Sports team performance, 92–93

Staff job-skills compensation, 173–176

Staffing, pay system. *See* Human resources administration

Status rewards, relative importance of, 16–17, 181–183, 203–204

Steers, R. M., 24, 238

Stock ownership. *See* Profit-sharing plans

Strategic compensation management. *See* Pay strategy
Suggestion system, employee, 115, 122
Sun Microsystems, 47, 271

T

Taco Bell, 111, 118
Takeovers, business, 128, 211, 249, 275
Tandem Computer, 271
Tannenbaum, A., 127
Task force, pay system. *See* Pay system design
Tax-advantaged pay practices, 273–276, 279–290
Teamwork: evaluation of, 92–93, 167–168; problem solving, 163; rewards, 21, 68, 77, 84, 98, 130, 154–156, 159–160, 236–237, 261–262, 266. *See also* Peer evaluation
Technical ladder. *See* Knowledge-based work
Technology. *See* High-technology industry
Tenure. *See* Seniority-based rewards
3M. *See* Minnesota Mining and Manufacturing (3M)
Timing: appraisal cycle, 100–103; participative decision making and, 224–225; payback period, 169; performance-reward, 19, 121, 123, 265–266
Top-to-bottom ratio. *See* Pay gap
Topping out, 168, 177
Tosi, H., 154
Tosi, L., 154
Toyota, 171
Trahan, J. T., 217, 219
Training costs, employee, 27
Trucking industry, 173
TRW, 47, 111, 112, 129, 159, 171, 194, 218
Tuller, M., 286
Turnover, employee: costs of, 25–27, 266; organizational goals for, 71, 194–195; retention *vs.*, 26–29, 49, 190–191, 193–194, 215

U

Unions, 196, 235, 282; incentive plans and, 60, 65; job descriptions and, 141; pay standardization and, 8; wage rates and, 7, 191, 233, 234
United Airlines, 196
United Auto Workers (UAW), 8
U.S. General Accounting Office, 111, 116
Upward mobility. *See* Mobility

V

Values, organizational, 142, 151-152, 164; core, 40-41. *See also* Culture, organizational
Varadarajan, P., 17, 203
Volvo, 155, 211
Von Glinow, M. A., 84, 92, 142, 261
Vroom, V. W., 13-14, 232

W

Wages. *See* Compensation levels; Pay practices
Wakeley, J. H., 110
Wall Street Journal, 94
Walton, R. E., 77, 163
Waterman, R. M., 10-11
Watson, T., 32
Weitzman, M. L., 34, 65, 124, 125, 126; *The Share Economy*, 274
Welbourne, T. M., 35, 181
Welch, J., 138, 200
Wells Fargo Bank, 81, 124
West Germany, 187, 286
White House Conference on Productivity, 66, 111
Whyte, W. F., 58
Wierton Steel, 127
Women workers, 216-217; comparable worth and, 276-279
Work in America (HEW), 65
Workers, lower-level, rewards to, 6-7, 125, 154
Workforce, the: all-salaried, 256-257, 283-284; changes in, 9-10,

64–65, 216–217; divided by pay issues, 61–62, 200, 208; problem solving by, 115, 122, 163–164; underutilization of, 7, 59–62, 177; utilization of, 8–9, 160–161

X

Xerox, 81, 112, 118, 122, 129, 142, 265

Y

Yankelovich, D., 43, 57, 66, 80
Young, K., 127

Z

Zager, R., 206

Printed in the United States
137942LV00001B/84/A